THE MAINE WOODS

THE
MAINE WOODS

by

Henry David Thoreau

Decorated by Clare Leighton

THOMAS Y. CROWELL COMPANY

New York, Established 1834

CONTENTS

CONTENTS

THE MAINE WOODS

KTAADN

ON the 31st of August, 1846, I left Concord in Massachusetts for Bangor and the backwoods of Maine, by way of the railroad and steamboat, intending to accompany a relative of mine engaged in the lumber-trade in Bangor, as far as a dam on the west branch of the Penobscot, in which property he was interested. From this place, which is about one hundred miles by the river above Bangor, thirty miles from the Houlton military road, and five miles beyond the last log-hut, I proposed to make excursions to Mount Ktaadn, the second highest mountain in New England, about thirty miles distant, and to some of the lakes of the Penobscot, either alone or with such company as I might pick up there. It is unusual to find a camp so far in the woods at that season, when lumbering operations have ceased, and I was glad to avail myself of the circumstance of a gang of men being employed there at that time in repairing the injuries caused by the great freshet in the spring. The mountain may be

approached more easily and directly on horse-
back and on foot from the northeast side, by
the Aroostook road, and the Wassataquoik
River; but in that case you see much less of the
wilderness, none of the glorious river and lake
scenery, and have no experience of the batteau
and the boatman's life. I was fortunate also in
the season of the year, for in the summer myriads
of black flies, mosquitoes, and midges, or, as
the Indians call them, "no-see-ems," make
travelling in the woods almost impossible; but
now their reign was nearly over.

Ktaadn, whose name is an Indian word signifying highest land, was first ascended by white
men in 1804. It was visited by Professor J. W.
Bailey of West Point in 1836; by Dr. Charles
T. Jackson, the State Geologist, in 1837; and
by two young men from Boston in 1845. All
these have given accounts of their expeditions.
Since I was there, two or three other parties have
made the excursion, and told their stories. Besides these, very few, even among backwoodsmen and hunters, have ever climbed it, and it
will be a long time before the tide of fashionable
travel sets that way. The mountainous region
of the State of Maine stretches from near the
White Mountains, northeasterly one hundred
and sixty miles, to the head of the Aroostook
River, and is about sixty miles wide. The wild
or unsettled portion is far more extensive. So

that some hours only of travel in this direction will carry the curious to the verge of a primitive forest, more interesting, perhaps, on all accounts, than they would reach by going a thousand miles westward.

The next forenoon, Tuesday, September 1st, I started with my companion in a buggy from Bangor for "up river," expecting to be overtaken the next day night at Mattawamkeag Point, some sixty miles off, by two more Bangoreans, who had decided to join us in a trip to the mountain. We had each a knapsack or bag filled with such clothing and articles as were indispensable, and my companion carried his gun.

Within a dozen miles of Bangor we passed through the villages of Stillwater and Oldtown, built at the falls of the Penobscot, which furnish the principal power by which the Maine woods are converted into lumber. The mills are built directly over and across the river. Here is a close jam, a hard rub, at all seasons; and then the once green tree, long since white, I need not say as the driven snow, but as a driven log, becomes lumber merely. Here your inch, your two and your three inch stuff begin to be, and Mr. Sawyer marks off those spaces which decide the destiny of so many prostrate forests. Through this steel riddle, more or less coarse, is the arrowy Maine forest, from Ktaadn and

Chesuncook, and the head-waters of the St. John, relentlessly sifted, till it comes out boards, clapboards, laths, and shingles such as the wind can take, still perchance to be slit and slit again till men get a size that will suit. Think how stood the white-pine tree on the shore of Chesuncook, its branches soughing with the four winds, and every individual needle trembling in the sunlight, — think how it stands with it now, — sold, perchance, to the New England Friction-Match Company! There were in 1837, as I read, two hundred and fifty saw mills on the Penobscot and its tributaries above Bangor, the greater part of them in this immediate neighborhood, and they sawed two hundred millions of feet of boards annually. To this is to be added the lumber of the Kennebec, Androscoggin, Saco, Passamaquoddy, and other streams. No wonder that we hear so often of vessels which are becalmed off our coast, being surrounded a week at a time by floating lumber from the Maine woods. The mission of men there seems to be, like so many busy demons, to drive the forest all out of the country, from every solitary beaver-swamp and mountain-side, as soon as possible.

At Oldtown we walked into a batteau-manufactory. The making of batteaux is quite a business here for the supply of the Penobscot River. We examined some on the stocks. They are light and shapely vessels, calculated for rapid and rocky streams, and to be carried over long portages on men's shoulders, from twenty to thirty feet long, and only four or four and a half wide, sharp at both ends like a canoe, though broadest forward on the bottom, and reaching seven or eight feet over the water, in order that they may slip over rocks as gently as possible. They are made very slight, only two boards to a side, commonly secured to a few light maple or other hard-wood knees, but inward are of the clearest and widest white-pine stuff, of which there is a great waste on account of their form, for the bottom is left perfectly flat, not only from side to side, but from end to end. Sometimes they become "hogging" even, after long use, and the boatmen then turn them over and straighten them by a weight at each end. They told us that one wore out in two years, or often in a single trip, on the rocks, and sold for from fourteen to sixteen dollars. There was something refreshing and wildly musical to my ears in the very name of the white man's canoe, reminding me of Charlevoix and Canadian Voyageurs. The batteau is a sort of mongrel between the canoe and the boat, a fur-trader's boat.

The ferry here took us past the Indian island. As we left the shore, I observed a short, shabby, washerwoman-looking Indian — they commonly

have the woe-begone look of the girl that cried
for spilt milk — just from "up river" — land
on the Oldtown side near a grocery, and, drawing up his canoe, take out a bundle of skins in
one hand, and an empty keg or half-barrel in
the other, and scramble up the bank with them.
This picture will do to put before the Indian's
history, that is, the history of his extinction. In
1837 there were three hundred and sixty-two
souls left of this tribe.   The island seemed
deserted to-day, yet I observed some new houses
among the weather-stained ones, as if the tribe
had still a design upon life; but generally they
have a very shabby, forlorn, and cheerless look,
being all back side and woodshed, not homesteads, even Indian homesteads, but instead of
home or abroad-steads, for their life is *domi aut
militiæ*, at home or at war, or now rather *venatus*,
that is, a hunting, and most of the latter.   The
church is the only trim-looking building, but
that is not Abenaki, that was Rome's doings.
Good Canadian it may be, but it is poor Indian.
These were once a powerful tribe.   Politics are all
the rage with them now.   I even thought that a
row of wigwams, with a dance of powwows, and
a prisoner tortured at the stake, would be more
respectable than this.

We landed in Milford, and rode along on the
east side of the Penobscot, having a more or less
constant view of the river, and the Indian islands

in it, for they retain all the islands as far up as
Nickatow, at the mouth of the East Branch.
They are generally well timbered, and are said
to be better soil than the neighboring shores.
The river seemed shallow and rocky, and inter-
rupted by rapids, rippling and gleaming in the
sun. We paused a moment to see a fish-hawk
dive for a fish down straight as an arrow, from
a great height, but he missed his prey this time.
It was the Houlton road on which we were now
travelling, over which some troops were marched
once towards Mars' Hill, though not to Mars'
field, as it proved. It is the main, almost the
only, road in these parts, as straight and well
made, and kept in as good repair, as almost any
you will find anywhere. Everywhere we saw
signs of the great freshet, — this house standing awry, and that where it was not founded,
but where it was found, at any rate, the next
day; and that other with a water-logged look,
as if it were still airing and drying its basement,
and logs with everybody's marks upon them,
and sometimes the marks of their having served
as bridges, strewn along the road. We crossed
the Sunkhaze, a summery Indian name, the
Olemmon, Passadumkeag, and other streams,
which make a greater show on the map than
they now did on the road. At Passadumkeag
we found anything but what the name implies,
— earnest politicians, to wit, — white ones, I

mean, — on the alert, to know how the election was likely to go; men who talked rapidly, with subdued voice, and a sort of factitious earnestness, you could not help believing, hardly waiting for an introduction, one on each side of your buggy, endeavoring to say much in little, for they see you hold the whip impatiently, but always saying little in much. Caucuses they have had, it seems, and caucuses they are to have again, — victory and defeat. Somebody may be elected, somebody may not. One man, a total stranger, who stood by our carriage in the dusk, actually frightened the horse with his asseverations, growing more solemnly positive as there was less in him to be positive about. So Passadumkeag did not look on the map. At sundown, leaving the river-road awhile for shortness, we went by way of Enfield, where we stopped for the night. This, like most of the localities bearing names on this road, was a place to name, which, in the midst of the unnamed and unincorporated wilderness, was to make a distinction without a difference, it seemed to me. Here, however, I noticed quite an orchard of healthy and well-grown apple-trees, in a bearing state, it being the oldest settler's house in this region, but all natural fruit, and comparatively worthless for want of a grafter. And so it is generally, lower down the river. It would be a good speculation, as well as a favor conferred on the settlers, for a Massachusetts boy to go down there with a trunk full of choice scions, and his grafting apparatus, in the spring.

The next morning we drove along through a high and hilly country, in view of Cold-Stream Pond, a beautiful lake four or five miles long, and came into the Houlton road again, here called the military road, at Lincoln, forty-five miles from Bangor, where there is quite a village for this country, — the principal one above Oldtown. Learning that there were several wigwams here, on one of the Indian islands, we left our horse and wagon, and walked through the forest half a mile to the river, to procure a guide to the mountain. It was not till after considerable search that we discovered their habitations, — small huts, in a retired place, where the scenery was unusually soft and beautiful, and the shore skirted with pleasant meadows and graceful elms. We paddled ourselves across to the island-side in a canoe, which we found on the shore. Near where we landed sat an Indian girl ten or twelve years old, on a rock in the water, in the sun, washing, and humming or moaning a song meanwhile. It was an aboriginal strain. A salmon-spear, made wholly of wood, lay on the shore, such as they might have used before white men came. It had an elastic piece of wood fastened to one side of its point, which slipped over and closed upon the fish, somewhat like the contrivance for holding a bucket at the end of a well-pole. As we walked up to the nearest house, we were met by a sally of a dozen wolfish-looking dogs, which may have been lineal descendants from the ancient Indian dogs, which the first voyageurs describe as "their wolves." I suppose they were. The occupant soon appeared, with a long pole in his hand, with which he beat off the dogs, while he parleyed with us. A stalwart, but dull and greasy-looking fellow, who told us, in his sluggish way, in answer to our questions, as if it were the first serious business he had to do that day, that there *were* Indians going "up river"—he and one other—to-day, before noon. And who was the other? Louis Neptune, who lives in the next house. Well, let us go over and see Louis together. The same doggish reception, and Louis Neptune makes his appearance,—a small, wiry man, with puckered and wrinkled face, yet he seemed the chief man of the two; the same, as I remembered, who had accompanied Jackson to the mountain in '37. The same questions were put to Louis, and the same information obtained, while the other Indian stood by. It appeared that they were going to start by noon, with two canoes, to go up to Chesuncook to hunt moose, —to be gone a month. "Well, Louis, suppose you get to the Point [to the Five Islands, just below Mattawamkeag], to camp, we walk on up the West Branch to-morrow, — four of us, — and wait for you at the dam, or this side. You overtake us to-morrow or next day, and take us into your canoes. We stop for you, you stop for us. We pay you for your trouble." "Ye!" replied Louis, "may be you carry some provision for all, — some pork, — some bread, — and so pay." He said, "Me sure get some moose;" and when I asked if he thought Pomola would let us go up, he answered that we must plant one bottle of rum on the top; he had planted good many; and when he looked again, the rum was all gone. He had been up two or three times: he had planted letter, — English, German, French, &c. These men were slightly clad in shirt and pantaloons, like laborers with us in warm weather. They did not invite us into their houses, but met us outside. So we left the Indians, thinking ourselves lucky to have secured such guides and companions.

There were very few houses along the road, yet they did not altogether fail, as if the law by which men are dispersed over the globe were a very stringent one, and not to be resisted with impunity or for slight reasons. There were even the germs of one or two villages just beginning to expand. The beauty of the road itself was remarkable. The various evergreens, many of which are rare with us, — delicate and beautiful specimens of the larch, arbor-vitæ, ball-spruce,

and fir-balsam, from a few inches to many feet
in height, — lined its sides, in some places like
a long, front yard, springing up from the smooth
grass-plots which uninterruptedly border it, and
are made fertile by its wash; while it was but
a step on either hand to the grim, untrodden
wilderness, whose tangled labyrinth of living,
fallen, and decaying trees only the deer and
moose, the bear and wolf, can easily penetrate.
More perfect specimens than any front-yard
plot can show, grew there to grace the passage
of the Houlton teams.

About noon we reached the Mattawamkeag,
fifty-six miles from Bangor by the way we had
come, and put up at a frequented house still on
the Houlton road, where the Houlton stage stops.
Here was a substantial covered bridge over the
Mattawamkeag, built, I think they said, some
seventeen years before. We had dinner, —
where, by the way, and even at breakfast, as well
as supper, at the public-houses on this road, the
front rank is composed of various kinds of "sweet
cakes," in a continuous line from one end of the
table to the other. I think I may safely say that
there was a row of ten or a dozen plates of this
kind set before us two here. To account for
which, they say that, when the lumberers come
out of the woods, they have a craving for cakes
and pies, and such sweet things, which there are
almost unknown, and this is the *supply* to satisfy

that *demand.* The supply is always equal to the demand, and these hungry men think a good deal of getting their money's worth. No doubt the balance of victuals is restored by the time they reach Bangor, — Mattawamkeag takes off the raw edge. Well, over this front rank, I say, you, coming from the "sweet cake" side, with a cheap philosophic indifference though it may be, have to assault what there is behind, which I do not by any means mean to insinuate is insufficient in quantity or quality to supply that other demand, of men, not from the woods, but from the towns, for venison and strong country fare. After dinner we strolled down to the "Point," formed by the junction of the two rivers, which is said to be the scene of an ancient battle between the Eastern Indians and the Mohawks, and searched there carefully for relics, though the men at the bar-room had never heard of such things; but we found only some flakes of arrow-head stone, some points of arrow-heads, one small leaden bullet, and some colored beads, the last to be referred, perhaps, to early fur-trader days. The Mattawamkeag, though wide, was a mere river's bed, full of rocks and shallows at this time, so that you could cross it almost dry-shod in boots; and I could hardly believe my companion, when he told me that he had been fifty or sixty miles up it in a batteau, through distant and still uncut forests. A batteau could hardly find a harbor now at its mouth. Deer and caribou, or reindeer, are taken here in the winter, in sight of the house.

Before our companions arrived, we rode on up the Houlton road seven miles, to Molunkus, where the Aroostook road comes into it, and where there is a spacious public house in the woods, called the "Molunkus House," kept by one Libbey, which looked as if it had its hall for dancing and for military drills. There was no other evidence of man but this huge shingle palace in this part of the world; but sometimes even this is filled with travellers. I looked off the piazza round the corner of the house up the Aroostook road, on which there was no clearing in sight. There was a man just adventuring upon it this evening in a rude, original, what you may call Aroostook wagon, — a mere seat, with a wagon swung under it, a few bags on it, and a dog asleep to watch them. He offered to carry a message for us to anybody in that country, cheerfully. I suspect that, if you should go to the end of the world, you would find somebody there going farther, as if just starting for home at sundown, and having a last word before he drove off. Here, too, *was* a small trader, whom I did not see at first, who kept a store — but no great store, certainly — in a small box over the way, behind the Molunkus sign-post. It looked like the balance-box of a patent hay-scales. As for his house, we could only conjecture where that was; he may have been a boarder in the Molunkus House. I saw him standing in his shop-door, — his shop was so small, that, if a traveller should make demonstrations of entering in, *he* would have to go out by the back way, and confer with his customer through a window, about his goods in the cellar, or, more probably, bespoken, and yet on the way. I should have gone in, for I felt a real impulse to trade, if I had not stopped to consider what would become of him. The day before, we had walked into a shop, over against an inn where we stopped, the puny beginning of trade, which would grow at last into a firm copartnership in the future town or city, — indeed, it was already "Somebody & Co.," I forget who. The woman came forward from the penetralia of the attached house, for "Somebody & Co." was in the burning, and she sold us percussion-caps, canalès and smooth, and knew their prices and qualities, and which the hunters preferred. Here was a little of everything in a small compass to satisfy the wants and the ambition of the woods, — a stock selected with what pains and care, and brought home in the wagon-box, or a corner of the Houlton team; but there seemed to me, as usual, a preponderance of children's toys, — dogs to bark, and cats to mew, and trumpets to blow, where natives there hardly are yet. As if a child, born into the

Maine woods, among the pine-cones and cedar-berries, could not do without such a sugar-man, or skipping-jack, as the young Rothschild has.

I think that there was not more than one house on the road to Molunkus, or for seven miles. At that place we got over the fence into a new field, planted with potatoes, where the logs were still burning between the hills; and, pulling up the vines, found good-sized potatoes, nearly ripe, growing like weeds, and turnips mixed with them. The mode of clearing and planting is, to fell the trees, and burn once what will burn, then cut them up into suitable lengths, roll into heaps, and burn again; then, with a hoe, plant potatoes where you can come at the ground between the stumps and charred logs; for a first crop the ashes sufficing for manure, and no hoeing being necessary the first year. In the fall, cut, roll, and burn again, and so on, till the land is cleared; and soon it is ready for grain, and to be laid down. Let those talk of poverty and hard times who will in the towns and cities; cannot the emigrant who can pay his fare to New York or Boston pay five dollars more to get here, — I paid three, all told, for my passage from Boston to Bangor, two hundred and fifty miles, — and be as rich as he pleases, where land virtually costs nothing, and houses only the labor of building, and he may begin life as Adam did? If he will still remember the distinction of poor and rich, let him bespeak him a narrower house forthwith.

When we returned to the Mattawamkeag, the Houlton stage had already put up there; and a Province man was betraying his greenness to the Yankees by his questions. Why Province money won't pass here at par, when States' money is good at Frederickton, — though this, perhaps, was sensible enough. From what I saw then, it appears that the Province man was now the only real Jonathan, or raw country bumpkin, left so far behind by his enterprising neighbors that he didn't know enough to put a question to them. No people can long continue provincial in character who have the propensity for politics and whittling, and rapid travelling, which the Yankees have, and who are leaving the mother country behind in the variety of their notions and inventions. The possession and exercise of practical talent merely are a sure and rapid means of intellectual culture and independence.

The last edition of Greenleaf's Map of Maine hung on the wall here, and, as we had no pocket-map, we resolved to trace a map of the lake country. So, dipping a wad of tow into the lamp, we oiled a sheet of paper on the oiled table-cloth, and, in good faith, traced what we afterwards ascertained to be a labyrinth of errors, carefully following the outlines of the imaginary

lakes which the map contains. The Map of the
Public Lands of Maine and Massachusetts is
the only one I have seen that at all deserves the
name. It was while we were engaged in this
operation that our companions arrived. They
had seen the Indians' fire on the Five Islands,
and so we concluded that all was right.

Early the next morning we had mounted our
packs, and prepared for a tramp up the West
Branch, my companion having turned his horse
out to pasture for a week or ten days, thinking
that a bite of fresh grass, and a taste of running
water, would do him as much good as backwoods
fare and new country influences his master.
Leaping over a fence, we began to follow an
obscure trail up the northern bank of the Penobscot. There was now no road further, the river
being the only highway, and but half a dozen
log-huts confined to its banks, to be met with
for thirty miles. On either hand, and beyond,
was a wholly uninhabited wilderness, stretching to Canada. Neither horse nor cow, nor
vehicle of any kind, had ever passed over this
ground; the cattle, and the few bulky articles
which the loggers use, being got up in the winter
on the ice, and down again before it breaks up.
The evergreen woods had a decidedly sweet and
bracing fragrance; the air was a sort of diet-
drink, and we walked on buoyantly in Indian
file, stretching our legs. Occasionally there was

a small opening on the bank, made for the purpose of log-rolling, where we got a sight of the
river, — always a rocky and rippling stream.
The roar of the rapids, the note of a whistler-
duck on the river, of the jay and chickadee
around us, and of the pigeon-woodpecker in the
openings, were the sounds that we heard. This
was what you might call a bran-new country;
the only roads were of Nature's making, and
the few houses were camps. Here, then, one
could no longer accuse institutions and society,
but must front the true source of evil.

There are three classes of inhabitants who
either frequent or inhabit the country which we
had now entered; — first, the loggers, who, for a
part of the year, the winter and spring, are far the
most numerous, but in the summer, except a few
explorers for timber, completely desert it; second,
the few settlers I have named, the only permanent
inhabitants, who live on the verge of it, and help
raise supplies for the former; third, the hunters,
mostly Indians, who range over it in their season.

At the end of three miles, we came to the Matta-
seunk stream and mill, where there was even a
rude wooden railroad running down to the Penobscot, the last railroad we were to see. We
crossed one tract, on the bank of the river, of
more than a hundred acres of heavy timber,
which had just been felled and burnt over, and
was still smoking. Our trail lay through the

midst of it, and was wellnigh blotted out. The
trees lay at full length, four or five feet deep, and
crossing each other in all directions, all black as
charcoal, but perfectly sound within, still good
for fuel or for timber; soon they would be cut
into lengths and burnt again. Here were thousands of cords, enough to keep the poor of Boston
and New York amply warm for a winter, which
only cumbered the ground and were in the settler's way. And the whole of that solid and interminable forest is doomed to be gradually
devoured thus by fire, like shavings, and no man
be warmed by it. At Crocker's log-hut, at the
mouth of Salmon River, seven miles from the
Point, one of the party commenced distributing
a store of small cent picture-books among the
children, to teach them to read, and also news-
papers, more or less recent, among the parents,
than which nothing can be more acceptable to a
backwoods people. It was really an important
item in our outfit, and, at times, the only cur-
rency that would circulate. I walked through
Salmon River with my shoes on, it being low
water, but not without wetting my feet. A few
miles farther we came to "Marm Howard's,"
at the end of an extensive clearing, where there
were two or three log-huts in sight at once, one
on the opposite side of the river, and a few graves,
even surrounded by a wooden paling, where
already the rude forefathers of *a* hamlet lie, and

a thousand years hence, perchance, some poet will write his "Elegy in a Country Churchyard." The "Village Hampdens," the "mute, inglorious Miltons," and Cromwells, "guiltless of" their "country's blood," were yet unborn.

"Perchance in this *wild* spot *there will be* laid
  Some heart once pregnant with celestial fire;
 Hands that the rod of empire might have swayed,
  Or waked to ecstasy the living lyre."

The next house was Fisk's, ten miles from the Point, at the mouth of the East Branch, opposite to the island Nickatow, or the Forks, the last of the Indian islands. I am particular to give the names of the settlers and the distances, since every log-hut in these woods is a public house, and such information is of no little consequence to those who may have occasion to travel this way. Our course here crossed the Penobscot, and followed the southern bank. One of the party, who entered the house in search of some one to set us over, reported a very neat dwelling, with plenty of books, and a new wife, just imported from Boston, wholly new to the woods. We found the East Branch a large and rapid stream at its mouth, and much deeper than it appeared. Having with some difficulty discovered the trail again, we kept up the south side of the West Branch, or main river, passing by some rapids called Rock-Ebeeme, the roar of which we heard through the woods, and, shortly after, in the thickest of the wood, some empty loggers' camps, still new, which were occupied the previous winter. Though we saw a few more afterwards, I will make one account serve for all. These were such houses as the lumberers of Maine spend the winter in, in the wilderness. There were the camps and the hovels for the cattle, hardly distinguishable, except that the latter had no chimney. These camps were about twenty feet long by fifteen wide, built of logs, — hemlock, cedar, spruce, or yellow birch, — one kind alone, or all together, with the bark on; two or three large ones first, one directly above another, and notched together at the ends, to the height of three or four feet, then of smaller logs resting upon transverse ones at the ends, each of the last successively shorter than the other, to form the roof. The chimney was an oblong square hole in the middle, three or four feet in diameter, with a fence of logs as high as the ridge. The interstices were filled with moss, and the roof was shingled with long and handsome splints of cedar, or spruce, or pine, rifted with a sledge and cleaver. The fire-place, the most important place of all, was in shape and size like the chimney, and directly under it, defined by a log fence or fender on the ground, and a heap of ashes, a foot or two deep, within, with solid benches of split logs running round it. Here the fire usually melts the snow, and dries

the rain before it can descend to quench it. The
faded beds of arbor-vitæ leaves extended under
the eaves on either hand. There was the place
for the water-pail, pork-barrel, and wash-basin,
and generally a dingy pack of cards left on a log.
Usually a good deal of whittling was expended
on the latch, which was made of wood, in the
form of an iron one. These houses are made
comfortable by the huge fires, which can be
afforded night and day. Usually the scenery
about them is drear and savage enough; and
the loggers' camp is as completely in the woods
as a fungus at the foot of a pine in a swamp; no
outlook but to the sky overhead; no more clearing than is made by cutting down the trees of
which it is built, and those which are necessary
for fuel. If only it be well sheltered and convenient to his work, and near a spring, he wastes
no thought on the prospect. They are very
proper forest houses, the stems of the trees collected together and piled up around a man to
keep out wind and rain, — made of living green
logs, hanging with moss and lichen, and with the
curls and fringes of the yellow-birch bark, and
dripping with resin, fresh and moist, and redo-
lent of swampy odors, with that sort of vigor
and perennialness even about them that toad-
stools suggest.[1] The logger's fare consists of tea,

[1] Springer, in his "Forest Life" (1851), says that they first re-
move the leaves and turf from the spot where they intend to build

molasses, flour, pork (sometimes beef), and
beans. A great proportion of the beans raised
in Massachusetts find their market here. On
expeditions it is only hard bread and pork, often
raw, slice upon slice, with tea or water, as the
case may be.

The primitive wood is always and everywhere
damp and mossy, so that I travelled constantly
with the impression that I was in a swamp; and
only when it was remarked that this or that tract,
judging from the quality of the timber on it,
would make a profitable clearing, was I reminded, that if the sun were let in it would make
a dry field, like the few I had seen, at once. The
best shod for the most part travel with wet feet.
If the ground was so wet and spongy at this, the
dryest part of a dry season, what must it be in
the spring? The woods hereabouts abounded
in beech and yellow birch, of which last there
were some very large specimens; also spruce,
cedar, fir, and hemlock; but we saw only the
stumps of the white pine here, some of them of

a camp, for fear of fire; also, that "the spruce-tree is generally
selected for camp-building, it being light, straight, and quite free
from sap;" that "the roof is finally covered with the boughs of
the fir, spruce, and hemlock, so that when the snow falls upon
the whole, the warmth of the camp is preserved in the coldest
weather;" and that they make the log seat before the fire, called
the "Deacon's Seat," of a spruce or fir split in halves, with three
or four stout limbs left on one side for legs, which are not likely
to get loose.

great size, these having been already culled out, being the only tree much sought after, even as low down as this. Only a little spruce and hemlock beside had been logged here. The Eastern wood which is sold for fuel in Massachusetts all comes from below Bangor. It was the pine alone, chiefly the white pine, that had tempted any but the hunter to precede us on this route.

Waite's farm, thirteen miles from the Point, is an extensive and elevated clearing, from which we got a fine view of the river, rippling and gleaming far beneath us. My companions had formerly had a good view of Ktaadn and the other mountains here, but to-day it was so smoky that we could see nothing of them. We could overlook an immense country of uninterrupted forest, stretching away up the East Branch toward Canada, on the north and northwest, and toward the Aroostook valley on the northeast; and imagine what wild life was stirring in its midst. Here was quite a field of corn for this region, whose peculiar dry scent we perceived a third of a mile off, before we saw it.

Eighteen miles from the Point brought us in sight of McCauslin's, or "Uncle George's," as he was familiarly called by my companions, to whom he was well known, where we intended to break our long fast. His house was in the midst of an extensive clearing of intervale, at the mouth of the Little Schoodic River, on the opposite or north bank of the Penobscot. So we collected on a point of the shore, that we might be seen, and fired our gun as a signal, which brought out his dogs forthwith, and thereafter their master, who in due time took us across in his batteau. This clearing was bounded abruptly, on all sides but the river, by the naked stems of the forest, as if you were to cut only a few feet square in the midst of a thousand acres of mowing, and set down a thimble therein. He had a whole heaven and horizon to himself, and the sun seemed to be journeying over his clearing only the livelong day. Here we concluded to spend the night, and wait for the Indians, as there was no stopping-place so convenient above. He had seen no Indians pass, and this did not often happen without his knowledge. He thought that his dogs sometimes gave notice of the approach of Indians half an hour before they arrived.

McCauslin was a Kennebec man, of Scotch descent, who had been a waterman twenty-two years, and had driven on the lakes and headwaters of the Penobscot five or six springs in succession, but was now settled here to raise supplies for the lumberers and for himself. He entertained us a day or two with true Scotch hospitality, and would accept no recompense for it. A man of a dry wit and shrewdness, and a general intelligence which I had not looked for

in the backwoods. In fact, the deeper you penetrate into the woods, the more intelligent, and,
in one sense, less countrified do you find the
inhabitants; for always the pioneer has been a
traveller, and, to some extent, a man of the
world; and, as the distances with which he is
familiar are greater, so is his information more
general and far reaching than the villagers'. If
I were to look for a narrow, uninformed, and
countrified mind, as opposed to the intelligence
and refinement which are thought to emanate
from cities, it would be among the rusty inhabitants of an old-settled country, on farms all run
out and gone to seed with life-everlasting, in the
towns about Boston, even on the high-road in
Concord, and not in the backwoods of Maine.

Supper was got before our eyes in the ample
kitchen, by a fire which would have roasted an
ox; many whole logs, four feet long, were consumed to boil our tea-kettle, — birch, or beech,
or maple, the same summer and winter; and the
dishes were soon smoking on the table, late the
arm-chair, against the wall, from which one of
the party was expelled. The arms of the chair
formed the frame on which the table rested;
and, when the round top was turned up against
the wall, it formed the back of the chair, and was
no more in the way than the wall itself. This,
we noticed, was the prevailing fashion in these
log-houses, in order to economize in room. There

were piping-hot wheaten cakes, the flour having been brought up the river in batteaux, — no Indian bread, for the upper part of Maine, it will be remembered, is a wheat country, — and ham, eggs, and potatoes, and milk and cheese, the produce of the farm; and also shad and salmon, tea sweetened with molasses, and sweet cakes, in contradistinction to the hot cakes not sweetened, the one white, the other yellow, to wind up with. Such we found was the prevailing fare, ordinary and extraordinary, along this river. Mountain cranberries (*Vaccinium Vitis-Idæa*), stewed and sweetened, were the common dessert. Everything here was in profusion, and the best of its kind. Butter was in such plenty that it was commonly used, before it was salted, to grease boots with.

In the night we were entertained by the sound of rain-drops on the cedar-splints which covered the roof, and awaked the next morning with a drop or two in our eyes. It had set in for a storm, and we made up our minds not to forsake such comfortable quarters with this prospect, but wait for Indians and fair weather. It rained and drizzled and gleamed by turns, the livelong day. What we did there, how we killed the time, would perhaps be idle to tell; how many times we buttered our boots, and how often a drowsy one was seen to sidle off to the bedroom. When it held up, I strolled up and down the bank, and gathered the harebell and cedar-berries, which grew there; or else we tried by turns the long-handled axe on the logs before the door. The axe-helves here were made to chop standing on the log, — a primitive log of course, — and were, therefore, nearly a foot longer than with us. One while we walked over the farm and visited his well-filled barns with McCauslin. There were one other man and two women only here. He kept horses, cows, oxen, and sheep. I think he said that he was the first to bring a plough and a cow so far; and he might have added the last, with only two exceptions. The potato-rot had found him out here, too, the previous year, and got half or two thirds of his crop, though the seed was of his own raising. Oats, grass, and potatoes were his staples; but he raised, also, a few carrots and turnips, and "a little corn for the hens," for this was all that he dared risk, for fear that it would not ripen. Melons, squashes, sweet-corn, beans, tomatoes, and many other vegetables, could not be ripened there.

The very few settlers along this stream were obviously tempted by the cheapness of the land mainly. When I asked McCauslin why more settlers did not come in, he answered, that one reason was, they could not buy the land, it belonged to individuals or companies who were afraid that their wild lands would be settled,

and so incorporated into towns, and they be
taxed for them; but to settling on the States'
land there was no such hindrance. For his own
part, he wanted no neighbors, — he did n't wish
to see any road by his house. Neighbors, even
the best, were a trouble and expense, especially
on the score of cattle and fences. They might
live across the river, perhaps, but not on the
same side.

The chickens here were protected by the dogs.
As McCauslin said, "The old one took it up
first, and she taught the pup, and now they had
got it into their heads that it would n't do to
have anything of the bird kind on the premises."
A hawk hovering over was not allowed to alight,
but barked off by the dogs circling underneath;
and a pigeon, or a "yellow-hammer," as they
called the pigeon-woodpecker, on a dead limb
or stump, was instantly expelled. It was the
main business of their day, and kept them constantly coming and going. One would rush out
of the house on the least alarm given by the other.

When it rained hardest, we returned to the
house, and took down a tract from the shelf.
There was the Wandering Jew, cheap edition
and fine print, the Criminal Calendar, and Par-
ish's Geography, and flash novels two or three.
Under the pressure of circumstances, we read a
little in these. With such aid, the press is not so
feeble an engine, after all. This house, which

was a fair specimen of those on this river, was
built of huge logs, which peeped out everywhere,
and were chinked with clay and moss. It contained four or five rooms. There were no sawed
boards, or shingles, or clapboards about it; and
scarcely any tool but the axe had been used in
its construction. The partitions were made of
long clapboard-like splints, of spruce or cedar,
turned to a delicate salmon color by the smoke.
The roof and sides were covered with the same,
instead of shingles and clapboards, and some of
a much thicker and larger size were used for the
floor. These were all so straight and smooth,
that they answered the purpose admirably; and
a careless observer would not have suspected
that they were not sawed and planed. The
chimney and hearth were of vast size, and made
of stone. The broom was a few twigs of arbor-
vitæ tied to a stick; and a pole was suspended
over the hearth, close to the ceilings, to dry stockings and clothes on. I noticed that the floor
was full of small, dingy holes, as if made with a
gimlet, but which were, in fact, made by the
spikes, nearly an inch long, which the lumberers
wear in their boots to prevent their slipping on
wet logs. Just above McCauslin's, there is a
rocky rapid, where logs jam in the spring; and
many "drivers" are there collected, who frequent his house for supplies; these were their
tracks which I saw.

At sundown McCauslin pointed away over the forest, across the river, to signs of fair weather amid the clouds, — some evening redness there. For even there the points of compass held; and there was a quarter of the heavens appropriated to sunrise and another to sunset.

The next morning, the weather proving fair enough for our purpose, we prepared to start, and, the Indians having failed us, persuaded McCauslin, who was not unwilling to revisit the scenes of his driving, to accompany us in their stead, intending to engage one other boatman on the way. A strip of cotton cloth for a tent, a couple of blankets, which would suffice for the whole party, fifteen pounds of hard bread, ten pounds of "clear" pork, and a little tea, made up "Uncle George's" pack. The last three articles were calculated to be provision enough for six men for a week, with what we might pick up. A tea-kettle, a frying-pan, and an axe, to be obtained at the last house, would complete our outfit.

We were soon out of McCauslin's clearing, and in the ever green woods again. The obscure trail made by the two settlers above, which even the woodman is sometimes puzzled to discern, erelong crossed a narrow, open strip in the woods overrun with weeds, called the Burnt Land, where a fire had raged formerly, stretching north-ward nine or ten miles, to Millinocket Lake. At the end of three miles, we reached Shad Pond, or Noliseemack, an expansion of the river. Hodge, the Assistant State Geologist, who passed through this on the 25th of June, 1837, says, "We pushed our boat through an acre or more of buck-beans, which had taken root at the bottom, and bloomed above the surface in the greatest profusion and beauty." Thomas Fowler's house is four miles from McCauslin's, on the shore of the pond, at the mouth of the Millinocket River, and eight miles from the lake of the same name, on the latter stream. This lake affords a more direct course to Ktaadn, but we preferred to follow the Penobscot and the Pamadumcook lakes. Fowler was just completing a new log-hut, and was sawing out a window through the logs, nearly two feet thick, when we arrived. He had begun to paper his house with spruce-bark, turned inside out, which had a good effect, and was in keeping with the circumstances. Instead of water we got here a draught of beer, which, it was allowed, would be better; clear and thin, but strong and stringent as the cedar-sap. It was as if we sucked at the very teats of Nature's pine-clad bosom in these parts, — the sap of all Millinocket botany commingled, — the topmost, most fantastic, and spiciest sprays of the primitive wood, and whatever invigorating and stringent gum or essence it afforded steeped and dissolved in it, — a lum-

berer's drink, which would acclimate and natu-
ralize a man at once, — which would make him
see green, and, if he slept, dream that he heard
the wind sough among the pines. Here was a
fife, praying to be played on, through which we
breathed a few tuneful strains, — brought hither
to tame wild beasts. As we stood upon the pile
of chips by the door, fish-hawks were sailing
overhead; and here, over Shad Pond, might
daily be witnessed the tyranny of the bald-eagle
over that bird. Tom pointed away over the
lake to a bald-eagle's nest, which was plainly
visible more than a mile off, on a pine, high above
the surrounding forest, and was frequented from
year to year by the same pair, and held sacred
by him. There were these two houses only there,
his low hut and the eagles' airy cart-load of
fagots. Thomas Fowler, too, was persuaded to
join us, for two men were necessary to manage
the batteau, which was soon to be our carriage,
and these men needed to be cool and skilful for
the navigation of the Penobscot. Tom's pack
was soon made, for he had not far to look for
his waterman's boots, and a red-flannel shirt.
This is the favorite color with lumbermen; and
red flannel is reputed to possess some mysterious
virtues, to be most healthful and convenient in
respect to perspiration. In every gang there will
be a large proportion of red birds. We took here
a poor and leaky batteau, and began to pole up

the Millinocket two miles, to the elder Fowler's, in order to avoid the Grand Falls of the Penobscot, intending to exchange our batteau there for a better. The Millinocket is a small, shallow, and sandy stream, full of what I took to be lamprey-eels' or suckers' nests, and lined with musquash cabins, but free from rapids, according to Fowler, excepting at its outlet from the lake. He was at this time engaged in cutting the native grass, — rush-grass and meadow-clover, as he called it, — on the meadows and small, low islands of this stream. We noticed flattened places in the grass on either side, where, he said, a moose had lain down the night before, adding, that there were thousands in these meadows.

Old Fowler's, on the Millinocket, six miles from McCauslin's, and twenty-four from the Point, is the last house. Gibson's, on the Sowadnehunk, is the only clearing above, but that had proved a failure, and was long since deserted. Fowler is the oldest inhabitant of these woods. He formerly lived a few miles from here, on the south side of the West Branch, where he built his house sixteen years ago, the first house built above the Five Islands. Here our new batteau was to be carried over the first portage of two miles, round the Grand Falls of the Penobscot, on a horse-sled made of saplings, to jump the numerous rocks in the way; but we had to wait a couple of hours for them to catch the horses, which were pastured at a distance, amid the stumps, and had wandered still farther off. The last of the salmon for this season had just been caught, and were still fresh in pickle, from which enough was extracted to fill our empty kettle, and so graduate our introduction to simpler forest fare. The week before they had lost nine sheep here out of their first flock, by the wolves. The surviving sheep came round the house, and seemed frightened, which induced them to go and look for the rest, when they found seven dead and lacerated, and two still alive. These last they carried to the house, and, as Mrs. Fowler said, they were merely scratched in the throat, and had no more visible wound than would be produced by the prick of a pin. She sheared off the wool from their throats, and washed them, and put on some salve, and turned them out, but in a few moments they were missing, and had not been found since. In fact, they were all poisoned, and those that were found swelled up at once, so that they saved neither skin nor wool. This realized the old fables of the wolves and the sheep, and convinced me that that ancient hostility still existed. Verily, the shepherd-boy did not need to sound a false alarm this time. There were steel traps by the door, of various sizes, for wolves, otter, and bears, with large claws instead of teeth, to catch in their sinews. Wolves are frequently killed with poisoned bait.

At length, after we had dined here on the usual backwoods fare, the horses arrived, and we hauled our batteau out of the water, and lashed it to its wicker carriage, and, throwing in our packs, walked on before, leaving the boat-men and driver, who was Tom's brother, to manage the concern. The route, which led through the wild pasture where the sheep were killed, was in some places the roughest ever travelled by horses, over rocky hills, where the sled bounced and slid along, like a vessel pitch-ing in a storm; and one man was as necessary to stand at the stern, to prevent the boat from being wrecked, as a helmsman in the roughest sea. The philosophy of our progress was some-thing like this: when the runners struck a rock three or four feet high, the sled bounced back and upwards at the same time; but, as the horses never ceased pulling, it came down on the top of the rock, and so we got over. This portage probably followed the trail of an ancient Indian carry round these falls. By two o'clock we, who had walked on before, reached the river above the falls, not far from the outlet of Quakish Lake, and waited for the batteau to come up. We had been here but a short time, when a thunder-shower was seen coming up from the west, over the still invisible lakes, and that pleasant wilder-

ness which we were so eager to become acquainted with; and soon the heavy drops began
to patter on the leaves around us. I had just
selected the prostrate trunk of a huge pine, five
or six feet in diameter, and was crawling under
it, when, luckily, the boat arrived. It would have
amused a sheltered man to witness the manner in
which it was unlashed, and whirled over, while
the first water-spout burst upon us. It was no
sooner in the hands of the eager company than it
was abandoned to the first revolutionary impulse,
and to gravity, to adjust it; and they might have
been seen all stooping to its shelter, and wriggling
under like so many eels, before it was fairly deposited on the ground. When all were under, we
propped up the lee side, and busied ourselves
there whittling tholepins for rowing, when we
should reach the lakes; and made the woods
ring, between the claps of thunder, with such
boat-songs as we could remember. The horses
stood sleek and shining with the rain, all drooping and crestfallen, while deluge after deluge
washed over us; but the bottom of a boat may
be relied on for a tight roof. At length, after
two hours' delay at this place, a streak of fair
weather appeared in the northwest, whither our
course now lay, promising a serene evening for
our voyage; and the driver returned with his
horses, while we made haste to launch our boat,
and commence our voyage in good earnest.

There were six of us, including the two boatmen. With our packs heaped up near the bows,
and ourselves disposed as baggage to trim the
boat, with instructions not to move in case we
should strike a rock, more than so many barrels
of pork, we pushed out into the first rapid, a
slight specimen of the stream we had to navigate. With Uncle George in the stern, and Tom
in the bows, each using a spruce pole about
twelve feet long, pointed with iron,[1] and poling
on the same side, we shot up the rapids like a
salmon, the water rushing and roaring around, so
that only a practised eye could distinguish a safe
course, or tell what was deep water and what
rocks, frequently grazing the latter on one or
both sides, with a hundred as narrow escapes as
ever the Argo had in passing through the Symple-
gades. I, who had had some experience in boating, had never experienced any half so exhilarating before. We were lucky to have exchanged
our Indians, whom we did not know, for these
men, who, together with Tom's brother, were
reputed the best boatmen on the river, and were
at once indispensable pilots and pleasant companions. The canoe is smaller, more easily upset, and sooner worn out; and the Indian is
said not to be so skilful in the management of
the batteau. He is, for the most part, less to be
relied on, and more disposed to sulks and whims.

[1] The Canadians call it *picquer de fond*.

The utmost familiarity with dead streams, or with the ocean, would not prepare a man for this peculiar navigation; and the most skilful boatman anywhere else would here be obliged to take out his boat and carry round a hundred times, still with great risk, as well as delay, where the practised batteau-man poles up with comparative ease and safety. The hardy "voyageur" pushes with incredible perseverance and success quite up to the foot of the falls, and then only carries round some perpendicular ledge, and launches again in

"The torrent's smoothness, ere it dash below,"

to struggle with the boiling rapids above. The Indians say that the river once ran both ways, one half up and the other down, but that, since the white man came, it all runs down, and now they must laboriously pole their canoes against the stream, and carry them over numerous portages. In the summer, all stores — the grindstone and the plough of the pioneer, flour, pork, and utensils for the explorer — must be conveyed up the river in batteaux; and many a cargo and many a boatman is lost in these waters. In the winter, however, which is very equable and long, the ice is the great highway, and the loggers' team penetrates to Chesuncook Lake, and still higher up, even two hundred miles above Bangor. Imagine the solitary sled-

track running far up into the snowy and ever
green wilderness, hemmed in closely for a hundred miles by the forest, and again stretching
straight across the broad surfaces of concealed
lakes!

We were soon in the smooth water of the
Quakish Lake, and took our turns at rowing
and paddling across it. It is a small, irregular,
but handsome lake, shut in on all sides by the
forest, and showing no traces of man but some
low boom in a distant cove, reserved for spring
use. The spruce and cedar on its shores, hung
with gray lichens, looked at a distance like the
ghosts of trees. Ducks were sailing here and
there on its surface, and a solitary loon, like a
more living wave, — a vital spot on the lake's
surface, — laughed and frolicked, and showed
its straight leg, for our amusement. Joe Merry
Mountain appeared in the northwest, as if it
were looking down on this lake especially; and
we had our first, but a partial view of Ktaadn,
its summit veiled in clouds, like a dark isthmus
in that quarter, connecting the heavens with the
earth. After two miles of smooth rowing across
this lake, we found ourselves in the river again,
which was a continuous rapid for one mile, to
the dam, requiring all the strength and skill of
our boatmen to pole up it.

This dam is a quite important and expensive
work for this country, whither cattle and horses

cannot penetrate in the summer, raising the whole river ten feet, and flooding, as they said, some sixty square miles by means of the innumerable lakes with which the river connects. It is a lofty and solid structure, with sloping piers some distance above, made of frames of logs filled with stones, to break the ice.[1] Here every log pays toll as it passes through the sluices.

We filed into the rude logger's camp at this place, such as I have described, without ceremony, and the cook, at that moment the sole occupant, at once set about preparing tea for his visitors. His fireplace, which the rain had converted into a mud-puddle, was soon blazing again, and we sat down on the log benches around it to dry us. On the well-flattened and somewhat faded beds of arbor-vitæ leaves, which stretched on either hand under the eaves behind us, lay an odd leaf of the Bible, some genealogical chapter out of the Old Testament; and, half buried by the leaves, we found Emerson's Address on West India Emancipation, which had been left here formerly by one of our company, and *had made two converts to the Liberty party here*, as I was told; also, an odd number of the Westminster Review, for 1834, and a pamphlet

---

[1] Even the Jesuit missionaries, accustomed to the St. Lawrence and other rivers of Canada, in their first expeditions to the Abenaquinois, speak of rivers *ferrées de rochers*, shod with rocks. See also No. 10 Relations, for 1647, p. 185.

entitled History of the Erection of the Monument on the grave of Myron Holly. This was the readable, or reading matter, in a lumberer's camp in the Maine woods, thirty miles from a road, which would be given up to the bears in a fortnight. These things were well thumbed and soiled. This gang was headed by one John Morrison, a good specimen of a Yankee; and was necessarily composed of men not bred to the business of dam-building, but who were Jacks-at-all-trades, handy with the axe, and other simple implements, and well skilled in wood and water craft. We had hot cakes for our supper even here, white as snowballs, but without butter, and the never-failing sweet cakes, with which we filled our pockets, foreseeing that we should not soon meet with the like again. Such delicate puff-balls seemed a singular diet for backwoodsmen. There was also tea without milk, sweetened with molasses. And so, exchanging a word with John Morrison and his gang when we had returned to the shore, and also exchanging our batteau for a better still, we made haste to improve the little daylight that remained. This camp, exactly twenty-nine miles from Mattawamkeag Point, by the way we had come, and about one hundred from Bangor by the river, was the last human habitation of any kind in this direction. Beyond, there was no trail; and the river and lakes, by batteaux and

canoes, was considered the only practicable
route. We were about thirty miles by the river
from the summit of Ktaadn, which was in sight,
though not more than twenty, perhaps, in a
straight line.

It being about the full of the moon, and a
warm and pleasant evening, we decided to row
five miles by moonlight to the head of the North
Twin Lake, lest the wind should rise on the
morrow. After one mile of river, or what the
boatmen call "thoroughfare," — for the river
becomes at length only the connecting link between the lakes, — and some slight rapid which
had been mostly made smooth water by the
dam, we entered the North Twin Lake just
after sundown, and steered across for the river
"thoroughfare," four miles distant. This is a
noble sheet of water, where one may get the impression which a new country and a "lake of
the woods" are fitted to create. There was the
smoke of no log-hut nor camp of any kind to
greet us, still less was any lover of nature or
musing traveller watching our batteau from the
distant hills; not even the Indian hunter was
there, for he rarely climbs them, but hugs the
river like ourselves. No face welcomed us but
the fine fantastic sprays of free and happy evergreen trees, waving one above another in their
ancient home. At first the red clouds hung over
the western shore as gorgeously as if over a city,

and the lake lay open to the light with even a
civilized aspect, as if expecting trade and commerce, and towns and villas. We could distinguish the inlet to the South Twin, which is said
to be the larger, where the shore was misty and
blue, and it was worth the while to look thus
through a narrow opening across the entire expanse of a concealed lake to its own yet more
dim and distant shore. The shores rose gently
to ranges of low hills covered with forests; and
though, in fact, the most valuable white pine
timber, even about this lake, had been culled
out, this would never have been suspected by
the voyager. The impression, which indeed cor-
responded with the fact, was, as if we were upon
a high table-land between the States and Canada,
the northern side of which is drained by the St.
John and Chaudiere, the southern by the Penobscot and Kennebec. There was no bold
mountainous shore, as we might have expected,
but only isolated hills and mountains rising here
and there from the plateau. The country is an
archipelago of lakes, — the lake-country of New
England. Their levels vary but a few feet, and
the boatmen, by short portages, or by none at
all, pass easily from one to another. They say
that at very high water the Penobscot and the
Kennebec flow into each other, or, at any rate,
that you may lie with your face in the one and
your toes in the other. Even the Penobscot and

St. John have been connected by a canal, so that
the lumber of the Allegash, instead of going
down the St. John, comes down the Penobscot;
and the Indian's tradition, that the Penobscot
once ran both ways for his convenience, is, in
one sense, partially realized to-day.

None of our party but McCauslin had been
above this lake, so we trusted to him to pilot us,
and we could not but confess the importance of
a pilot on these waters. While it is river, you
will not easily forget which way is up stream;
but when you enter a lake, the river is completely
lost, and you scan the distant shores in vain to
find where it comes in. A stranger is, for the
time at least, lost, and must set about a voyage
of discovery first of all to find the river. To
follow the windings of the shore when the lake
is ten miles, or even more, in length, and of an
irregularity which will not soon be mapped, is a
wearisome voyage, and will spend his time and
his provisions. They tell a story of a gang of
experienced woodmen sent to a location on this
stream, who were thus lost in the wilderness of
lakes. They cut their way through thickets,
and carried their baggage and their boats over
from lake to lake, sometimes several miles.
They carried into Millinocket Lake, which is
on another stream, and is ten miles square, and
contains a hundred islands. They explored its
shores thoroughly, and then carried into another,

and another, and it was a week of toil and anxiety before they found the Penobscot River again, and then their provisions were exhausted, and they were obliged to return.

While Uncle George steered for a small island near the head of the lake, now just visible, like a speck on the water, we rowed by turns swiftly over its surface, singing such boat-songs as we could remember. The shores seemed at an indefinite distance in the moonlight. Occasionally we paused in our singing and rested on our oars, while we listened to hear if the wolves howled, for this is a common serenade, and my companions affirmed that it was the most dismal and unearthly of sounds; but we heard none this time. If we did not *hear*, however, we did *listen*, not without a reasonable expectation; that at least I have to tell, — only some utterly uncivilized, big-throated owl hooted loud and dismally in the drear and boughy wilderness, plainly not nervous about his solitary life, nor afraid to hear the echoes of his voice there. We remembered also that possibly moose were silently watching us from the distant coves, or some surly bear or timid caribou had been startled by our singing. It was with new emphasis that we sang there the Canadian boat-song, —

> "Row, brothers, row, the stream runs fast,
> The Rapids are near and the daylight 's past!" —

which describes precisely our own adventure, and was inspired by the experience of a similar kind of life, — for the rapids were ever near, and the daylight long past; the woods on shore looked dim, and many an Utawas' tide here emptied into the lake.

> "Why should we yet our sail unfurl?
> There is not a breath the blue wave to curl!
> But, when the wind blows off the shore,
> O sweetly we'll rest our weary oar."

> "Utawas' tide! this trembling moon,
> Shall see us float o'er thy surges soon."

At last we glided past the "green isle" which had been our landmark, all joining in the chorus; as if by the watery links of rivers and of lakes we were about to float over unmeasured zones of earth, bound on unimaginable adventures, —

> "Saint of this green isle! hear our prayers,
> O grant us cool heavens and favoring airs!"

About nine o'clock we reached the river, and ran our boat into a natural haven between some rocks, and drew her out on the sand. This camping-ground McCauslin had been familiar with in his lumbering days, and he now struck it unerringly in the moonlight, and we heard the sound of the rill which would supply us with cool water emptying into the lake. The first business was to make a fire, an operation which was a little delayed by the wetness of the fuel and the ground, owing to the heavy showers of the afternoon. The fire is the main comfort of the camp, whether in summer or winter, and is about as ample at one season as at another. It is as well for cheerfulness as for warmth and dryness. It forms one side of the camp; one bright side at any rate. Some were dispersed to fetch in dead trees and boughs, while Uncle George felled the birches and beeches which stood convenient, and soon we had a fire some ten feet long by three or four high, which rapidly dried the sand before it. This was calculated to burn all night. We next proceeded to pitch our tent; which operation was performed by sticking our two spike-poles into the ground in a slanting direction, about ten feet apart, for rafters, and then drawing our cotton cloth over them, and tying it down at the ends, leaving it open in front, shed-fashion. But this evening the wind carried the sparks on to the tent and burned it. So we hastily drew up the batteau just within the edge of the woods before the fire, and propping up one side three or four feet high, spread the tent on the ground to lie on; and with the corner of a blanket, or what more or less we could get to put over us, lay down with our heads and bodies under the boat, and our feet and legs on the sand toward the fire. At first we lay awake, talking of our course, and finding ourselves in so convenient a posture for studying the heavens, with

the moon and stars shining in our faces, our conversation naturally turned upon astronomy, and
we recounted by turns the most interesting dis-
coveries in that science. But at length we
composed ourselves seriously to sleep. It was
interesting, when awakened at midnight, to watch
the grotesque and field-like forms and motions
of some one of the party, who, not being able to
sleep, had got up silently to arouse the fire, and
add fresh fuel, for a change; now stealthily
lugging a dead tree from out the dark, and heaving it on, now stirring up the embers with his
fork, or tiptoeing about to observe the stars,
watched, perchance, by half the prostrate party
in breathless silence; so much the more intense
because they were awake, while each supposed
his neighbor sound asleep. Thus aroused, I too
brought fresh fuel to the fire, and then rambled
along the sandy shore in the moonlight, hoping
to meet a moose, come down to drink, or else a
wolf. The little rill tinkled the louder, and
peopled all the wilderness for me; and the glassy
smoothness of the sleeping lake, laving the shores
of a new world, with the dark, fantastic rocks
rising here and there from its surface, made a
scene not easily described. It has left such an
impression of stern, yet gentle, wildness on my
memory as will not soon be effaced. Not far
from midnight we were one after another awakened by rain falling on our extremities; and as

each was made aware of the fact by cold or wet,
he drew a long sigh and then drew up his legs,
until gradually we had all sidled round from
lying at right angles with the boat, till our bodies
formed an acute angle with it, and were wholly
protected. When next we awoke, the moon and
stars were shining again, and there were signs
of dawn in the east. I have been thus particular
in order to convey some idea of a night in the
woods.

We had soon launched and loaded our boat,
and, leaving our fire blazing, were off again
before breakfast. The lumberers rarely trouble
themselves to put out their fires, such is the
dampness of the primitive forest; and this is
one cause, no doubt, of the frequent fires in
Maine, of which we hear so much on smoky
days in Massachusetts. The forests are held
cheap after the white pine has been culled out;
and the explorers and hunters pray for rain only
to clear the atmosphere of smoke. The woods
were so wet to-day, however, that there was no
danger of our fire spreading. After poling up
half a mile of river, or thoroughfare, we rowed
a mile across the foot of Pamadumcook Lake,
which is the name given on the map to this whole
chain of lakes, as if there was but one, though
they are, in each instance, distinctly separated
by a reach of the river, with its narrow and
rocky channel and its rapids. This lake, which

is one of the largest, stretched northwest ten
miles, to hills and mountains in the distance.
McCauslin pointed to some distant, and as yet
inaccessible, forests of white pine, on the sides
of a mountain in that direction. The Joe Merry
Lakes, which lay between us and Moosehead,
on the west, were recently, if they are not still,
"surrounded by some of the best timbered land
in the State." By another thoroughfare we
passed into Deep Cove, a part of the same lake,
which makes up two miles, toward the northeast, and rowing two miles across this, by another
short thoroughfare, entered Ambejijis Lake.

At the entrance to a lake we sometimes observed what is technically called "fencing stuff,"
or the unhewn timbers of which booms are
formed, either secured together in the water, or
laid up on the rocks and lashed to trees, for spring
use. But it was always startling to discover so
plain a trail of civilized man there. I remember
that I was strangely affected, when we were
returning, by the sight of a ring-bolt well drilled
into a rock, and fastened with lead, at the head
of this solitary Ambejijis Lake.

It was easy to see that driving logs must be an
exciting as well as arduous and dangerous business. All winter long the logger goes on piling
up the trees which he has trimmed and hauled
in some dry ravine at the head of a stream, and
then in the spring he stands on the bank and

whistles for Rain and Thaw, ready to wring the perspiration out of his shirt to swell the tide, till suddenly, with a whoop and halloo from him, shutting his eyes, as if to bid farewell to the existing state of things, a fair proportion of his winter's work goes scrambling down the country, followed by his faithful dogs, Thaw and Rain and Freshet and Wind, the whole pack in full cry, toward the Orono Mills. Every log is marked with the owner's name, cut in the sapwood with an axe or bored with an auger, so deep as not to be worn off in the driving, and yet not so as to injure the timber; and it requires consider-able ingenuity to invent new and simple marks where there are so many owners. They have quite an alphabet of their own, which only the practised can read. One of my companions read off from his memorandum-book some marks of his own logs, among which there were crosses, belts, crow's feet, girdles, &c., as, "Y — girdle — crowfoot," and various other devices. When the logs have run the gantlet of innumerable rapids and falls, each on its own account, with more or less jamming and bruising, those bearing various owners' marks being mixed up together, — since all must take advantage of the same freshet, — they are collected together at the heads of the lakes, and surrounded by a boom fence of floating logs, to prevent their being dispersed by the wind, and are thus towed all together, like a flock of sheep, across the lake, where there is no current, by a windlass, or boom-head, such as we sometimes saw standing on an island or headland, and, if circumstances permit, with the aid of sails and oars. Sometimes, notwithstanding, the logs are dispersed over many miles of lake surface in a few hours by winds and freshets, and thrown up on distant shores, where the driver can pick up only one or two at a time, and return with them to the thoroughfare; and before he gets his flock well through Ambejijis or Pamadumcook, he makes many a wet and uncomfortable camp on the shore. He must be able to navigate a log as if it were a canoe, and be as indifferent to cold and wet as a muskrat. He uses a few efficient tools, — a lever, commonly of rock maple, six or seven feet long, with a stout spike in it, strongly feruled on, and a long spike-pole, with a screw at the end of the spike to make it hold. The boys along shore learn to walk on floating logs as city boys on sidewalks. Sometimes the logs are thrown up on rocks in such positions as to be irrecoverable but by another freshet as high, or they jam together at rapids and falls, and accumulate in vast piles, which the driver must start at the risk of his life. Such is the lumber business, which depends on many accidents, as the early freezing of the rivers, that the teams may get up in season, a sufficient freshet in the spring, to fetch the logs down, and many others.[1] I quote Michaux on Lumbering on the Kennebec, then the source of the best white-pine lumber carried to England. "The persons engaged in this branch of industry are generally emigrants from New Hampshire. . . . In the summer they unite in small companies, and traverse these vast solitudes in every direction, to ascertain the places in which the pines abound. After cutting the grass and converting it into hay for the nourishment of the cattle to be employed in their labor, they return home. In the beginning of the winter they enter the forests again, establish themselves in huts covered with the bark of the canoe-birch, or the arbor-vitæ; and, though the cold is so intense that the mercury sometimes remains for several weeks from 40° to 50° [Fahr.] below the point of congelation, they persevere, with unabated courage, in their work." According to Springer, the company consists of choppers, swampers, — who make roads, — barker and loader, teamster, and cook. "When the trees are felled, they cut

---

[1] "A steady current or pitch of water is preferable to one either rising or diminishing; as, when rising rapidly, the water at the middle of the river is considerably higher than at the shores, — so much so as to be distinctly perceived by the eye of a spectator on the banks, presenting an appearance like a turnpike road. The lumber, therefore, is always sure to incline from the centre of the channel toward either shore." — Springer.

them into logs from fourteen to eighteen feet
long, and, by means of their cattle, which they
employ with great dexterity, drag them to the
river, and after stamping on them a mark of
property, roll them on its frozen bosom. At
the breaking of the ice, in the spring, they float
down with the current. . . . The logs that are
not drawn the first year," adds Michaux, "are
attacked by large worms, which form holes about
two lines in diameter, in every direction; but,
if stripped of their bark, they will remain unin-
jured for thirty years."

Ambejijis, this quiet Sunday morning, struck
me as the most beautiful lake we had seen. It
is said to be one of the deepest. We had the
fairest view of Joe Merry, Double Top, and
Ktaadn, from its surface. The summit of the
latter had a singularly flat, table-land appearance, like a short highway, where a demigod
might be let down to take a turn or two in an
afternoon, to settle his dinner. We rowed a
mile and a half to near the head of the lake, and,
pushing through a field of lily-pads, landed, to
cook our breakfast, by the side of a large rock,
known to McCauslin. Our breakfast consisted
of tea, with hard bread and pork, and fried
salmon, which we ate with forks neatly whittled
from alder-twigs, which grew there, off strips of
birch-bark for plates. The tea was black tea,
without milk to color or sugar to sweeten it, and

two tin dippers were our tea-cups. This bever-
age is as indispensable to the loggers as to any
gossiping old women in the land, and they, no
doubt, derive great comfort from it. Here was
the site of an old logger's camp, remembered by
McCauslin, now overgrown with weeds and
bushes. In the midst of a dense underwood we
noticed a whole brick, on a rock, in a small run,
clean and red and square as in a brick-yard,
which had been brought thus far formerly for
tamping. Some of us afterward regretted that
we had not carried this on with us to the top of
the mountain, to be left there for our mark. It
would certainly have been a simple evidence of
civilized man. McCauslin said that large wooden
crosses, made of oak, still sound, were sometimes found standing in this wilderness, which
were set up by the first Catholic missionaries
who came through to the Kennebec.

In the next nine miles, which were the extent
of our voyage, and which it took us the rest of
the day to get over, we rowed across several
small lakes, poled up numerous rapids and
thoroughfares, and carried over four portages.
I will give the names and distances, for the benefit of future tourists. First, after leaving Ambejijis Lake, we had a quarter of a mile of rapids
to the portage, or carry of ninety rods around
Ambejijis Falls; then a mile and a half through
Passamagamet Lake, which is narrow and river-

like, to the falls of the same name, — Ambejijis stream coming in on the right; then two miles through Katepskonegan Lake to the portage of ninety rods around Katepskonegan Falls, which name signifies "carrying-place," — Passamaga-met stream coming in on the left; then three miles through Pockwockomus Lake, a slight expansion of the river, to the portage of forty rods around the falls of the same name, — Katep-skonegan stream coming in on the left; then three quarters of a mile through Aboljacarmegus Lake, similar to the last, to the portage of forty rods around the falls of the same name; then half a mile of rapid water to the Sowadnehunk dead-water, and the Aboljacknagesic stream.

This is generally the order of names as you ascend the river: First, the lake, or, if there is no expansion, the dead-water; then the falls; then the stream emptying into the lake, or river above, all of the same name. First we came to Passamagamet Lake, then to Passamagamet Falls, then to Passamagamet stream, emptying in. This order and identity of names, it will be perceived, is quite philosophical, since the dead-water or lake is always at least partially pro-duced by the stream emptying in above; and the first fall below, which is the outlet of that lake, and where that tributary water makes its first plunge, also naturally bears the same name.

At the portage around Ambejijis Falls I

observed a pork-barrel on the shore, with a hole
eight or nine inches square cut in one side, which
was set against an upright rock; but the bears,
without turning or upsetting the barrel, had
gnawed a hole in the opposite side, which looked
exactly like an enormous rat hole, big enough to
put their heads in; and at the bottom of the
barrel were still left a few mangled and slabbered
slices of pork. It is usual for the lumberers to
leave such supplies as they cannot conveniently
carry along with them at carries or camps, to
which the next comers do not scruple to help
themselves, they being the property, commonly,
not of an individual, but a company, who can
afford to deal liberally.

I will describe particularly how we got over
some of these portages and rapids, in order that
the reader may get an idea of the boatman's life.
At Ambejijis Falls, for instance, there was the
roughest path imaginable cut through the woods;
at first up hill, at an angle of nearly forty-five
degrees, over rocks and logs without end. This
was the manner of the portage. We first carried
over our baggage, and deposited it on the shore
at the other end; then returning to the batteau,
we dragged it up the hill by the painter, and
onward, with frequent pauses, over half the
portage. But this was a bungling way, and
would soon have worn out the boat. Commonly,
three men walk over with a batteau weighing

from three to five or six hundred pounds on their heads and shoulders, the tallest standing under the middle of the boat, which is turned over, and one at each end, or else there are two at the bows. More cannot well take hold at once. But this requires some practice, as well as strength, and is in any case extremely laborious, and wearing to the constitution, to follow. We were, on the whole, rather an invalid party, and could render our boatmen but little assistance. Our two men at length took the batteau upon their shoulders, and, while two of us steadied it, to prevent it from rocking and wearing into their shoulders, on which they placed their hats folded, walked bravely over the remaining distance, with two or three pauses. In the same manner they accomplished the other portages. With this crushing weight they must climb and stumble along over fallen trees and slippery rocks of all sizes, where those who walked by the sides were continually brushed off, such was the narrowness of the path. But we were fortunate not to have to cut our path in the first place. Before we launched our boat, we scraped the bottom smooth again, with our knives, where it had rubbed on the rocks, to save friction.

To avoid the difficulties of the portage, our men determined to "warp up" the Passamagamet Falls; so while the rest walked over the portage with the baggage, I remained in the

batteau, to assist in warping up. We were soon
in the midst of the rapids, which were more
swift and tumultuous than any we had poled up,
and had turned to the side of the stream for the
purpose of warping, when the boatmen, who felt
some pride in their skill, and were ambitious to
do something more than usual, for my benefit,
as I surmised, took one more view of the rapids,
or rather the falls; and, in answer to our question, whether we could n't get up there, the
other answered that he guessed he 'd try it. So
we pushed again into the midst of the stream,
and began to struggle with the current. I sat
in the middle of the boat to trim it, moving
slightly to the right or left as it grazed a rock.
With an uncertain and wavering motion we
wound and bolted our way up, until the bow
was actually raised two feet above the stern at
the steepest pitch; and then, when everything
depended upon his exertions, the bowman's
pole snapped in two; but before he had time to
take the spare one, which I reached him, he had
saved himself with the fragment upon a rock;
and so we got up by a hair's breadth; and Uncle
George exclaimed that that was never done
before; and he had not tried it if he had not
known whom he had got in the bow, nor he in
the bow, if he had not known him in the stern.
At this place there was a regular portage cut
through the woods, and our boatmen had never

known a batteau to ascend the falls. As near as I can remember, there was a perpendicular fall here, at the worst place of the whole Penobscot River, two or three feet at least. I could not sufficiently admire the skill and coolness with which they performed this feat, never speaking to each other. The bowman, not looking behind, but knowing exactly what the other is about, works as if he worked alone. Now sounding in vain for a bottom in fifteen feet of water, while the boat falls back several rods, held straight only with the greatest skill and exertion; or, while the sternman obstinately holds his ground, like a turtle, the bowman springs from side to side with wonderful suppleness and dexterity, scanning the rapids and the rocks with a thousand eyes; and now, having got a bite at last, with a lusty shove, which makes his pole bend and quiver, and the whole boat tremble, he gains a few feet upon the river. To add to the danger, the poles are liable at any time to be caught between the rocks, and wrenched out of their hands, leaving them at the mercy of the rapids, — the rocks, as it were, lying in wait, like so many alligators, to catch them in their teeth, and jerk them from your hands, before you have stolen an effectual shove against their palates. The pole is set close to the boat, and the prow is made to overshoot, and just turn the corners of the rocks, in the

very teeth of the rapids. Nothing but the length
and lightness, and the slight draught of the batteau, enables them to make any headway. The
bowman must quickly choose his course; there
is no time to deliberate. Frequently the boat is
shoved between rocks where both sides touch,
and the waters on either hand are a perfect
maelstrom.

Half a mile above this, two of us tried our
hands at poling up a slight rapid; and we were
just surmounting the last difficulty when an
unlucky rock confounded our calculations; and
while the batteau was sweeping round irrecover-
ably amid the whirlpool, we were obliged to
resign the poles to more skilful hands.

Katepskonegan is one of the shallowest and
weediest of the lakes, and looked as if it might
abound in pickerel. The falls of the same name,
where we stopped to dine, are considerable and
quite picturesque. Here Uncle George had seen
trout caught by the barrelful; but they would
not rise to our bait at this hour. Half-way over
this carry, thus far in the Maine wilderness on
its way to the Provinces, we noticed a large,
flaming, Oak Hall hand-bill, about two feet
long, wrapped round the trunk of a pine, from
which the bark had been stript, and to which it
was fast glued by the pitch. This should be
recorded among the advantages of this mode of
advertising, that so, possibly, even the bears

and wolves, moose, deer, otter, and beaver, not to mention the Indian, may learn where they can fit themselves according to the latest fashion, or, at least, recover some of their own lost garments. We christened this, the Oak Hall carry.

The forenoon was as serene and placid on this wild stream in the woods, as we are apt to imagine that Sunday in summer usually is in Massachusetts. We were occasionally startled by the scream of a bald-eagle, sailing over the stream in front of our batteau; or of the fish-hawks, on whom he levies his contributions. There were, at intervals, small meadows of a few acres on the sides of the stream, waving with uncut grass, which attracted the attention of our boatmen, who regretted that they were not nearer to their clearings, and calculated how many stacks they might cut. Two or three men sometimes spend the summer by themselves, cutting the grass in these meadows, to sell to the loggers in the winter, since it will fetch a higher price on the spot than in any market in the State. On a small isle, covered with this kind of rush, or cut grass, on which we landed, to consult about our further course, we noticed the recent track of a moose, a large, roundish hole, in the soft wet ground, evincing the great size and weight of the animal that made it. They are fond of the water, and visit all these island-meadows, swimming as easily from island to island as they make their

way through the thickets on land. Now and
then we passed what McCauslin called a pokelogan, an Indian term for what the drivers might
have reason to call a poke-logs-in, an inlet that
leads nowhere. If you get in, you have got to get
out again the same way. These, and the frequent "run-rounds" which come into the river
again, would embarrass an inexperienced voyager not a little.

The carry around Pockwockomus Falls was
exceedingly rough and rocky, the batteau having
to be lifted directly from the water up four or
five feet on to a rock, and launched again down
a similar bank. The rocks on this portage were
covered with the *dents* made by the spikes in
the lumberers' boots while staggering over under
the weight of their batteaux; and you could see
where the surface of some large rocks on which
they had rested their batteaux was worn quite
smooth with use. As it was, we had carried
over but half the usual portage at this place for
this stage of the water, and launched our boat
in the smooth wave just curving to the fall,
prepared to struggle with the most violent rapid
we had to encounter. The rest of the party
walked over the remainder of the portage, while
I remained with the boatmen to assist in warping up. One had to hold the boat while the
others got in to prevent it from going over the
falls. When we had pushed up the rapids as

far as possible, keeping close to the shore, Tom
seized the painter and leaped out upon a rock
just visible in the water, but he lost his footing,
notwithstanding his spiked boots, and was
instantly amid the rapids; but recovering himself by good luck, and reaching another rock,
he passed the painter to me, who had followed
him, and took his place again in the bows.
Leaping from rock to rock in the shoal water,
close to the shore, and now and then getting a
bite with the rope round an upright one, I held
the boat while one reset his pole, and then all
three forced it upward against any rapid. This
was "warping up." When a part of us walked
round at such a place, we generally took the
precaution to take out the most valuable part
of the baggage, for fear of being swamped.

As we poled up a swift rapid for half a mile
above Aboljacarmegus Falls, some of the party
read their own marks on the huge logs which
lay piled up high and dry on the rocks on either
hand, the relics probably of a jam which had
taken place here in the Great Freshet in the
spring. Many of these would have to wait for
another great freshet, perchance, if they lasted
so long, before they could be got off. It was
singular enough to meet with property of theirs
which they had never seen, and where they had
never been before, thus detained by freshets and
rocks when on its way to them. Methinks that

must be where all my property lies, cast up on the rocks on some distant and unexplored stream, and waiting for an unheard-of freshet to fetch it down. O make haste, ye gods, with your winds and rains, and start the jam before it rots!

The last half-mile carried us to the Sowadne-hunk dead-water, so called from the stream of the same name, signifying "running between mountains," an important tributary which comes in a mile above. Here we decided to camp, about twenty miles from the Dam, at the mouth of Murch Brook and the Aboljacknagesic, mountain streams, broad off from Ktaadn, and about a dozen miles from its summit; having made fifteen miles this day.

We had been told by McCauslin that we should here find trout enough: so, while some prepared the camp, the rest fell to fishing. Seizing the birch-poles which some party of Indians, or white hunters, had left on the shore, and baiting our hooks with pork, and with trout, as soon as they were caught, we cast our lines into the mouth of the Aboljacknagesic, a clear, swift, shallow stream, which came in from Ktaadn. Instantly a shoal of white chivin (*Leucisci pulchelli*), silvery roaches, cousin-trout, or what not, large and small, prowling thereabouts, fell upon our bait, and one after another were landed amidst the bushes. Anon their cousins, the true trout, took their turn, and alternately the speckled

trout, and the silvery roaches, swallowed the
bait as fast as we could throw in; and the finest
specimens of both that I have ever seen, the
largest one weighing three pounds, were heaved
upon the shore, though at first in vain, to wriggle
down into the water again, for we stood in the
boat; but soon we learned to remedy this evil:
for one, who had lost his hook, stood on shore
to catch them as they fell in a perfect shower
around him, — sometimes, wet and slippery,
full in his face and bosom, as his arms were out-
stretched to receive them.   While yet alive,
before their tints had faded, they glistened like
the fairest flowers, the product of primitive
rivers; and he could hardly trust his senses,
as he stood over them, that these jewels should
have swam away in that Aboljacknagesic water
for so long, so many dark ages; — these bright
fluviatile flowers, seen of Indians only, made
beautiful, the Lord only knows why, to swim
there! I could understand better, for this, the
truth of mythology, the fables of Proteus, and
all those beautiful sea-monsters, — how all history, indeed, put to a terrestrial use, is mere
history; but put to a celestial, is mythology
always.

But there is the rough voice of Uncle George,
who commands at the frying-pan, to send over
what you 've got, and then you may stay till
morning. The pork sizzles, and cries for fish.

Luckily for the foolish race, and this particularly foolish generation of trout, the night shut down at last, not a little deepened by the dark side of Ktaadn, which, like a permanent shadow, reared itself from the eastern bank. Lescarbot, writing in 1609, tells us that the Sieur Champdoré, who, with one of the people of the Sieur de Monts, ascended some fifty leagues up the St. John in 1608, found the fish so plenty, "qu'en mettant la chaudière sur le feu ils en avoient pris suffisamment pour eux dîsner avant que l'eau fust chaude." Their descendants here are no less numerous. So we accompanied Tom into the woods to cut cedar-twigs for our bed. While he went ahead with the axe, and lopt off the smallest twigs of the flat-leaved cedar, the arbor-vitæ of the gardens, we gathered them up, and returned with them to the boat, until it was loaded. Our bed was made with as much care and skill as a roof is shingled; beginning at the foot, and laying the twig end of the cedar upward, we advanced to the head, a course at a time, thus successively covering the stub-ends, and producing a soft and level bed. For us six it was about ten feet long by six in breadth. This time we lay under our tent, having pitched it more prudently with reference to the wind and the flame, and the usual huge fire blazed in front. Supper was eaten off a large log, which some freshet had thrown up. This night we had a dish of arbor-vitæ or cedar tea, which the lumberer sometimes uses when other herbs fail, —

> "A quart of arbor-vitæ,
>   To make him strong and mighty,"

but I had no wish to repeat the experiment. It had too medicinal a taste for my palate. There was the skeleton of a moose here, whose bones some Indian hunters had picked on this very spot.

In the night I dreamed of trout-fishing; and, when at length I awoke, it seemed a fable that this painted fish swam there so near my couch, and rose to our hooks the last evening, and I doubted if I had not dreamed it all. So I arose before dawn to test its truth, while my companions were still sleeping. There stood Ktaadn with distinct and cloudless outline in the moonlight; and the rippling of the rapids was the only sound to break the stillness. Standing on the shore, I once more cast my line into the stream, and found the dream to be real and the fable true. The speckled trout and silvery roach, like flying-fish, sped swiftly through the moonlight air, describing bright arcs on the dark side of Ktaadn, until moonlight, now fading into daylight, brought satiety to my mind, and the minds of my companions, who had joined me.

By six o'clock, having mounted our packs and a good blanketful of trout, ready dressed, and swung up such baggage and provision as we

wished to leave behind, upon the tops of saplings, to be out of the reach of bears, we started
for the summit of the mountain, distant, as
Uncle George said the boatmen called it, about
four miles, but as I judged, and as it proved,
nearer fourteen. He had never been any nearer
the mountain than this, and there was not the
slightest trace of man to guide us farther in this
direction. At first, pushing a few rods up the
Aboljacknagesic, or "open-land stream," we
fastened our batteau to a tree, and travelled up
the north side, through burnt lands, now partially
overgrown with young aspens, and other shrub-
bery; but soon, recrossing this stream, where it
was about fifty or sixty feet wide, upon a jam
of logs and rocks, — and you could cross it by
this means almost anywhere, — we struck at
once for the highest peak, over a mile or more
of comparatively open land, still very gradually
ascending the while. Here it fell to my lot, as
the oldest mountain-climber, to take the lead.
So, scanning the woody side of the mountain,
which lay still at an indefinite distance, stretched
out some seven or eight miles in length before
us, we determined to steer directly for the base
of the highest peak, leaving a large slide, by
which, as I have since learned, some of our predecessors ascended, on our left. This course
would lead us parallel to a dark seam in the
forest, which marked the bed of a torrent, and

over a slight spur, which extended southward from the main mountain, from whose bare summit we could get an outlook over the country, and climb directly up the peak, which would then be close at hand. Seen from this point, a bare ridge at the extremity of the open land, Ktaadn presented a different aspect from any mountain I have seen, there being a greater proportion of naked rock rising abruptly from the forest; and we looked up at this blue barrier as if it were some fragment of a wall which anciently bounded the earth in that direction. Setting the compass for a northeast course, which was the bearing of the southern base of the highest peak, we were soon buried in the woods.

We soon began to meet with traces of bears and moose, and those of rabbits were everywhere visible. The tracks of moose, more or less recent, to speak literally, covered every square rod on the sides of the mountain; and these animals are probably more numerous there now than ever before, being driven into this wilderness, from all sides, by the settlements. The track of a full-grown moose is like that of a cow, or larger, and of the young, like that of a calf. Sometimes we found ourselves travelling in faint paths, which they had made, like cow-paths in the woods, only far more indistinct, being rather openings, affording imperfect vistas through the dense underwood,

than trodden paths; and everywhere the twigs
had been browsed by them, clipt as smoothly as
if by a knife. The bark of trees was stript up
by them to the height of eight or nine feet, in
long, narrow strips, an inch wide, still showing
the distinct marks of their teeth. We expected
nothing less than to meet a herd of them every
moment, and our Nimrod held his shooting-iron
in readiness; but we did not go out of our way
to look for them, and, though numerous, they
are so wary that the unskilful hunter might
range the forest a long time before he could get
sight of one. They are sometimes dangerous
to encounter, and will not turn out for the hunter,
but furiously rush upon him and trample him
to death, unless he is lucky enough to avoid
them by dodging round a tree. The largest are
nearly as large as a horse, and weigh sometimes
one thousand pounds; and it is said that they
can step over a five-feet gate in their ordinary
walk. They are described as exceedingly awk-
ward-looking animals, with their long legs and
short bodies, making a ludicrous figure when in
full run, but making great headway nevertheless.
It seemed a mystery to us how they could thread
these woods, which it required all our suppleness
to accomplish, — climbing, stooping, and winding, alternately. They are said to drop their
long and branching horns, which usually spread
five or six feet, on their backs, and make their

way easily by the weight of their bodies. Our
boatmen said, but I know not with how much
truth, that their horns are apt to be gnawed
away by vermin while they sleep. Their flesh,
which is more like beef than venison, is common
in Bangor market.

We had proceeded on thus seven or eight
miles, till about noon, with frequent pauses to
refresh the weary ones, crossing a considerable
mountain stream, which we conjectured to be
Murch Brook, at whose mouth we had camped,
all the time in woods, without having once seen
the summit, and rising very gradually, when the
boatmen, beginning to despair a little, and fearing that we were leaving the mountain on one
side of us, for they had not entire faith in the
compass, McCauslin climbed a tree, from the
top of which he could see the peak, when it
appeared that we had not swerved from a right
line, the compass down below still ranging with
his arm, which pointed to the summit. By the
side of a cool mountain rill, amid the woods,
where the water began to partake of the purity
and transparency of the air, we stopped to cook
some of our fishes, which we had brought thus
far in order to save our hard bread and pork,
in the use of which we had put ourselves on short
allowance. We soon had a fire blazing, and
stood around it, under the damp and sombre
forest of firs and birches, each with a sharpened

stick, three or four feet in length, upon which
he had spitted his trout, or roach, previously
well gashed and salted, our sticks radiating like
the spokes of a wheel from one centre, and each
crowding his particular fish into the most desir-
able exposure, not with the truest regard always
to his neighbor's rights. Thus we regaled ourselves, drinking meanwhile at the spring, till
one man's pack, at least, was considerably lightened, when we again took up our line of march.

At length we reached an elevation sufficiently
bare to afford a view of the summit, still distant
and blue, almost as if retreating from us. A
torrent, which proved to be the same we had
crossed, was seen tumbling down in front, literally from out of the clouds. But this glimpse at
our whereabouts was soon lost, and we were
buried in the woods again. The wood was
chiefly yellow birch, spruce, fir, mountain-ash,
or round-wood, as the Maine people call it, and
moose-wood. It was the worst kind of travelling;
sometimes like the densest scrub-oak patches
with us. The cornel, or bunch-berries, were
very abundant, as well as Solomon's seal and
moose-berries. Blueberries were distributed
along our whole route; and in one place the
bushes were drooping with the weight of the
fruit, still as fresh as ever. It was the 7th of
September. Such patches afforded a grateful
repast, and served to bait the tired party for-

ward. When any lagged behind, the cry of "blueberries" was most effectual to bring them up. Even at this elevation we passed through a moose-yard, formed by a large flat rock, four or five rods square, where they tread down the snow in winter. At length, fearing that if we held the direct course to the summit we should not find any water near our camping-ground, we gradually swerved to the west, till, at four o'clock, we struck again the torrent which I have mentioned, and here, in view of the summit, the weary party decided to camp that night.

While my companions were seeking a suitable spot for this purpose, I improved the little daylight that was left, in climbing the mountain alone. We were in a deep and narrow ravine, sloping up to the clouds, at an angle of nearly forty-five degrees, and hemmed in by walls of rock, which were at first covered with low trees, then with impenetrable thickets of scraggy birches and spruce-trees, and with moss, but at last bare of all vegetation but lichens, and almost continually draped in clouds. Following up the course of the torrent which occupied this, — and I mean to lay some emphasis on this word *up*, — pulling myself up by the side of perpendicular falls of twenty or thirty feet, by the roots of firs and birches, and then, perhaps, walking a level rod or two in the thin stream, for it took up the whole road, ascending by huge

steps, as it were, a giant's stairway, down which
a river flowed, I had soon cleared the trees, and
paused on the successive shelves, to look back
over the country. The torrent was from fifteen
to thirty feet wide, without a tributary, and seemingly not diminishing in breadth as I advanced;
but still it came rushing and roaring down, with
a copious tide, over and amidst masses of bare
rock, from the very clouds, as though a water-
spout had just burst over the mountain. Leaving this at last, I began to work my way, scarcely
less arduous than Satan's anciently through
Chaos, up the nearest, though not the highest
peak. At first scrambling on all fours over the
tops of ancient black spruce-trees (*Abies nigra*),
old as the flood, from two to ten or twelve feet
in height, their tops flat and spreading, and their
foliage blue, and nipt with cold, as if for centuries
they had ceased growing upward against the
bleak sky, the solid cold. I walked some good
rods erect upon the tops of these trees, which
were overgrown with moss and mountain-cran-
berries. It seemed that in the course of time
they had filled up the intervals between the huge
rocks, and the cold wind had uniformly levelled
all over. Here the principle of vegetation was
hard put to it. There was apparently a belt of
this kind running quite round the mountain,
though, perhaps, nowhere so remarkable as
here. Once, slumping through, I looked down

ten feet, into a dark and cavernous region, and saw the stem of a spruce, on whose top I stood, as on a mass of coarse basket-work, fully nine inches in diameter at the ground. These holes were bears' dens, and the bears were even then at home. This was the sort of garden I made my way *over*, for an eighth of a mile, at the risk, it is true, of treading on some of the plants, not seeing any path *through* it, — certainly the most treacherous and porous country I ever travelled.

> "Nigh foundered on he fares,
>   Treading the crude consistence, half on foot,
>   Half flying."

But nothing could exceed the toughness of the twigs, — not one snapped under my weight, for they had slowly grown. Having slumped, scrambled, rolled, bounced, and walked, by turns, over this scraggy country, I arrived upon a side-hill, or rather side-mountain, where rocks, gray, silent rocks, were the flocks and herds that pastured, chewing a rocky cud at sunset. They looked at me with hard gray eyes, without a bleat or a low. This brought me to the skirt of a cloud, and bounded my walk that night. But I had already seen that Maine country when I turned about, waving, flowing, rippling, down below.

When I returned to my companions, they had selected a camping-ground on the torrent's edge, and were resting on the ground; one was on the sick list, rolled in a blanket, on a damp shelf of rock. It was a savage and dreary scenery enough; so wildly rough, that they looked long to find a level and open space for the tent. We could not well camp higher, for want of fuel; and the trees here seemed so evergreen and sappy, that we almost doubted if they would acknowledge the influence of fire; but fire prevailed at last, and blazed here, too, like a good citizen of the world. Even at this height we met with frequent traces of moose, as well as of bears. As here was no cedar, we made our bed of coarser feathered spruce; but at any rate the feathers were plucked from the live tree. It was, perhaps, even a more grand and desolate place for a night's lodging than the summit would have been, being in the neighborhood of those wild trees, and of the torrent. Some more aerial and finer-spirited winds rushed and roared through the ravine all night, from time to time arousing our fire, and dispersing the embers about. It was as if we lay in the very nest of a young whirlwind. At midnight, one of my bedfellows, being startled in his dreams by the sudden blazing up to its top of a fir-tree, whose green boughs were dried by the heat, sprang up, with a cry, from his bed, thinking the world on fire, and drew the whole camp after him.

In the morning, after whetting our appetite

on some raw pork, a wafer of hard bread, and a dipper of condensed cloud or waterspout, we all together began to make our way up the falls, which I have described; this time choosing the right hand, or highest peak, which was not the one I had approached before. But soon my companions were lost to my sight behind the mountain ridge in my rear, which still seemed ever retreating before me, and I climbed alone over huge rocks, loosely poised, a mile or more, still edging toward the clouds; for though the day was clear elsewhere, the summit was concealed by mist. The mountain seemed a vast aggregation of loose rocks, as if some time it had rained rocks, and they lay as they fell on the mountain sides, nowhere fairly at rest, but leaning on each other, all rocking-stones, with cavities between, but scarcely any soil or smoother shelf. They were the raw materials of a planet dropped from an unseen quarry, which the vast chemistry of nature would anon work up, or work down, into the smiling and verdant plains and valleys of earth. This was an undone extremity of the globe; as in lignite we see coal in the process of formation.

At length I entered within the skirts of the cloud which seemed forever drifting over the summit, and yet would never be gone, but was generated out of that pure air as fast as it flowed away; and when, a quarter of a mile farther, I reached the summit of the ridge, which those who have seen in clearer weather say is about five miles long, and contains a thousand acres of table-land, I was deep within the hostile ranks of clouds, and all objects were obscured by them. Now the wind would blow me out a yard of clear sunlight, wherein I stood; then a gray, dawning light was all it could accomplish, the cloud-line ever rising and falling with the wind's intensity. Sometimes it seemed as if the summit would be cleared in a few moments, and smile in sunshine: but what was gained on one side was lost on another. It was like sitting in a chimney and waiting for the smoke to blow away. It was, in fact, a cloud-factory, — these were the cloud-works, and the wind turned them off done from the cool, bare rocks. Occasionally, when the windy columns broke in to me, I caught sight of a dark, damp crag to the right or left; the mist driving ceaselessly between it and me. It reminded me of the creations of the old epic and dramatic poets, of Atlas, Vulcan, the Cyclops, and Prometheus. Such was Caucasus and the rock where Prometheus was bound. Æschylus had no doubt visited such scenery as this. It was vast, Titanic, and such as man never inhabits. Some part of the beholder, even some vital part, seems to escape through the loose grating of his ribs as he ascends. He is more lone than you can imagine. There is less

of substantial thought and fair understanding
in him, than in the plains where men inhabit.
His reason is dispersed and shadowy, more thin
and subtile, like the air. Vast, Titanic, inhuman
Nature has got him at disadvantage, caught him
alone, and pilfers him of some of his divine fac-
ulty. She does not smile on him as in the plains.
She seems to say sternly, why came ye here
before your time? This ground is not prepared for you. Is it not enough that I smile in
the valleys? I have never made this soil for
thy feet, this air for thy breathing, these rocks
for thy neighbors. I cannot pity nor fondle thee
here, but forever relentlessly drive thee hence
to where I *am* kind. Why seek me where I
have not called thee, and then complain because you find me but a stepmother? Shouldst
thou freeze or starve, or shudder thy life away,
here is no shrine, nor altar, nor any access to
my ear.

> "Chaos and ancient Night, I come no spy
> With purpose to explore or to disturb
> The secrets of your realm, but . . .
> . . . . as my way
> Lies through your spacious empire up to light."

The tops of mountains are among the unfin-
ished parts of the globe, whither it is a slight
insult to the gods to climb and pry into their
secrets, and try their effect on our humanity.
Only daring and insolent men, perchance, go

there. Simple races, as savages, do not climb
mountains, — their tops are sacred and mysterious tracts never visited by them. Pomola is
always angry with those who climb to the summit
of Ktaadn.

According to Jackson, who, in his capacity of
geological surveyor of the State, has accurately
measured it, — the altitude of Ktaadn is 5,300
feet, or a little more than one mile above the
level of the sea, — and he adds, "It is then
evidently the highest point in the State of Maine,
and is the most abrupt granite mountain in New
England." The peculiarities of that spacious
table-land on which I was standing, as well as
the remarkable semi-circular precipice or basin
on the eastern side, were all concealed by the
mist. I had brought my whole pack to the top,
not knowing but I should have to make my
descent to the river, and possibly to the settled
portion of the State alone, and by some other
route, and wishing to have a complete outfit
with me. But at length, fearing that my companions would be anxious to reach the river
before night, and knowing that the clouds might
rest on the mountain for days, I was compelled
to descend. Occasionally, as I came down, the
wind would blow me a vista open, through which
I could see the country eastward, boundless
forests, and lakes, and streams, gleaming in the
sun, some of them emptying into the East

Branch. There were also new mountains in sight in that direction. Now and then some small bird of the sparrow family would flit away before me, unable to command its course, like a fragment of the gray rock blown off by the wind.

I found my companions where I had left them, on the side of the peak, gathering the mountain cranberries, which filled every crevice between the rocks, together with blueberries, which had a spicier flavor the higher up they grew, but were not the less agreeable to our palates. When the country is settled, and roads are made, these cranberries will perhaps become an article of commerce. From this elevation, just on the skirts of the clouds, we could overlook the country, west and south, for a hundred miles. There it was, the State of Maine, which we had seen on the map, but not much like that, — immeasurable forest for the sun to shine on, that eastern *stuff* we hear of in Massachusetts. No clearing, no house. It did not look as if a solitary traveller had cut so much as a walking-stick there. Countless lakes, — Moosehead in the southwest, forty miles long by ten wide, like a gleaming silver platter at the end of the table; Chesuncook, eighteen long by three wide, without an island; Millinocket, on the south, with its hundred islands; and a hundred others without a name; and mountains also, whose names, for the most part, are known only to the Indians.

The forest looked like a firm grass sward, and the effect of these lakes in its midst has been well compared, by one who has since visited this same spot, to that of a "mirror broken into a thousand fragments, and wildly scattered over the grass, reflecting the full blaze of the sun." It was a large farm for somebody, when cleared. According to the Gazetteer, which was printed before the boundary question was settled, this single Penobscot county, in which we were, was larger than the whole State of Vermont, with its fourteen counties; and this was only a part of the wild lands of Maine. We are concerned now, however, about natural, not political limits. We were about eighty miles, as the bird flies, from Bangor, or one hundred and fifteen, as we had rode, and walked, and paddled. We had to console ourselves with the reflection that this view was probably as good as that from the peak, as far as it went; and what were a mountain without its attendant clouds and mists? Like ourselves, neither Bailey nor Jackson had obtained a clear view from the summit.

Setting out on our return to the river, still at an early hour in the day, we decided to follow the course of the torrent, which we supposed to be Murch Brook, as long as it would not lead us too far out of our way. We thus travelled about four miles in the very torrent itself, continually crossing and recrossing it, leaping from

rock to rock, and jumping with the stream down
falls of seven or eight feet, or sometimes sliding
down on our backs in a thin sheet of water. This
ravine had been the scene of an extraordinary
freshet in the spring, apparently accompanied by
a slide from the mountain. It must have been
filled with a stream of stones and water, at least
twenty feet above the present level of the torrent. For a rod or two, on either side of its
channel, the trees were barked and splintered
up to their tops, the birches bent over, twisted,
and sometimes finely split, like a stablebroom;
some, a foot in diameter, snapped off, and whole
clumps of trees bent over with the weight of
rocks piled on them. In one place we noticed a
rock, two or three feet in diameter, lodged
nearly twenty feet high in the crotch of a tree.
For the whole four miles, we saw but one rill
emptying in, and the volume of water did not
seem to be increased from the first. We travelled
thus very rapidly with a downward impetus, and
grew remarkably expert at leaping from rock to
rock, for leap we must, and leap we did, whether
there was any rock at the right distance or not.
It was a pleasant picture when the foremost
turned about and looked up the winding ravine,
walled in with rocks and the green forest, to
see, at intervals of a rod or two, a red-shirted or
green-jacketed mountaineer against the white
torrent, leaping down the channel with his pack

on his back, or pausing upon a convenient rock in the midst of the torrent to mend a rent in his clothes, or unstrap the dipper at his belt to take a draught of the water. At one place we were startled by seeing, on a little sandy shelf by the side of the stream, the fresh print of a man's foot, and for a moment realized how Robinson Crusoe felt in a similar case; but at last we remembered that we had struck this stream on our way up, though we could not have told where, and one had descended into the ravine for a drink. The cool air above, and the continual bathing of our bodies in mountain water, alternate foot, sitz, douche, and plunge baths, made this walk exceedingly refreshing, and we had travelled only a mile or two, after leaving the torrent, before every thread of our clothes was as dry as usual, owing perhaps to a peculiar quality in the atmosphere.

After leaving the torrent, being in doubt about our course, Tom threw down his pack at the foot of the loftiest spruce tree at hand, and shinned up the bare trunk, some twenty feet, and then climbed through the green tower, lost to our sight, until he held the topmost spray in his hand.[1] McCauslin, in his younger days, had

---

[1] "The spruce-tree," says Springer in '51, "is generally selected, principally for the superior facilities which its numerous limbs afford the climber. To gain the first limbs of this tree, which are from twenty to forty feet from the ground, a smaller

marched through the wilderness with a body of troops, under General Somebody, and with one other man did all the scouting and spying service. The General's word was, "Throw down the top of that tree," and there was no tree in the Maine woods so high that it did not lose its top in such a case. I have heard a story of two men being lost once in these woods, nearer to the settlements than this, who climbed the loftiest pine they could find, some six feet in diameter at the ground, from whose top they discovered a solitary clearing and its smoke. When at this height, some two hundred feet from the ground, one of them became dizzy, and fainted in his companion's arms, and the latter had to accomplish the descent with him, alternately fainting and reviving, as best he could. To Tom we cried, Where away does the summit bear? where the burnt lands? The last he could only conjecture; he descried, however, a little meadow and pond, lying probably in our course, which we concluded to steer for. On reaching this secluded meadow, we found fresh tracks of

tree is undercut and lodged against it, clambering up which the top of the spruce is reached. In some cases, when a very elevated position is desired, the spruce-tree is lodged against the trunk of some lofty pine, up which we ascend to a height twice that of the surrounding forest."

To indicate the direction of pines, he throws down a branch, and a man at the ground takes the bearing.

moose on the shore of the pond, and the water
was still unsettled as if they had fled before us.
A little farther, in a dense thicket, we seemed
to be still on their trail. It was a small meadow,
of a few acres, on the mountain side, concealed
by the forest, and perhaps never seen by a white
man before, where one would think that the
moose might browse and bathe, and rest in
peace. Pursuing this course, we soon reached
the open land, which went sloping down some
miles toward the Penobscot.

Perhaps I most fully realized that this was
primeval, untamed, and forever untameable
Nature, or whatever else men call it, while
coming down this part of the mountain. We
were passing over "Burnt Lands," burnt by
lightning, perchance, though they showed no
recent marks of fire, hardly so much as a charred
stump, but looked rather like a natural pasture
for the moose and deer, exceedingly wild and
desolate, with occasional strips of timber crossing them, and low poplars springing up, and
patches of blueberries here and there. I found
myself traversing them familiarly, like some
pasture run to waste, or partially reclaimed by
man; but when I reflected what man, what
brother or sister or kinsman of our race made
it and claimed it, I expected the proprietor to
rise up and dispute my passage. It is difficult to
conceive of a region uninhabited by man. We

habitually presume his presence and influence everywhere. And yet we have not seen pure Nature, unless we have seen her thus vast and drear and inhuman, though in the midst of cities. Nature was here something savage and awful, though beautiful. I looked with awe at the ground I trod on, to see what the Powers had made there, the form and fashion and material of their work. This was that Earth of which we have heard, made out of Chaos and Old Night. Here was no man's garden, but the unhand-selled globe. It was not lawn, nor pasture, nor mead, nor woodland, nor lea, nor arable, nor waste-land. It was the fresh and natural surface of the planet Earth, as it was made for ever and ever, — to be the dwelling of man, we say — so Nature made it, and man may use it if he can. Man was not to be associated with it. It was Matter, vast, terrific, — not his Mother Earth that we have heard of, not for him to tread on, or be buried in, — no, it were being too familiar even to let his bones lie there, — the home, this, of Necessity and Fate. There was there felt the presence of a force not bound to be kind to man. It was a place for heathen-ism and superstitious rites, — to be inhabited by men nearer of kin to the rocks and to wild animals than we. We walked over it with a certain awe, stopping, from time to time, to pick the blueberries which grew there, and had a smart and spicy taste. Perchance where *our* wild pines stand, and leaves lie on their forest floor, in Concord, there were once reapers, and husbandmen planted grain; but here not even the surface had been scarred by man, but it was a specimen of what God saw fit to make this world. What is it to be admitted to a museum, to see a myriad of particular things, compared with being shown some star's surface, some hard matter in its home! I stand in awe of my body, this matter to which I am bound has become so strange to me. I fear not spirits, ghosts, of which I am one, — *that* my body might, — but I fear bodies, I tremble to meet them. What is this Titan that has possession of me? Talk of mysteries! — Think of our life in nature, — daily to be shown matter, to come in contact with it, — rocks, trees, wind on our cheeks! the *solid* earth! the *actual* world! the *common sense! Contact! Contact! Who* are we? *where* are we?

Erelong we recognized some rocks and other features in the landscape which we had purposely impressed on our memories, and, quickening our pace, by two o'clock we reached the batteau.[1] Here we had expected to dine on trout, but in this glaring sunlight they were slow to take the bait, so we were compelled to make

[1] The bears had not touched things on our possessions. They sometimes tear a batteau to pieces for the sake of the tar with which it is besmeared.

the most of the crumbs of our hard bread and our pork, which were both nearly exhausted. Meanwhile we deliberated whether we should go up the river a mile farther, to Gibson's clearing, on the Sowadnehunk, where there was a deserted log-hut, in order to get a half-inch auger, to mend one of our spike-poles with. There were young spruce-trees enough around us, and we had a spare spike, but nothing to make a hole with. But as it was uncertain whether we should find any tools left there, we patched up the broken pole, as well as we could, for the downward voyage, in which there would be but little use for it. Moreover, we were unwilling to lose any time in this expedition, lest the wind should rise before we reached the larger lakes, and detain us; for a moderate wind produces quite a sea on these waters, in which a batteau will not live for a moment; and on one occasion McCauslin had been delayed a week at the head of the North Twin, which is only four miles across. We were nearly out of provisions, and ill prepared in this respect for what might possibly prove a week's journey round by the shore, fording innumerable streams, and threading a trackless forest, should any accident happen to our boat.

It was with regret that we turned our backs on Chesuncook, which McCauslin had formerly logged on, and the Allegash lakes. There were still longer rapids and portages above; among

the last the Rippogenus Portage, which he described as the most difficult on the river, and
three miles long. The whole length of the Penobscot is two hundred and seventy-five miles, and
we are still nearly one hundred miles from its
source. Hodge, the assistant State Geologist,
passed up this river in 1837, and by a portage
of only one mile and three-quarters crossed over
into the Allegash, and so went down that into
the St. John, and up the Madawaska to the
Grand Portage across to the St. Lawrence. His
is the only account that I know, of an expedition through to Canada in this direction. He
thus describes his first sight of the latter river,
which, to compare small things with great, is
like Balboa's first sight of the Pacific from the
mountains of the Isthmus of Darien. "When
we first came in sight of the St. Lawrence," he
says, "from the top of a high hill, the view was
most striking, and much more interesting to me
from having been shut up in the woods for the
two previous months. Directly before us lay
the broad river, extending across nine or ten
miles, its surface broken by a few islands and
reefs, and two ships riding at anchor near the
shore. Beyond, extended ranges of uncultivated
hills, parallel with the river. The sun was just
going down behind them, and gilding the whole
scene with its parting rays."

About four o'clock, the same afternoon, we

commenced our return voyage, which would require but little if any poling. In shooting rapids the boatmen use large and broad paddles, instead of poles, to guide the boat with. Though we glided so swiftly, and often smoothly, down, where it had cost us no slight effort to get up, our present voyage was attended with far more danger: for if we once fairly struck one of the thousand rocks by which we were surrounded the boat would be swamped in an instant. When a boat is swamped under these circumstances, the boatmen commonly find no difficulty in keeping afloat at first, for the current keeps both them and their cargo up for a long way down the stream; and if they can swim, they have only to work their way gradually to the shore. The greatest danger is of being caught in an eddy behind some larger rock, where the water rushes up stream faster than elsewhere it does down, and being carried round and round under the surface till they are drowned. McCauslin pointed out some rocks which had been the scene of a fatal accident of this kind. Sometimes the body is not thrown out for several hours. He himself had performed such a circuit once, only his legs being visible to his companions; but he was fortunately thrown out in season to recover his breath.[1] In shooting the

[1] I cut this from a newspaper. "On the 11th (instant?) [May, '49], on Rappogenes Falls, Mr. John Delantee, of Orono, Me.,

rapids, the boatman has this problem to solve: to choose a circuitous and safe course amid a thousand sunken rocks, scattered over a quarter or half a mile, at the same time that he is moving steadily on at the rate of fifteen miles an hour. Stop he cannot; the only question is, where will he go? The bowman chooses the course with all his eyes about him, striking broad off with his paddle, and drawing the boat by main force into her course. The sternman faithfully follows the bow.

We were soon at the Aboljacarmegus Falls. Anxious to avoid the delay, as well as the labor, of the portage here, our boatmen went forward first to reconnoitre, and concluded to let the batteau down the falls, carrying the baggage only over the portage. Jumping from rock to rock until nearly in the middle of the stream, we were ready to receive the boat and let her down over the first fall, some six or seven feet perpendicular. The boatmen stand upon the edge of a shelf of rock, where the fall is perhaps nine or ten feet perpendicular, in from one to two feet of rapid water, one on each side of the boat, and let it slide gently over, till the bow is run out ten or twelve feet in the air; then, letting it drop squarely, while one holds the painter,

was drowned while running logs. He was a citizen of Orono, and was twenty-six years of age. His companions found his body, enclosed it in bark, and buried it in the solemn woods."

the other leaps in, and his companion following, they are whirled down the rapids to a new fall, or to smooth water. In a very few minutes they had accomplished a passage in safety, which would be as foolhardy for the unskilful to attempt as the descent of Niagara itself. It seemed as if it needed only a little familiarity, and a little more skill, to navigate down such falls as Niagara itself with safety. At any rate, I should not despair of such men in the rapids above table-rock, until I saw them actually go over the falls, so cool, so collected, so fertile in resources are they. One might have thought that these were falls, and that falls were not to be waded through with impunity, like a mud-puddle. There was really danger of their losing their sublimity in losing their power to harm us. Familiarity breeds contempt. The boatman pauses, perchance, on some shelf beneath a table-rock under the fall, standing in some cove of back-water two feet deep, and you hear his rough voice come up through the spray, coolly giving directions how to launch the boat this time.

Having carried round Pockwockomus Falls, our oars soon brought us to the Katepskonegan, or Oak Hall carry, where we decided to camp half-way over, leaving our batteau to be carried over in the morning on fresh shoulders. One shoulder of each of the boatmen showed a red

spot as large as one's hand, worn by the batteau
on this expedition; and this shoulder, as it did
all the work, was perceptibly lower than its
fellow, from long service. Such toil soon wears
out the strongest constitution. The drivers are
accustomed to work in the cold water in the
spring, rarely ever dry; and if one falls in all over
he rarely changes his clothes till night, if then,
even. One who takes this precaution is called
by a particular nickname, or is turned off. None
can lead this life who are not almost amphibious.
McCauslin said soberly, what is at any rate a
good story to tell, that he had seen where six men
were wholly under water at once, at a jam, with
their shoulders to handspikes. If the log did not
start, then they had to put out their heads to
breathe. The driver works as long as he can
see, from dark to dark, and at night has not time
to eat his supper and dry his clothes fairly,
before he is asleep on his cedar bed. We lay
that night on the very bed made by such a party,
stretching our tent over the poles which were
still standing, but reshingling the damp and
faded bed with fresh leaves.

In the morning we carried our boat over and
launched it, making haste lest the wind should
rise. The boatmen ran down Passamagamet,
and, soon after, Ambejijis Falls, while we walked
round with the baggage. We made a hasty
breakfast at the head of Ambejijis Lake, on the

remainder of our pork, and were soon rowing across its smooth surface again, under a pleasant sky, the mountain being now clear of clouds, in the northeast. Taking turns at the oars, we shot rapidly across Deep Cove, the foot of Pamadumcook, and the North Twin, at the rate of six miles an hour, the wind not being high enough to disturb us, and reached the Dam at noon. The boatmen went through one of the log sluices in the batteau, where the fall was ten feet at the bottom, and took us in below. Here was the longest rapid in our voyage, and perhaps the running this was as dangerous and arduous a task as any. Shooting down sometimes at the rate, as we judged, of fifteen miles an hour, if we struck a rock we were split from end to end in an instant. Now, like a bait bobbing for some river monster, amid the eddies, now darting to this side of the stream, now to that, gliding swift and smooth near to our destruction, or striking broad off with the paddle and drawing the boat to right or left with all our might, in order to avoid a rock. I suppose that it was like running the rapids of the Saute de St. Marie, at the outlet of Lake Superior, and our boatmen probably displayed no less dexterity than the Indians there do. We soon ran through this mile, and floated in Quakish Lake.

After such a voyage, the troubled and angry waters, which once had seemed terrible and not to be trifled with, appeared tamed and subdued; they had been bearded and worried in their channels, pricked and whipped into submission with the spike-pole and paddle, gone through and through with impunity, and all their spirit and their danger taken out of them, and the most swollen and impetuous rivers seemed but playthings henceforth. I began, at length, to understand the boatman's familiarity with, and contempt for, the rapids. "Those Fowler boys," said Mrs. McCauslin, "are perfect ducks for the water." They had run down to Lincoln, according to her, thirty or forty miles, in a batteau, in the night, for a doctor, when it was so dark that they could not see a rod before them, and the river was swollen so as to be almost a continuous rapid, so that the doctor *cried*, when they brought him up by daylight, "Why, Tom, how did you see to steer?" "We did n't steer much, — only kept her straight." And yet they met with no accident. It is true, the more difficult rapids are higher up than this.

When we reached the Millinocket opposite to Tom's house, and were waiting for his folks to set us over, for we had left our batteau above the Grand Falls, we discovered two canoes, with two men in each, turning up this stream from Shad Pond, one keeping the opposite side of a small island before us, while the other approached the side where we were standing, examining the

banks carefully for muskrats as they came along.
The last proved to be Louis Neptune and his
companion, now, at last, on their way up to
Chesuncook after moose; but they were so dis-
guised that we hardly knew them. At a little
distance they might have been taken for Quak-
ers, with their broad-brimmed hats, and over-
coats with broad capes, the spoils of Bangor,
seeking a settlement in this Sylvania, — or,
nearer at hand, for fashionable gentlemen the
morning after a spree. Met face to face, these
Indians in their native woods looked like the
sinister and slouching fellows whom you meet
picking up strings and paper in the streets of a
city. There is, in fact, a remarkable and unex-
pected resemblance between the degraded savage and the lowest classes in a great city. The
one is no more a child of nature than the other.
In the progress of degradation the distinction of
races is soon lost. Neptune at first was only
anxious to know what we "kill," seeing some
partridges in the hands of one of the party, but
we had assumed too much anger to permit of
a reply. We thought Indians had some honor
before. But — "Me been sick. O, me unwell
now. You make bargain, then me go." They
had in fact been delayed so long by a drunken
frolic at the Five Islands, and they had not yet
recovered from its effects. They had some
young musquash in their canoes, which they

dug out of the banks with a hoe, for food, not for their skins, for musquash are their principal food on these expeditions. So they went on up the Millinocket, and we kept down the bank of the Penobscot, after recruiting ourselves with a draught of Tom's beer, leaving Tom at his home.

Thus a man shall lead his life away here on the edge of the wilderness, on Indian Millinocket stream, in a new world, far in the dark of a continent, and have a flute to play at evening here, while his strains echo to the stars, amid the howling of wolves; shall live, as it were, in the primitive age of the world, a primitive man. Yet he shall spend a sunny day, and in this century be my contemporary; perchance shall read some scattered leaves of literature, and sometimes talk with me. Why read history, then, if the ages and the generations are now? He lives three thousand years deep into time, an age not yet described by poets. Can you well go further back in history than this? Ay! ay! — for there turns up but now into the mouth of Millinocket stream a still more ancient and primitive man, whose history is not brought down even to the former. In a bark vessel sewn with the roots of the spruce, with hornbeam paddles, he dips his way along. He is but dim and misty to me, obscured by the æons that lie between the bark-canoe and the batteau. He builds no house of logs, but a wigwam of skins. He eats no hot bread and sweet cake, but musquash and moose-meat and the fat of bears. He glides up the Millinocket and is lost to my sight, as a more distant and misty cloud is seen flitting by behind a nearer, and is lost in space. So he goes about his destiny, the red face of man.

After having passed the night, and buttered our boots for the last time, at Uncle George's, whose dogs almost devoured him for joy at his return, we kept on down the river the next day, about eight miles on foot, and then took a batteau, with a man to pole it, to Mattawamkeag, ten more. At the middle of that very night, to make a swift conclusion to a long story, we dropped our buggy over the half-finished bridge at Oldtown, where we heard the confused din and clink of a hundred saws, which never rest, and at six o'clock the next morning one of the party was steaming his way to Massachusetts.

What is most striking in the Maine wilderness is the continuousness of the forest, with fewer open intervals or glades than you had imagined. Except the few burnt-lands, the narrow intervals on the rivers, the bare tops of the high mountains, and the lakes and streams, the forest is uninterrupted. It is even more grim and wild than you had anticipated, a damp and intricate wilderness, in the spring everywhere wet and miry. The aspect of the country, indeed, is uni-

versally stern and savage, excepting the distant
views of the forest from hills, and the lake pros-
pects, which are mild and civilizing in a degree.
The lakes are something which you are unpre-
pared for; they lie up so high, exposed to the
light, and the forest is diminished to a fine fringe
on their edges, with here and there a blue
mountain, like amethyst jewels set around some
jewel of the first water, — so anterior, so superior,
to all the changes that are to take place on their
shores, even now civil and refined, and fair as
they can ever be. These are not the artificial
forests of an English king, — a royal preserve
merely. Here prevail no forest laws but those
of nature. The aborigines have never been dis-
possessed, nor nature disforested.

It is a country full of evergreen trees, of mossy
silver birches and watery maples, the ground
dotted with insipid, small, red berries, and
strewn with damp and moss-grown rocks, — a
country diversified with innumerable lakes and
rapid streams, peopled with trout and various
species of *leucisci*, with salmon, shad, and pickerel, and other fishes; the forest resounding at
rare intervals with the note of the chicadee, the
blue-jay, and the woodpecker, the scream of the
fish-hawk and the eagle, the laugh of the loon,
and the whistle of ducks along the solitary
streams; at night, with the hooting of owls and
howling of wolves; in summer, swarming with

myriads of black flies and mosquitoes, more formidable than wolves to the white man. Such is the home of the moose, the bear, the caribou, the wolf, the beaver, and the Indian. Who shall describe the inexpressible tenderness and immortal life of the grim forest, where Nature, though it be mid-winter, is ever in her spring, where the moss-grown and decaying trees are not old, but seem to enjoy a perpetual youth; and blissful, innocent Nature, like a serene infant, is too happy to make a noise, except by a few tinkling, lisping birds and trickling rills?

What a place to live, what a place to die and be buried in! There certainly men would live forever, and laugh at death and the grave. There they could have no such thoughts as are associated with the village graveyard, — that make a grave out of one of those moist evergreen hummocks!

> Die and be buried who will,
> I mean to live here still;
> My nature grows ever more young
> The primitive pines among.

I am reminded by my journey how exceedingly new this country still is. You have only to travel for a few days into the interior and back parts even of many of the old States, to come to that very America which the Northmen, and Cabot, and Gosnold, and Smith, and Raleigh visited. If Columbus was the first to discover

the islands, Americus Vespucius and Cabot, and
the Puritans, and we their descendants, have
discovered only the shores of America. While
the republic has already acquired a history world-
wide, America is still unsettled and unexplored.
Like the English in New Holland, we live only
on the shores of a continent even yet, and hardly
know where the rivers come from which float our
navy. The very timber and boards and shingles
of which our houses are made, grew but yesterday in a wilderness where the Indian still hunts
and the moose runs wild. New York has her
wilderness within her own borders; and though
the sailors of Europe are familiar with the sound-
ings of her Hudson, and Fulton long since invented the steamboat on its waters, an Indian is
still necessary to guide her scientific men to its
head-waters in the Adirondac country.

Have we even so much as discovered and
settled the shores? Let a man travel on foot
along the coast, from the Passamaquoddy to the
Sabine, or to the Rio Bravo, or to wherever the
end is now, if he is swift enough to overtake it,
faithfully following the windings of every inlet
and of every cape, and stepping to the music of
the surf, — with a desolate fishing-town once a
week, and a city's port once a month to cheer
him, and putting up at the light-houses, when
there are any, — and tell me if it looks like a
discovered and settled country, and not rather,

for the most part, like a desolate island, and No-man's Land.

We have advanced by leaps to the Pacific, and left many a lesser Oregon and California unexplored behind us. Though the railroad and the telegraph have been established on the shores of Maine, the Indian still looks out from her interior mountains over all these to the sea. There stands the city of Bangor, fifty miles up the Penobscot, at the head of navigation for vessels of the largest class, the principal lumber depot on this continent, with a population of twelve thousand, like a star on the edge of night, still hewing at the forests of which it is built, already overflowing with the luxuries and refinement of Europe, and sending its vessels to Spain, to England, and to the West Indies for its groceries, — and yet only a few axe-men have gone "up river," into the howling wilderness which feeds it. The bear and deer are still found within its limits; and the moose, as he swims the Penobscot, is entangled amid its shipping, and taken by foreign sailors in its harbor. Twelve miles in the rear, twelve miles of railroad, are Orono and the Indian Island, the home of the Penobscot tribe, and then commence the batteau and the canoe, and the military road; and sixty miles above, the country is virtually unmapped and unexplored, and there still waves the virgin forest of the New World.

CHESUNCOOK

A T 5 P. M., September 13th, 1853, I left Boston, in the steamer for Bangor, by the outside course. It was a warm and still night, — warmer, probably, on the water than on the land, — and the sea was as smooth as a small lake in summer, merely rippled. The passengers went singing on the deck, as in a parlor, till ten o'clock. We passed a vessel on her beam-ends on a rock just outside the islands, and some of us thought that she was the "rapt ship" which ran

> "on her side so low
> That she drank water, and her keel ploughed air,"

not considering that there was no wind, and that she was under bare poles. Now we have left the islands behind and are off Nahant. We behold those features which the discoverers saw, apparently unchanged. Now we see the Cape Ann lights, and now pass near a small village-like fleet of mackerel-fishers at anchor, probably off Gloucester. They salute us with a shout from their low decks; but I understand their "Good evening" to mean "Don't run against me, Sir." From the wonders of the deep we go below to

yet deeper sleep.   And then the absurdity of
being waked up in the night by a man who wants
the job of blacking your boots!   It is more in-
evitable than sea-sickness, and may have something to do with it.   It is like the ducking you
get on crossing the line the first time.   I trusted
that these old customs were abolished.   They
might with the same propriety insist on blacking
your face.   I heard of one man who complained
that somebody had stolen his boots in the night;
and when he found them, he wanted to know
what they had done to them, — they had spoiled
them, — he never put that stuff on them; and
the bootblack narrowly escaped paying damages.

Anxious to get out of the whale's belly, I rose
early, and joined some old salts, who were smoking by a dim light on a sheltered part of the deck.
We were just getting into the river.   They knew
all about it, of course.   I was proud to find that
I had stood the voyage so well, and was not in
the least digested.   We brushed up and watched
the first signs of dawn through an open port;
but the day seemed to hang fire.   We inquired
the time; none of my companions had a chro-
nometer.   At length an African prince rushed by
observing, "Twelve o'clock, gentlemen!" and
blew out the light.   It was moon-rise.   So I
slunk down into the monster's bowels again.

The first land we make is Manhegan Island,
before dawn, and next St. George's Islands, see-

ing two or three lights. Whitehead, with its
bare rocks and funereal bell, is interesting. Next
I remember that the Camden Hills attracted my
eyes, and afterward the hills about Frankfort.
We reached Bangor about noon.

When I arrived, my companion that was to
be had gone up river, and engaged an Indian,
Joe Aitteon, a son of the Governor, to go with
us to Chesuncook Lake. Joe had conducted
two white men a-moose-hunting in the same
direction the year before. He arrived by cars
at Bangor that evening, with his canoe and a
companion, Sabattis Solomon, who was going
to leave Bangor the following Monday with Joe's
father, by way of the Penobscot, and join Joe
in moose-hunting at Chesuncook, when we had
done with him. They took supper at my friend's
house and lodged in his barn, saying that they
should fare worse than that in the woods. They
only made Watch bark a little, when they came
to the door in the night for water, for he does not
like Indians.

The next morning Joe and his canoe were put
on board the stage for Moosehead Lake, sixty
and odd miles distant, an hour before we started
in an open wagon. We carried hard bread,
pork, smoked beef, tea, sugar, etc., seemingly
enough for a regiment; the sight of which
brought together reminded me by what ignoble
means we had maintained our ground hitherto.

We went by the Avenue Road, which is quite straight and very good, northwestward toward Moosehead Lake, through more than a dozen flourishing towns, with almost every one its academy, — not one of which, however, is on my General Atlas, published, alas! in 1824; so much are they before the age, or I behind it! The earth must have been considerably lighter to the shoulders of General Atlas then.

It rained all this day and till the middle of the next forenoon, concealing the landscape almost entirely; but we had hardly got out of the streets of Bangor before I began to be exhilarated by the sight of the wild fir and spruce-tops, and those of other primitive evergreens, peering through the mist in the horizon. It was like the sight and odor of cake to a schoolboy. He who rides and keeps the beaten track studies the fences chiefly. Near Bangor, the fence-posts, on account of the frosts' heaving them in the clayey soil, were not planted in the ground, but were mortised into a transverse horizontal beam lying on the surface. Afterwards, the prevailing fences were log ones, with sometimes a Virginia fence, or else rails slanted over crossed stakes, — and these zigzagged or played leap-frog all the way to the lake, keeping just ahead of us. After getting out of the Penobscot Valley, the country was unexpectedly level, or consisted of very even and equal swells, for twenty or thirty miles, never rising above the general level, but affording, it is said, a very good prospect in clear weather, with frequent views of Ktaadn, — straight roads and long hills. The houses were far apart, commonly small and of one story, but framed. There was very little land under cultivation, yet the forest did not often border the road. The stumps were frequently as high as one's head, showing the depth of the snows. The white hay-caps, drawn over small stacks of beans or corn in the fields, on account of the rain, were a novel sight to me. We saw large flocks of pigeons, and several times came within a rod or two of partridges in the road. My companion said, that, in one journey out of Bangor, he and his son had shot sixty partridges from his buggy. The mountain-ash was now very handsome, as also the wayfarer's tree or hobble-bush, with its ripe purple berries mixed with red. The Canada thistle, an introduced plant, was the prevailing weed all the way to the lake, — the road-side in many places, and fields not long cleared, being densely filled with it as with a crop, to the exclusion of everything else. There were also whole fields full of ferns, now rusty and withering, which in older countries are commonly confined to wet ground. There were very few flowers, even allowing for the lateness of the season. It chanced that I saw no asters in bloom along the road for fifty miles, though

they were so abundant then in Massachusetts, —
except in one place one or two of the Aster
acuminatus, — and no golden-rods till within
twenty miles of Monson, where I saw a three-
ribbed one. There were many late buttercups,
however, and the two fire-weeds, Erechthites
and Epilobium, commonly where there had
been a burning, and at last the pearly everlasting.
I noticed occasionally very long troughs which
supplied the road with water, and my companion
said that three dollars annually were granted
by the State to one man in each school-district,
who provided and maintained a suitable water-
trough by the roadside, for the use of travellers,
— a piece of intelligence as refreshing to me as
the water itself. That legislature did not sit in
vain. It was an Oriental act, which made me
wish that I was still farther down East, —
another Maine law, which I hope we may get in
Massachusetts. That State is banishing bar-
rooms from its highways, and conducting the
mountain-springs thither.

The country was first decidedly mountainous
in Garland, Sangerville, and onwards, twenty-
five or thirty miles from Bangor. At Sangerville, where we stopped at mid-afternoon to
warm and dry ourselves, the landlord told us
that he had found a wilderness where we found
him. At a fork in the road between Abbot and
Monson, about twenty miles from Moosehead

Lake, I saw a guide-post surmounted by a pair of Moose-horns, spreading four or five feet, with the word "Monson" painted on one blade, and the name of some other town on the other. They are sometimes used for ornamental hat-trees, together with deer's horns, in front entries; but, after the experience which I shall relate, I trust that I shall have a better excuse for killing a moose than that I may hang my hat on his horns. We reached Monson, fifty miles from Bangor, and thirteen from the lake, after dark.

At four o'clock the next morning, in the dark, and still in the rain, we pursued our journey. Close to the academy in this town they have erected a sort of gallows for the pupils to practise on. I thought that they might as well hang at once all who need to go through such exercises in so new a country, where there is nothing to hinder their living an outdoor life. Better omit Blair, and take the air. The country about the south end of the lake is quite mountainous, and the road began to feel the effects of it. There is one hill which, it is calculated, it takes twenty-five minutes to ascend. In many places the road was in that condition called *repaired*, having just been whittled into the required semi-cylindrical form with the shovel and scraper, with all the softest inequalities in the middle, like a hog's back with the bristles up, and Jehu was expected to keep astride of the spine. As you looked off each side of the bare sphere into the horizon, the ditches were awful to behold, — a vast hollowness, like that between Saturn and his ring. At a tavern hereabouts the hostler greeted our horse as an old acquaintance, though he did not remember the driver. He said that he had taken care of that little mare for a short time, a year or two before, at the Mount Kineo House, and thought she was not in as good condition as then. Every man to his trade. I am not acquainted with a single horse in the world, not even the one that kicked me.

Already we had thought that we saw Moosehead Lake from a hill-top, where an extensive fog filled the distant lowlands, but we were mistaken. It was not till we were within a mile or two of its south end that we got our first view of it, — a suitably wild-looking sheet of water, sprinkled with small, low islands, which were covered with shaggy spruce and other wild wood, — seen over the infant port of Greenville, with mountains on each side and far in the north, and a steamer's smoke-pipe rising above a roof. A pair of moose-horns ornamented a corner of the public house where we left our horse, and a few rods distant lay the small steamer Moosehead, Captain King. There was no village, and no summer road any farther in this direction, — but a winter road, that is, one passable only when deep snow covers its inequalities, from Greenville up the east side of the lake to Lily Bay, about twelve miles.

I was here first introduced to Joe. He had ridden all the way on the outside of the stage, the day before, in the rain, giving way to ladies, and was well wetted. As it still rained, he asked if we were going to "put it through." He was a good-looking Indian, twenty-four years old, apparently of unmixed blood, short and stout, with a broad face and reddish complexion, and eyes, methinks, narrower and more turned-up at the outer corners than ours, answering to the description of his race. Besides his underclothing, he wore a red-flannel shirt, woollen pants, and a black Kossuth hat, the ordinary dress of the lumberman, and, to a considerable extent, of the Penobscot Indian. When, afterward, he had occasion to take off his shoes and stockings, I was struck with the smallness of his feet. He had worked a good deal as a lumberman, and appeared to identify himself with that class. He was the only one of the party who possessed an India-rubber jacket. The top strip or edge of his canoe was worn nearly through by friction on the stage.

At eight o'clock the steamer, with her bell and whistle, scaring the moose, summoned us on board. She was a well-appointed little boat, commanded by a gentlemanly captain, with

patent life-seats and metallic life-boat, and dinner on board, if you wish. She is chiefly used
by lumberers for the transportation of themselves,
their boats, and supplies, but also by hunters
and tourists. There was another steamer,
named Amphitrite, laid up close by; but, apparently, her name was not more trite than her
hull. There were also two or three large sail-
boats in port. These beginnings of commerce
on a lake in the wilderness are very interesting,
— these larger white birds that come to keep
company with the gulls. There were but few
passengers, and not one female among them:
a St. Francis Indian, with his canoe and moose-
hides, two explorers for lumber, three men who
landed at Sandbar Island, and a gentleman who
lives on Deer Island, eleven miles up the lake,
and owns also Sugar Island, between which and
the former the steamer runs; these, I think,
were all beside ourselves. In the saloon was
some kind of musical instrument, cherubim, or
seraphim, to soothe the angry waves; and
there, very properly, was tacked up the map of
the public lands of Maine and Massachusetts,
a copy of which I had in my pocket.

The heavy rain confining us to the saloon
awhile, I discoursed with the proprietor of
Sugar Island on the condition of the world in
Old Testament times. But at length, leaving
this subject as fresh as we found it, he told me

that he had lived about this lake twenty or
thirty years, and yet had not been to the head of
it, for twenty-one years. He faces the other way.
The explorers had a fine new birch on board,
larger than ours, in which they had come up the
Piscataquis from Howland, and they had had
several messes of trout already. They were
going to the neighborhood of Eagle and Chamberlain Lakes, or the headwaters of the St. John,
and offered to keep us company as far as we
went. The lake to-day was rougher than I
found the ocean, either going or returning, and
Joe remarked that it would swamp his birch.
Off Lily Bay it is a dozen miles wide, but it is
much broken by islands. The scenery is not
merely wild, but varied and interesting; mountains were seen, farther or nearer, on all sides
but the northwest, their summits now lost in
the clouds; but Mount Kineo is the principal
feature of the lake, and more exclusively belongs to it. After leaving Greenville, at the foot,
which is the nucleus of a town some eight or
ten years old, you see but three or four houses
for the whole length of the lake, or about forty
miles, three of them the public houses at which
the steamer is advertised to stop, and the shore
is an unbroken wilderness. The prevailing wood
seemed to be spruce, fir, birch, and rock-maple.
You could easily distinguish the hard wood from
the soft, or "black growth," as it is called, at

a great distance, — the former being smooth, round-topped, and light green, with a bowery and cultivated look.

Mount Kineo, at which the boat touched, is a peninsula with a narrow neck, about midway the lake on the east side. The celebrated precipice is on the east or land side of this, and is so high and perpendicular that you can jump from the top, many hundred feet, into the water, which makes up behind the point. A man on board told us that an anchor had been sunk ninety fathoms at its base before reaching bottom! Probably it will be discovered erelong that some Indian maiden jumped off it for love once, for true love never could have found a path more to its mind. We passed quite close to the rock here, since it is a very bold shore, and I observed marks of a rise of four or five feet on it. The St. Francis Indian expected to take in his boy here, but he was not at the landing. The father's sharp eyes, however, detected a canoe with his boy in it far away under the mountain, though no one else could see it. "Where is the canoe?" asked the captain, "I don't see it"; but he held on, nevertheless, and by and by it hove in sight.

We reached the head of the lake about noon. The weather had, in the meanwhile, cleared up, though the mountains were still capped with clouds. Seen from this point, Mount Kineo,

and two other allied mountains ranging with it
northeasterly, presented a very strong family
likeness, as if all cast in one mould. The steamer
here approached a long pier projecting from the
northern wilderness, and built of some of its
logs, — and whistled, where not a cabin nor a
mortal was to be seen. The shore was quite
low, with flat rocks on it, overhung with black
ash, arbor-vitæ, etc., which at first looked as if
they did not care a whistle for us. There was
not a single cabman to cry "Coach!" or inveigle
us to the United States Hotel. At length a Mr.
Hinckley, who has a camp at the other end of
the "carry," appeared with a truck drawn by
an ox and a horse over a rude log-railway through
the woods. The next thing was to get our canoe
and effects over the carry from this lake, one of
the heads of the Kennebec, into the Penobscot
River. This railway from the lake to the river
occupied the middle of a clearing two or three
rods wide and perfectly straight through the
forest. We walked across while our baggage
was drawn behind. My companion went ahead
to be ready for partridges, while I followed,
looking at the plants.

This was an interesting botanical locality for
one coming from the South to commence with;
for many plants which are rather rare, and one
or two which are not found at all, in the eastern
part of Massachusetts, grew abundantly between

the rails, — as Labrador tea, Kalmia glauca,
Canada blueberry (which was still in fruit, and
a second time in bloom), Clintonia and Linnæa borealis, which last a lumberer called *moxon*,
creeping snowberry, painted trillium, large-
flowered bellwort, etc. I fancied that the Aster
radula, Diplopappus umbellatus, Solidago lance-
olatus, red trumpet-weed, and many others
which were conspicuously in bloom on the shore
of the lake and on the carry, had a peculiarly
wild and primitive look there. The spruce and
fir trees crowded to the track on each side to
welcome us, the arbor-vitæ, with its changing
leaves, prompted us to make haste, and the sight
of the canoe-birch gave us spirits to do so. Sometimes an evergreen just fallen lay across the
track with its rich burden of cones, looking, still,
fuller of life than our trees in the most favorable
positions. You did not expect to find such *spruce*
trees in the wild woods, but they evidently attend to their toilets each morning even there.
Through such a front-yard did we enter that
wilderness.

There was a very slight rise above the lake, —
the country appearing like, and perhaps being,
partly a swamp, — and at length a gradual
descent to the Penobscot, which I was surprised
to find here a large stream, from twelve to fifteen
rods wide, flowing from west to east, or at right
angles with the lake, and not more than two

and a half miles from it. The distance is nearly
twice too great on the Map of the Public Lands,
and on Colton's Map of Maine, and Russell
Stream is placed too far down. Jackson makes
Moosehead Lake to be nine hundred and sixty
feet above high water in Portland harbor. It
is higher than Chesuncook, for the lumberers
consider the Penobscot, where we struck it,
twenty-five feet lower than Moosehead, — though
eight miles above it is said to be the highest,
so that the water can be made to flow either
way, and the river falls a good deal between here
and Chesuncook. The carryman called this
about one hundred and forty miles above Bangor
by the river, or two hundred from the ocean,
and fifty-five miles below Hilton's, on the Canada
road, the first clearing above, which is four and
a half miles from the source of the Penobscot.

At the north end of the carry, in the midst of
a clearing of sixty acres or more, there was a log
camp of the usual construction, with something
more like a house adjoining, for the accommoda-
tion of the carryman's family and passing lumberers. The bed of withered fir-twigs smelled
very sweet, though really very dirty. There was
also a store-house on the bank of the river, containing pork, flour, iron, batteaux, and birches,
locked up.

We now proceeded to get our dinner, which
always turned out to be tea, and to pitch canoes,

for which purpose a large iron pot lay permanently on the bank. This we did in company with the explorers. Both Indians and whites use a mixture of rosin and grease for this purpose, — that is, for the pitching, not the dinner. Joe took a small brand from the fire and blew the heat and flame against the pitch on his birch, and so melted and spread it. Sometimes he put his mouth over the suspected spot and sucked, to see if it admitted air; and at one place, where we stopped, he set his canoe high on crossed stakes, and poured water into it. I narrowly watched his motions, and listened attentively to his observations, for we had employed an Indian mainly that I might have an opportunity to study his ways. I heard him swear once, mildly, during this operation, about his knife being as dull as a hoe, — an accomplishment which he owed to his intercourse with the whites; and he remarked, "We ought to have some tea before we start; we shall be hungry before we kill that moose."

At mid-afternoon we embarked on the Penobscot. Our birch was nineteen and a half feet long by two and a half at the widest part, and fourteen inches deep within, both ends alike, and painted green, which Joe thought affected the pitch and made it leak. This, I think, was a middling-sized one. That of the explorers was much larger, though probably not much longer.

This carried us three with our baggage, weighing in all between five hundred and fifty and six
hundred pounds. We had two heavy, though
slender, rock-maple paddles, one of them of
bird's-eye maple. Joe placed birch-bark on the
bottom for us to sit on, and slanted cedar splints
against the cross-bars to protect our backs,
while he himself sat upon a cross-bar in the
stern. The baggage occupied the middle or
widest part of the canoe. We also paddled by
turns in the bows, now sitting with our legs
extended, now sitting upon our legs, and now
rising upon our knees; but I found none of
these positions endurable, and was reminded of
the complaints of the old Jesuit missionaries of
the torture they endured from long confinement
in constrained positions in canoes, in their long
voyages from Quebec to the Huron country;
but afterwards I sat on the cross-bars, or stood
up, and experienced no inconvenience.

It was dead-water for a couple of miles. The
river had been raised about two feet by the rain,
and lumberers were hoping for a flood sufficient
to bring down the logs that were left in the spring.
Its banks were seven or eight feet high, and
densely covered with white and black spruce,
— which, I think, must be the commonest trees
thereabouts, — fir, arbor-vitæ, canoe, yellow, and
black birch, rock, mountain, and a few red
maples, beech, black and mountain ash, the

large-toothed aspen, many civil-looking elms, now imbrowned, along the stream, and at first a few hemlocks also. We had not gone far before I was startled by seeing what I thought was an Indian encampment, covered with a red flag, on the bank, and exclaimed, "Camp!" to my comrades. I was slow to discover that it was a red maple changed by the frost. The immediate shores were also densely covered with the speckled alder, red osier, shrubby-willows or sallows, and the like. There were a few yellow-lily-pads still left, half-drowned, along the sides, and sometimes a white one. Many fresh tracks of moose were visible where the water was shallow, and on the shore, and the lily-stems were freshly bitten off by them.

After paddling about two miles, we parted company with the explorers, and turned up Lobster Stream, which comes in on the right, from the southeast. This was six or eight rods wide, and appeared to run nearly parallel with the Penobscot. Joe said that it was so called from small fresh-water lobsters found in it. It is the Matahumkeag of the maps. My companion wished to look for moose signs, and intended, if it proved worth the while, to camp up that way, since the Indian advised it. On account of the rise of the Penobscot the water ran up this stream quite to the pond of the same name, one or two miles. The Spencer Moun-

tains, east of the north end of Moosehead Lake,
were now in plain sight in front of us. The
kingfisher flew before us, the pigeon woodpecker was seen and heard, and nuthatches and
chicadees close at hand. Joe said that they
called the chicadee *kecunnilessu* in his language.
I will not vouch for the spelling of what possibly
was never spelt before, but I pronounced after
him till he said it would do. We passed close
to a woodcock, which stood perfectly still on the
shore, with feathers puffed up, as if sick. This
Joe said they called *nipsquecohossus*. The kingfisher was *skuscumonsuck;* bear was *wassus;*
Indian Devil, *lunxus;* the mountain-ash, *upahsis*. This was very abundant and beautiful.
Moose-tracks were not so fresh along this stream,
except in a small creek about a mile up it, where
a large log had lodged in the spring, marked
"W—cross—girdle—crow-foot." We saw a pair
of moose-horns on the shore, and I asked Joe
if a moose had shed them; but he said there
was a head attached to them, and I knew that
they did not shed their heads more than once in
their lives.

After ascending about a mile and a half, to
within a short distance of Lobster Lake, we
returned to the Penobscot. Just below the
mouth of the Lobster we found quick water, and
the river expanded to twenty or thirty rods in
width. The moose-tracks were quite numerous

and fresh here. We noticed in a great many
places narrow and well-trodden paths by which
they had come down to the river, and where
they had slid on the steep and clayey bank.
Their tracks were either close to the edge of the
stream, those of the calves distinguishable from
the others, or in shallow water; the holes made
by their feet in the soft bottom being visible for
a long time. They were particularly numerous
where there was a small bay, or *pokelogan*, as it
is called, bordered by a strip of meadow, or
separated from the river by a low peninsula
covered with coarse grass, wool-grass, etc.,
wherein they had waded back and forth and
eaten the pads. We detected the remains of
one in such a spot. At one place, where we
landed to pick up a summer duck, which my
companion had shot, Joe peeled a canoe-birch
for bark for his hunting-horn. He then asked
if we were not going to get the other duck, for
his sharp eyes had seen another fall in the bushes
a little farther along, and my companion obtained it. I now began to notice the bright red
berries of the tree-cranberry, which grows eight
or ten feet high, mingled with the alders and
cornel along the shore. There was less hard
wood than at first.

After proceeding a mile and three-quarters
below the mouth of the Lobster, we reached,
about sun-down, a small island at the head of

what Joe called the Moosehorn Dead-water (the Moosehorn, in which he was going to hunt that night, coming in about three miles below), and on the upper end of this we decided to camp. On a point at the lower end lay the carcass of a moose killed a month or more before. We concluded merely to prepare our camp, and leave our baggage here, that all might be ready when we returned from moose-hunting. Though I had not come a-hunting, and felt some compunctions about accompanying the hunters, I wished to see a moose near at hand, and was not sorry to learn how the Indian managed to kill one. I went as reporter or chaplain to the hunters, — and the chaplain has been known to carry a gun himself. After clearing a small space amid the dense spruce and fir trees, we covered the damp ground with a shingling of fir-twigs, and, while Joe was preparing his birch-horn and pitching his canoe, — for this had to be done whenever we stopped long enough to build a fire, and was the principal labor which he took upon himself at such times, — we collected fuel for the night, large wet and rotting logs, which had lodged at the head of the island, for our hatchet was too small for effective chopping; but we did not kindle a fire, lest the moose should smell it. Joe set up a couple of forked stakes, and prepared half a dozen poles, ready to cast one of our blankets over in case it rained in the night, which precaution, however, was omitted the next night. We also plucked the ducks which had been killed for breakfast.

While we were thus engaged in the twilight, we heard faintly, from far down the stream, what sounded like two strokes of a woodchopper's axe, echoing dully through the grim solitude. We are wont to liken many sounds, heard at a distance in the forest, to the stroke of an axe, because they resemble each other under those circumstances, and that is the one we commonly hear there. When we told Joe of this, he exclaimed, "By George, I'll bet that was a moose! They make a noise like that." These sounds affected us strangely, and by their very resemblance to a familiar one, where they probably had so different an origin, enchanced the impression of solitude and wildness.

At starlight we dropped down the stream, which was a dead-water for three miles, or as far as the Moosehorn; Joe telling us that we must be very silent, and he himself making no noise with his paddle, while he urged the canoe along with effective impulses. It was a still night, and suitable for this purpose, — for if there is wind, the moose will smell you, — and Joe was very confident that he should get some. The harvest moon had just risen, and its level rays began to light up the forest on our right, while we glided downward in the shade on the same side, against the little breeze that was stirring. The lofty, spiring tops of the spruce and fir were very black against the sky, and more distinct than by day, close bordering this broad avenue on each side; and the beauty of the scene, as the moon rose above the forest, it would not be easy to describe. A bat flew over our heads, and we heard a few faint notes of birds from time to time, perhaps the myrtle-bird for one, or the sudden plunge of a musquash, or saw one crossing the stream before us, or heard the sound of a rill emptying in, swollen by the recent rain. About a mile below the island, when the solitude seemed to be growing more complete every moment, we suddenly saw the light and heard the crackling of a fire on the bank, and discovered the camp of the two explorers; they standing before it in their red shirts, and talking aloud of the adventures and profits of the day. They were just then speaking of a bargain, in which, as I understood, somebody had cleared twenty-five dollars. We glided by without speaking, close under the bank, within a couple of rods of them; and Joe, taking his horn, imitated the call of the moose, till we suggested that they might fire on us. This was the last we saw of them, and we never knew whether they detected or suspected us.

I have often wished since that I was with them. They search for timber over a given section,

climbing hills and often high trees to look off, —
explore the streams by which it is to be driven,
and the like, — spend five or six weeks in the
woods, they two alone, a hundred miles or more
from any town, — roaming about, and sleeping
on the ground where night overtakes them, —
depending chiefly on the provisions they carry
with them, though they do not decline what
game they come across, — and then in the fall
they return and make report to their employers,
determining the number of teams that will be
required the following winter. Experienced men
get three or four dollars a day for this work. It
is a solitary and adventurous life, and comes
nearest to that of the trapper of the West, perhaps. They work ever with a gun as well as an
axe, let their beards grow, and live without
neighbors, not on an open plain, but far within
a wilderness.

This discovery accounted for the sounds which
we had heard, and destroyed the prospect of
seeing moose yet awhile. At length, when we
had left the explorers far behind, Joe laid down
his paddle, drew forth his birch horn, — a
straight one, about fifteen inches long and three
or four wide at the mouth, tied round with strips
of the same bark, — and standing up, imitated
the call of the moose, — *ugh-ugh-ugh*, or *oo-oo-
oo-oo*, and then a prolonged *oo-o-o-o-o-o-o-o*, and
listened attentively for several minutes. We

asked him what kind of noise he expected to hear. He said, that, if a moose heard it, he guessed we should find out; we should hear him coming half a mile off; he would come close to, perhaps into, the water, and my companion must wait till he got fair sight, and then aim just behind the shoulder.

The moose venture out to the river-side to feed and drink at night. Earlier in the season the hunters do not use a horn to call them out, but steal upon them as they are feeding along the sides of the stream, and often the first notice they have of one is the sound of the water dropping from its muzzle. An Indian whom I heard imitate the voice of the moose, and also that of the caribou and the deer, using a much longer horn than Joe's, told me that the first could be heard eight or ten miles, sometimes; it was a loud sort of bellowing sound, clearer and more sonorous than the lowing of cattle, — the caribou's a sort of snort, — and the small deer's like that of a lamb.

At length we turned up the Moosehorn, where the Indians at the carry had told us that they killed a moose the night before. This is a very meandering stream, only a rod or two in width, but comparatively deep, coming in on the right, fitly enough named Moosehorn, whether from its windings or its inhabitants. It was bordered here and there by narrow meadows between the stream and the endless forest, affording favorable places for the moose to feed, and to call them out on. We proceeded half a mile up this, as through a narrow, winding canal, where the tall, dark spruce and firs and arbor-vitæ towered on both sides in the moonlight, forming a perpendicular forest-edge of great height, like the spires of a Venice in the forest. In two places stood a small stack of hay on the bank, ready for the lumberer's use in the winter, looking strange enough there. We thought of the day when this might be a brook winding through smooth-shaven meadows on some gentleman's grounds; and seen by moonlight then, excepting the forest that now hems it in, how little changed it would appear!

Again and again Joe called the moose, placing the canoe close by some favorable point of meadow for them to come out on, but listened in vain to hear one come rushing through the woods and concluded that they had been hunted too much thereabouts. We saw, many times, what to our imaginations looked like a gigantic moose, with his horns peering from out the forest-edge; but we saw the forest only, and not its inhabitants, that night. So at last we turned about. There was now a little fog on the water, though it was a fine, clear night above. There were very few sounds to break the stillness of the forest. Several times we heard the hooting

of a great horned-owl, as at home, and told Joe
that he would call out the moose for him, for
he made a sound considerably like the horn, —
but Joe answered, that the moose had heard
that sound a thousand times, and knew better;
and oftener still we were startled by the plunge
of a musquash. Once, when Joe had called
again, and we were listening for moose, we heard,
come faintly echoing, or creeping from far,
through the moss-clad aisles, a dull, dry, rushing
sound, with a solid core to it, yet as if half smothered under the grasp of the luxuriant and fungus-
like forest, like the shutting of a door in some
distant entry of the damp and shaggy wilderness. If we had not been there, no mortal had
heard it. When we asked Joe in a whisper what
it was, he answered, — "Tree fall." There is
something singularly grand and impressive in
the sound of a tree falling in a perfectly calm
night like this, as if the agencies which over-
throw it did not need to be excited, but worked
with a subtle, deliberate, and conscious force,
like a boa-constrictor, and more effectively then
than even in a windy day. If there is any such
difference, perhaps it is because trees with the
dews of the night on them are heavier than by
day.

Having reached the camp, about ten o'clock,
we kindled our fire and went to bed. Each of
us had a blanket, in which he lay on the fir-

twigs, with his extremities toward the fire, but nothing over his head. It was worth the while to lie down in a country where you could afford such great fires; that was one whole side, and the bright side of our world. We had first rolled up a large log some eighteen inches through and ten feet long, for a back-log, to last all night, and then piled on the trees to the height of three or four feet, no matter how green or damp. In fact, we burned as much wood that night as would, with economy and an air-tight stove, last a poor family in one of our cities all winter. It was very agreeable, as well as independent, thus lying in the open air, and the fire kept our uncovered extremities warm enough. The Jesuit missionaries used to say, that, in their journeys with the Indians in Canada, they lay on a bed which had never been shaken up since the creation, unless by earthquakes. It is surprising with what impunity and comfort one who has always lain in a warm bed in a close apartment, and studiously avoided drafts of air, can lie down on the ground without a shelter, roll himself in a blanket, and sleep before a fire, in a frosty, autumn night, just after a long rain-storm, and even come soon to enjoy and value the fresh air.

I lay awake awhile, watching the ascent of the sparks through the firs, and sometimes their descent in half-extinguished cinders on my blanket. They were as interesting as fireworks, going up in endless, successive crowds, each after an explosion, in an eager, serpentine course, some to five or six rods above the tree-tops before they went out. We do not suspect how much our chimneys have concealed; and now air-tight stoves have come to conceal all the rest. In the course of the night, I got up once or twice and put fresh logs on the fire, making my companions curl up their legs.

When we awoke in the morning, (Saturday, September 17,) there was considerable frost whitening the leaves. We heard the sound of the chicadee, and a few faintly lisping birds, and also of ducks in the water about the island. I took a botanical account of stock of our domains before the dew was off, and found that the ground-hemlock, or American yew, was the prevailing under-shrub. We breakfasted on tea, hard bread, and ducks.

Before the fog had fairly cleared away, we paddled down the stream again, and were soon past the mouth of the Moosehorn. These twenty miles of the Penobscot, between Moosehead and Chesuncook Lakes, are comparatively smooth, and a great part dead-water; but from time to time it is shallow and rapid, with rocks or gravel-beds, where you can wade across. There is no expanse of water, and no break in the forest, and the meadow is a mere edging here and there. There are no hills near the river nor within sight, except one or two distant mountains seen in a few places. The banks are from six to ten feet high, but once or twice rise gently to higher ground. In many places the forest on the bank was but a thin strip, letting the light through from some alder-swamp or meadow behind. The conspicuous berry-bearing bushes and trees along the shore were the red osier, with its whitish fruit, hobble-bush, mountain-ash, tree-cranberry, choke-cherry, now ripe, alternate cornel, and naked viburnum. Following Joe's example, I ate the fruit of the last, and also of the hobble-bush, but found them rather insipid and seedy. I looked very narrowly at the vegetation, as we glided along close to the shore, and frequently made Joe turn aside for me to pluck a plant, that I might see by comparison what was primitive about my native river. Horehound, horsemint, and the sensitive fern grew close to the edge, under the willows and alders, and wool-grass on the islands, as along the Assabet River in Concord. It was too late for flowers, except a few asters, golden-rods, etc. In several places we noticed the slight frame of a camp, such as we had prepared to set up, amid the forest by the river-side, where some lumberers or hunters had passed a night, — and sometimes steps cut in the muddy or clayey bank in front of it.

We stopped to fish for trout at the mouth of a

small stream called Ragmuff, which came in
from the west, about two miles below the Moosehorn. Here were the ruins of an old lumbering-
camp, and a small space, which had formerly
been cleared and burned over, was now densely
overgrown with the red cherry and raspberries.
While we were trying for trout, Joe, Indian-like,
wandered off up the Ragmuff on his own errands,
and when we were ready to start was far beyond
call. So we were compelled to make a fire and
get our dinner here, not to lose time. Some dark
reddish birds, with grayer females, (perhaps
purple finches,) and myrtle-birds in their summer dress, hopped within six or eight feet of us
and our smoke. Perhaps they smelled the frying
pork. The latter bird, or both, made the lisping
notes which I had heard in the forest. They
suggested that the few small birds found in the
wilderness are on more familiar terms with the
lumberman and hunter than those of the orchard
and clearing with the farmer. I have since
found the Canada jay, and partridges, both the
black and the common, equally tame there,
as if they had not yet learned to mistrust man
entirely. The chicadee, which is at home alike
in the primitive woods and in our wood-lots,
still retains its confidence in the towns to a remarkable degree.

Joe at length returned, after an hour and a
half, and said that he had been two miles up

the stream exploring, and had seen a moose, but, not having the gun, he did not get him. We made no complaint, but concluded to look out for Joe the next time. However, this may have been a mere mistake, for we had no reason to complain of him afterwards. As we continued down the stream, I was surprised to hear him whistling "O Susanna," and several other such airs, while his paddle urged us along. Once he said, "Yes, Sir-ee." His common word was "Sartain." He paddled, as usual, on one side only, giving the birch an impulse by using the side as a fulcrum. I asked him how the ribs were fastened to the side rails. He answered, "I don't know, I never noticed." Talking with him about subsisting wholly on what the woods yielded, game, fish, berries, etc., I suggested that his ancestors did so; but he answered, that he had been brought up in such a way that he could not do it. "Yes," said he, "that's the way they got a living, like wild fellows, wild as bears. By George! I shan't go into the woods without provision, — hard bread, pork, etc." He had brought on a barrel of hard bread and stored it at the carry for his hunting. However, though he was a Governor's son, he had not learned to read.

At one place below this, on the east side, where the bank was higher and drier than usual, rising gently from the shore to a slight elevation,

some one had felled the trees over twenty or
thirty acres, and left them drying in order to
burn. This was the only preparation for a house
between the Moosehead carry and Chesuncook,
but there was no hut nor inhabitants there yet.
The pioneer thus selects a site for his house,
which will, perhaps, prove the germ of a town.

My eyes were all the while on the trees, distinguishing between the black and white spruce
and the fir. You paddle along in a narrow canal
through an endless forest, and the vision I have
in my mind's eye, still, is of the small, dark, and
sharp tops of tall fir and spruce trees, and pagoda-
like arbor-vitæs, crowded together on each side,
with various hard woods, intermixed. Some of
the arbor-vitæs were at least sixty feet high.
The hard woods, occasionally occurring exclusively, were less wild to my eye. I fancied
them ornamental grounds, with farm-houses in
the rear. The canoe and yellow birch, beech,
maple, and elm are Saxon and Norman; but
the spruce and fir, and pines generally, are
Indian. The soft engravings which adorn the
annuals give no idea of a stream in such a wilderness as this. The rough sketches in Jackson's
Reports on the Geology of Maine answer much
better. At one place we saw a small grove of
slender sapling white-pines, the only collection
of pines that I saw on this voyage. Here
and there, however, was a fully-grown, tall and

slender, but defective one, what lumbermen call a *konchus* tree, which they ascertain with their axes, or by the knots. I did not learn whether this word was Indian or English. It reminded me of the Greek κόγχη, a conch or shell, and I amused myself with fancying that it might signify the dead sound which the trees yield when struck. All the rest of the pines had been driven off.

How far men go for the material of their houses! The inhabitants of the most civilized cities, in all ages, send into far, primitive forests, beyond the bounds of their civilization, where the moose and bear and savage dwell, for their pine-boards for ordinary use. And, on the other hand, the savage soon receives from cities, iron arrow-points, hatchets, and guns, to point his savageness with.

The solid and well-defined fir-tops, like sharp and regular spear-heads, black against the sky, gave a peculiar, dark, and sombre look to the forest. The spruce-tops have a similar, but more ragged outline, — their shafts also merely feathered below. The firs were somewhat oftener regular and dense pyramids. I was struck by this universal spiring upward of the forest evergreens. The tendency is to slender, spiring tops, while they are narrower below. Not only the spruce and fir, but even the arbor-vitæ and white-pine, unlike the soft, spreading

second-growth, of which I saw none, all spire
upwards, lifting a dense spear-head of cones
to the light and air, at any rate, while their
branches struggle after as they may; as Indians
lift the ball over the heads of the crowd in their
desperate game. In this they resemble grasses,
as also palms somewhat. The hemlock is commonly a tent-like pyramid from the ground to
its summit.

After passing through some long rips, and by
a large island, we reached an interesting part
of the river called the Pine Stream Dead-Water,
about six miles below Ragmuff, where the river
expanded to thirty rods in width and had many
islands in it, with elms and canoe-birches, now
yellowing, along the shore, and we got our first
sight of Ktaadn.

Here, about two o'clock, we turned up a small
branch three or four rods wide, which comes in
on the right from the south, called Pine Stream,
to look for moose signs. We had gone but a few
rods before we saw very recent signs along the
water's edge, the mud lifted up by their feet
being quite fresh, and Joe declared that they
had gone along there but a short time before.
We soon reached a small meadow on the east
side, at an angle in the stream, which was, for
the most part, densely covered with alders. As
we were advancing along the edge of this, rather
more quietly than usual, perhaps, on account of

the freshness of the signs, — the design being to camp up this stream, if it promised well, — I heard a slight crackling of twigs deep in the alders, and turned Joe's attention to it; whereupon he began to push the canoe back rapidly; and we had receded thus half a dozen rods, when we suddenly spied two moose standing just on the edge of the open part of the meadow which we had passed, not more than six or seven rods distant, looking round the alders at us. They made me think of great frightened rabbits, with their long ears and half-inquisitive, half-frightened looks; the true denizens of the forest, (I saw at once,) filling a vacuum which now first I discovered had not been filled for me, — *moose-men*, *wood-eaters*, the word is said to mean, — clad in a sort of Vermont gray, or homespun. Our Nimrod, owing to the retrograde movement, was now the farthest from the game; but being warned of its neighborhood, he hastily stood up, and, while we ducked, fired over our heads one barrel at the foremost, which alone he saw, though he did not know what kind of creature it was; whereupon this one dashed across the meadow and up a high bank on the northeast, so rapidly as to leave but an indistinct impression of its outlines on my mind. At the same instant, the other, a young one, but as tall as a horse, leaped out into the stream, in full sight, and there stood cowering for a moment, or rather

its disproportionate lowness behind gave it that
appearance, and uttering two or three trumpet-
ing squeaks. I have an indistinct recollection of
seeing the old one pause an instant on the top
of the bank in the woods, look toward its shiver-
ing young, and then dash away again. The
second barrel was levelled at the calf, and when
we expected to see it drop in the water, after a
little hesitation, it, too, got out of the water, and
dashed up the hill, though in a somewhat different direction. All this was the work of a few
seconds, and our hunter, having never seen a
moose before, did not know but they were deer,
for they stood partly in the water, nor whether
he had fired at the same one twice or not. From
the style in which they went off, and the fact
that he was not used to standing up and firing
from a canoe, I judged that we should not see
anything more of them. The Indian said that
they were a cow and her calf, — a yearling, or
perhaps two years old, for they accompany their
dams so long; but, for my part, I had not
noticed much difference in their size. It was
but two or three rods across the meadow to the
foot of the bank, which, like all the world thereabouts, was densely wooded; but I was surprised to notice, that, as soon as the moose had
passed behind the veil of the woods, there was no
sound of footsteps to be heard from the soft,
damp moss which carpets that forest, and long

before we landed, perfect silence reigned. Joe said, "If you wound 'em moose, me sure get 'em."

We all landed at once. My companion reloaded; the Indian fastened his birch, threw off his hat, adjusted his waistband, seized the hatchet, and set out. He told me afterward, casually, that before we landed he had seen a drop of blood on the bank, when it was two or three rods off. He proceeded rapidly up the bank and through the woods, with a peculiar, elastic, noiseless, and stealthy tread, looking to right and left on the ground, and stepping in the faint tracks of the wounded moose, now and then pointing in silence to a single drop of blood on the handsome, shining leaves of the Clintonia Borealis, which, on every side, covered the ground, or to a dry fern-stem freshly broken, all the while chewing some leaf or else the spruce gum. I followed, watching his motions more than the trail of the moose. After following the trail about forty rods in a pretty direct course, stepping over fallen trees and winding between standing ones, he at length lost it, for there were many other moose-tracks there, and returning once more to the last blood-stain, traced it a little way and lost it again, and, too soon, I thought, for a good hunter, gave it up entirely. He traced a few steps, also, the tracks of the calf;. but, seeing no blood, soon relinquished the search.

I observed, while he was tracking the moose, a certain reticence or moderation in him. He did not communicate several observations of interest which he made, as a white man would have done, though they may have leaked out afterward. At another time, when we heard a slight crackling of twigs and he landed to reconnoitre, he stepped lightly and gracefully, stealing through the bushes with the least possible noise, in a way in which no white man does, — as it were, finding a place for his foot each time.

About half an hour after seeing the moose, we pursued our voyage up Pine-Stream, and soon, coming to a part which was very shoal and also rapid, we took out the baggage, and proceeded to carry it round, while Joe got up with the canoe alone. We were just completing our portage and I was absorbed in the plants, admiring the leaves of the aster macrophyllus, ten inches wide, and plucking the seeds of the great round-leaved orchis, when Joe exclaimed from the stream that he had killed a moose. He had found the cow-moose lying dead, but quite warm, in the middle of the stream, which was so shallow that it rested on the bottom, with hardly a third of its body above water. It was about an hour after it was shot, and it was swollen with water. It had run about a hundred rods and sought the stream again, cutting off a slight bend. No doubt, a better hunter would have tracked it to this spot at once. I was surprised at its great size, horse-like, but Joe said it was not a large cow-moose. My companion went in search of the calf again. I took hold of the ears of the moose, while Joe pushed his canoe down stream toward a favorable shore, and so we made out, though with some difficulty, its long nose frequently sticking in the bottom, to drag it into still shallower water. It was a brownish black, or perhaps a dark iron-gray, on the back and sides, but lighter beneath and in front. I took the cord which served for the canoe's painter, and with Joe's assistance measured it carefully, the greatest distances first, making a knot each time. The painter being wanted, I reduced these measures that night with equal care to lengths and fractions of my umbrella, beginning with the smallest measures, and untying the knots as I proceeded; and when we arrived at Chesuncook the next day, finding a two-foot rule there, I reduced the last to feet and inches; and, moreover, I made myself a two-foot rule of a thin and narrow strip of black ash which would fold up conveniently to six inches. All this pains I took because I did not wish to be obliged to say merely that the moose was very large. Of the various dimensions which I obtained I will mention only two. The distance from the tips of the hoofs of the fore-feet, stretched out, to the top of the back between the shoulders, was seven feet and five inches. I

can hardly believe my own measure, for this is
about two feet greater than the height of a tall
horse. [Indeed, I am now satisfied that this
measurement was incorrect, but the other measures given here I can warrant to be correct,
having proved them in a more recent visit to
those woods.] The extreme length was eight
feet and two inches. Another cow-moose,
which I have since measured in those woods
with a tape, was just six feet from the tip of the
hoof to the shoulders, and eight feet long as she
lay.

When afterward I asked an Indian at the
carry how much taller the male was, he answered,
"Eighteen inches," and made me observe the
height of a cross-stake over the fire, more than
four feet from the ground, to give me some idea
of the depth of his chest. Another Indian, at
Oldtown, told me that they were nine feet high
to the top of the back, and that one which he
tried weighed eight hundred pounds. The length
of the spinal projections between the shoulders
is very great. A white hunter, who was the best
authority among hunters that I could have, told
me that the male was *not* eighteen inches taller
than the female; yet he agreed that he was
sometimes nine feet high to the top of the back,
and weighed a thousand pounds. Only the
male has horns, and they rise two feet or more
above the shoulders, — spreading three or four,

and sometimes six feet, — which would make him in all, sometimes, eleven feet high ! According to this calculation, the moose is as tall, though it may not be as large, as the great Irish elk, Megaceros Hibernicus, of a former period, of which Mantell says that it "very far exceeded in magnitude any living species, the skeleton" being "upward of ten feet high from the ground to the highest point of the antlers." Joe said, that, though the moose shed the whole horn annually, each new horn has an additional prong; but I have noticed that they sometimes have more prongs on one side than on the other. I was struck with the delicacy and tenderness of the hoofs, which divide very far up, and the one half could be pressed very much behind the other, thus probably making the animal surer-footed on the uneven ground and slippery moss-covered logs of the primitive forest. They were very unlike the stiff and battered feet of our horses and oxen. The bare, horny part of the fore-foot was just six inches long, and the two portions could be separated four inches at the extremities.

The moose is singularly grotesque and awkward to look at. Why should it stand so high at the shoulders ? Why have so long a head ? Why have no tail to speak of ? for in my examination I overlooked it entirely. Naturalists say it is an inch and a half long. It reminded me at

once of the camelopard, high before and low
behind, — and no wonder, for, like it, it is fitted
to browse on trees. The upper lip projected
two inches beyond the lower for this purpose.
This was the kind of man that was at home
there; for, as near as I can learn, that has never
been the residence, but rather the hunting-
ground, of the Indian. The moose will perhaps
one day become extinct; but how naturally
then, when it exists only as a fossil relic, and
unseen as that, may the poet or sculptor invent
a fabulous animal with similar branching and
leafy horns, — a sort of fucus or lichen in bone,
— to be the inhabitant of such a forest as this!

Here, just at the head of the murmuring
rapids, Joe now proceeded to skin the moose
with a pocket-knife, while I looked on; and a
tragical business it was, — to see that still warm
and palpitating body pierced with a knife, to
see the warm milk stream from the rent udder,
and the ghastly naked red carcass appearing
from within its seemly robe, which was made
to hide it. The ball had passed through the
shoulder-blade diagonally and lodged under the
skin on the opposite side, and was partially flattened. My companion keeps it to show to his
grandchildren. He has the shanks of another
moose which he has since shot, skinned and
stuffed, ready to be made into boots by putting
in a thick leather sole. Joe said, if a moose

stood fronting you, you must not fire, but advance toward him, for he will turn slowly and give you a fair shot. In the bed of this narrow, wild, and rocky stream, between two lofty walls of spruce and firs, a mere cleft in the forest which the stream had made, this work went on. At length Joe had stripped off the hide and dragged it trailing to the shore, declaring that it weighed a hundred pounds, though probably fifty would have been nearer the truth. He cut off a large mass of the meat to carry along, and another, together with the tongue and nose, he put with the hide on the shore to lie there all night, or till we returned. I was surprised that he thought of leaving this meat thus exposed by the side of the carcass, as the simplest course, not fearing that any creature would touch it; but nothing did. This could hardly have happened on the bank of one of our rivers in the eastern part of Massachusetts; but I suspect that fewer small wild animals are prowling there than with us. Twice, however, in this excursion I had a glimpse of a species of large mouse.

This stream was so withdrawn, and the moose-tracks were so fresh, that my companions, still bent on hunting, concluded to go farther up it and camp, and then hunt up or down at night. Half a mile above this, at a place where I saw the aster puniceus and the beaked hazel, as we paddled along, Joe, hearing a slight rustling amid the alders, and seeing something black about two rods off, jumped up and whispered, "Bear!" but before the hunter had discharged his piece, he corrected himself to "Beaver!" — "Hedgehog!" The bullet killed a large hedge-hog more than two feet and eight inches long. The quills were rayed out and flattened on the hinder part of its back, even as if it had lain on that part, but were erect and long between this and the tail. Their points, closely examined, were seen to be finely bearded or barbed, and shaped like an awl, that is, a little concave, to give the barbs effect. After about a mile of still water, we prepared our camp on the right side, just at the foot of a considerable fall. Little chopping was done that night, for fear of scaring the moose. We had moose-meat fried for supper. It tasted like tender beef, with perhaps more flavor, — sometimes like veal.

After supper, the moon having risen, we proceeded to hunt a mile up this stream, first "carry-ing" about the falls. We made a picturesque sight, wending single-file along the shore, climb-ing over rocks and logs, — Joe, who brought up the rear, twirling his canoe in his hands as if it were a feather, in places where it was difficult to get along without a burden. We launched the canoe again from the ledge over which the stream fell, but after half a mile of still water, suitable for hunting, it became rapid again, and we were compelled to make our way along the shore, while Joe endeavored to get up in the birch alone, though it was still very difficult for him to pick his way amid the rocks in the night. We on the shore found the worst of walking, a perfect chaos of fallen and drifted trees, and of bushes projecting far over the water, and now and then we made our way across the mouth of a small tributary on a kind of net-work of alders. So we went tumbling on in the dark, being on the shady side, effectually scaring all the moose and bears that might be thereabouts. At length we came to a standstill, and Joe went forward to reconnoitre; but he reported that it was still a continuous rapid as far as he went, or half a mile, with no prospect of improvement, as if it were coming down from a mountain. So we turned about, hunting back to the camp through the still water. It was a splendid moonlight night, and I, getting sleepy as it grew late, — for I had nothing to do, — found it difficult to realize where I was. This stream was much more unfrequented than the main one, lumbering operations being no longer carried on in this quarter. It was only three or four rods wide, but the firs and spruce through which it trickled seemed yet taller by contrast. Being in this dreamy state, which the moonlight enhanced, I did not clearly discern the shore, but seemed, most of the time, to be floating through orna-

mental grounds, — for I associated the fir-tops
with such scenes; — very high up some Broadway, and beneath or between their tops I thought
I saw an endless succession of porticos and columns, cornices and façades, verandas and
churches. I did not merely fancy this, but in my
drowsy state such was the illusion. I fairly lost
myself in sleep several times, still dreaming of
that architecture and the nobility that dwelt
behind and might issue from it; but all at once
I would be aroused and brought back to a sense
of my actual position by the sound of Joe's
birch horn in the midst of all this silence calling
the moose, *ugh, ugh, oo-oo-oo-oo-oo-oo*, and I prepared to hear a furious moose come rushing and
crashing through the forest, and see him burst
out on to the little strip of meadow by our side.

But, on more accounts than one, I had had
enough of moose-hunting. I had not come to
the woods for this purpose, nor had I foreseen it,
though I had been willing to learn how the
Indian manœuvred; but one moose killed was
as good, if not as bad, as a dozen. The afternoon's tragedy, and my share in it, as it affected
the innocence, destroyed the pleasure of my
adventure. It is true, I came as near as is possible to come to being a hunter and miss it, myself; and as it is, I think that I could spend a
year in the woods, fishing and hunting, just
enough to sustain myself, with satisfaction.

This would be next to living like a philosopher on the fruits of the earth which you had raised, which also attracts me. But this hunting of the moose merely for the satisfaction of killing him, — not even for the sake of his hide, — without making any extraordinary exertion or running any risk yourself, is too much like going out by night to some woodside pasture and shooting your neighbor's horses. These are God's own horses, poor, timid creatures, that will run fast enough as soon as they smell you, though they *are* nine feet high. Joe told us of some hunters who a year or two before had shot down several oxen by night, somewhere in the Maine woods, mistaking them for moose. And so might any of the hunters; and what is the difference in the sport, but the name? In the former case, having killed one of God's and *your own* oxen, you strip off its hide, — because that is the common trophy, and, moreover, you have heard that it may be sold for moccasins, — cut a steak from its haunches, and leave the huge carcass to smell to heaven for you. It is no better, at least, than to assist at a slaughter-house.

This afternoon's experience suggested to me how base or coarse are the motives which commonly carry men into the wilderness. The explorers and lumberers generally are all hirelings, paid so much a day for their labor, and as such they have no more love for wild nature than

wood-sawyers have for forests. Other white
men and Indians who come here are for the
most part hunters, whose object is to slay as
many moose and other wild animals as possible.
But, pray, could not one spend some weeks or
years in the solitude of this vast wilderness with
other employments than these, — employments
perfectly sweet and innocent and ennobling?
For one that comes with a pencil to sketch, or
sing, a thousand come with an axe or rifle.
What a coarse and imperfect use Indians and
hunters make of Nature! No wonder that their
race is so soon exterminated. I already, and for
weeks afterward, felt my nature the coarser for
this part of my woodland experience, and was
reminded that our life should be lived as tenderly
and daintily as one would pluck a flower.

With these thoughts, when we reached our
camping-ground, I decided to leave my companions to continue moose-hunting down the
stream, while I prepared the camp, though they
requested me not to chop much nor make a
large fire, for fear I should scare their game. In
the midst of the damp fir-wood, high on the
mossy bank, about nine o'clock of this bright
moonlight night, I kindled a fire, when they
were gone, and, sitting on the fir-twigs, within
sound of the falls, examined by its light the
botanical specimens which I had collected that
afternoon, and wrote down some of the reflec-

tions which I have here expanded; or I walked along the shore and gazed up the stream, where the whole space above the falls was filled with mellow light. As I sat before the fire on my fir-twig seat, without walls above or around me, I remembered how far on every hand that wilderness stretched, before you came to cleared or cultivated fields, and wondered if any bear or moose was watching the light of my fire; for Nature looked sternly upon me on account of the murder of the moose.

Strange that so few ever come to the woods to see how the pine lives and grows and spires, lifting its evergreen arms to the light, — to see its perfect success; but most are content to behold it in the shape of many broad boards brought to market, and deem *that* its true success! But the pine is no more lumber than man is, and to be made into boards and houses is no more its true and highest use than the truest use of a man is to be cut down and made into manure. There is a higher law affecting our relation to pines as well as to men. A pine cut down, a dead pine, is no more a pine than a dead human carcass is a man. Can he who has discovered only some of the values of whalebone and whale oil be said to have discovered the true use of the whale? Can he who slays the elephant for his ivory be said to have "seen the elephant"? These are petty and accidental uses;

just as if a stronger race were to kill us in order to make buttons and flageolets of our bones; for everything may serve a lower as well as a higher use. Every creature is better alive than dead, men and moose and pine-trees, and he who understands it aright will rather preserve its life than destroy it.

Is it the lumberman, then, who is the friend and lover of the pine, stands nearest to it, and understands its nature best? Is it the tanner who has barked it, or he who has boxed it for turpentine, whom posterity will fable to have been changed into a pine at last? No! no! it is the poet; he it is who makes the truest use of the pine, — who does not fondle it with an axe, nor tickle it with a saw, nor stroke it with a plane, — who knows whether its heart is false without cutting into it, — who has not bought the stumpage of the township on which it stands. All the pines shudder and heave a sigh when *that* man steps on the forest floor. No, it is the poet, who loves them as his own shadow in the air, and lets them stand. I have been into the lumberyard, and the carpenter's shop, and the tannery, and the lampblack-factory, and the turpentine clearing; but when at length I saw the tops of the pines waving and reflecting the light at a distance high over all the rest of the forest, I realized that the former were not the highest use of the pine. It is not their bones or hide or tallow that I love most. It is the living spirit of the tree, not its spirit of turpentine, with which I sympathize, and which heals my cuts. It is as immortal as I am, and perchance will go to as high a heaven, there to tower above me still.

Erelong, the hunters returned, not having seen a moose, but, in consequence of my suggestions, bringing a quarter of the dead one, which, with ourselves, made quite a load for the canoe.

After breakfasting on moose-meat, we returned down Pine Stream on our way to Chesuncook Lake, which was about five miles distant. We could see the red carcass of the moose lying in Pine Stream when nearly half a mile off. Just below the mouth of this stream were the most considerable rapids between the two lakes, called Pine Stream Falls, where were large flat rocks washed smooth, and at this time you could easily wade across above them. Joe ran down alone while we walked over the portage, my companion collecting spruce gum for his friends at home, and I looking for flowers. Near the lake, which we were approaching with as much expectation as if it had been a university, — for it is not often that the stream of our life opens into such expansions, — were islands, and a low and meadowy shore with scattered trees, birches, white and yellow, slanted over the water, and maples,

— many of the white birches killed, apparently by inundations. There was considerable native grass; and even a few cattle — whose movements we heard, though we did not see them, mistaking them at first for moose — were pastured there.

On entering the lake, where the stream runs southeasterly, and for some time before, we had a view of the mountains about Ktaadn, (*Katah-dinauquoh* one says they are called,) like a cluster of blue fungi of rank growth, apparently twenty-five or thirty miles distant, in a southeast direction, their summits concealed by clouds. Joe called some of them the *Souadnehunk* mountains. This is the name of a stream there, which another Indian told us meant "Running between mountains." Though some lower summits were afterwards uncovered, we got no more complete view of Ktaadn while we were in the woods. The clearing to which we were bound was on the right of the mouth of the river, and was reached by going round a low point, where the water was shallow to a great distance from the shore. Chesuncook Lake extends northwest and southeast, and is called eighteen miles long and three wide, without an island. We had entered the northwest corner of it, and when near the shore could see only part way down it. The principal mountains visible from the land here were those already mentioned, between southeast and east, and a few summits a little west of north, but generally the north and north-west horizon about the St. John and the British boundary was comparatively level.

Ansell Smith's, the oldest and principal clearing about this lake, appeared to be quite a harbor for *batteaux* and canoes; seven or eight of the former were lying about, and there was a small scow for hay, and a capstan on a platform, now high and dry, ready to be floated and anchored to tow rafts with. It was a very primitive kind of harbor, where boats were drawn up amid the stumps, — such a one, methought, as the Argo might have been launched in. There were five other huts with small clearings on the opposite side of the lake, all at this end and visible from this point. One of the Smiths told me that it was so far cleared that they came here to live and built the present house four years before, though the family had been here but a few months.

I was interested to see how a pioneer lived on this side of the country. His life is in some respects more adventurous than that of his brother in the West; for he contends with winter as well as the wilderness, and there is a greater interval of time at least between him and the army which is to follow. Here immigration is a tide which may ebb when it has swept away the pines; there it is not a tide, but an inundation, and roads and other improvements come steadily rushing after.

As we approached the log-house, a dozen rods from the lake, and considerably elevated above it, the projecting ends of the logs lapping over each other irregularly several feet at the corners gave it a very rich and picturesque look, far removed from the meanness of weather-boards. It was a very spacious, low building, about eighty feet long, with many large apartments. The walls were well clayed between the logs, which were large and round, except on the upper and under sides, and as visible inside as out, successive bulging cheeks gradually lessening upwards and tuned to each other with the axe, like Pandean pipes. Probably the musical forest-gods had not yet cast them aside; they never do till they are split or the bark is gone. It was a style of architecture not described by Vitruvius, I suspect, though possibly hinted at in the biography of Orpheus; none of your frilled or fluted columns, which have cut such a false swell, and support nothing but a gable end and their builder's pretensions, — that is, with the multitude; and as for "ornamentation," one of those words with a dead tail which architects very properly use to describe their flourishes, there were the lichens and mosses and fringes of bark, which nobody troubled himself about. We certainly leave the hand-

somest paint and clapboards behind in the woods,
when we strip off the bark and poison ourselves
with white-lead in the towns. We get but half
the spoils of the forest. For beauty, give me
trees with the fur on. This house was designed
and constructed with the freedom of stroke of
a forester's axe, without other compass and
square than Nature uses. Wherever the logs
were cut off by a window or door, that is, were
not kept in place by alternate overlapping, they
were held one upon another by very large pins,
driven in diagonally on each side, where branches
might have been, and then cut off so close up
and down as not to project beyond the bulge of
the log, as if the logs clasped each other in their
arms. These logs were posts, studs, boards,
clapboards, laths, plaster, and nails, all in one.
Where the citizen uses a mere sliver or board,
the pioneer uses the whole trunk of a tree. The
house had large stone chimneys, and was roofed
with spruce-bark. The windows were imported, all but the casings. One end was a
regular logger's camp, for the boarders, with
the usual fir floor and log benches. Thus this
house was but a slight departure from the hollow tree, which the bear still inhabits, — being a
hollow made with trees piled up, with a coating
of bark like its original.

The cellar was a separate building, like an
ice-house, and it answered for a refrigerator at

this season, our moose-meat being kept there.
It was a potato-hole with a permanent roof.
Each structure and institution here was so
primitive that you could at once refer it to its
source; but our buildings commonly suggest
neither their origin nor their purpose. There
was a large, and what farmers would call handsome, barn, part of whose boards had been
sawed by a whip-saw; and the saw-pit, with
its great pile of dust, remained before the house.
The long split shingles on a portion of the barn
were laid a foot to the weather, suggesting what
kind of weather they have there. Grant's barn
at Caribou Lake was said to be still larger, the
biggest ox-nest in the woods, fifty feet by a
hundred. Think of a monster barn in that
primitive forest lifting its gray back above the
tree-tops! Man makes very much such a nest
for his domestic animals, of withered grass and
fodder, as the squirrels and many other wild
creatures do for themselves.

There was also a blacksmith's shop, where
plainly a good deal of work was done. The
oxen and horses used in lumbering operations
were shod, and all the iron-work of sleds, etc.,
was repaired or made here. I saw them load a
batteau at the Moosehead carry, the next Tuesday, with about thirteen hundred weight of bar
iron for this shop. This reminded me how
primitive and honorable a trade was Vulcan's.

I do not hear that there was any carpenter or tailor among the gods. The smith seems to have preceded these and every other mechanic at Chesuncook as well as on Olympus, and his family is the most widely dispersed, whether he be christened John or Ansell.

Smith owned two miles down the lake by half a mile in width. There were about one hundred acres cleared here. He cut seventy tons of English hay this year on this ground, and twenty more on another clearing, and he uses it all himself in lumbering operations. The barn was crowded with pressed hay and a machine to press it. There was a large garden full of roots, — turnips, beets, carrots, potatoes, etc., all of great size. They said that they were worth as much here as in New York. I suggested some currants for sauce, especially as they had no apple-trees set out, and showed how easily they could be obtained.

There was the usual long-handled axe of the primitive woods by the door, three and a half feet long, — for my new black-ash rule was in constant use, — and a large, shaggy dog, whose nose, report said, was full of porcupine quills. I can testify that he looked very sober. This is the usual fortune of pioneer dogs, for they have to face the brunt of the battle for their race, and act the part of Arnold Winkelried without intending it. If he should invite one of his

town friends up this way, suggesting moose-
meat and unlimited freedom, the latter might
pertinently inquire, "What is that sticking in
your nose?" When a generation or two have
used up all the enemies' darts, their successors
lead a comparatively easy life. We owe to our
fathers analogous blessings. Many old people
receive pensions for no other reason, it seems to
me, but as a compensation for having lived a
long time ago. No doubt our town dogs still
talk, in a snuffling way, about the days that
tried dogs' noses. How they got a cat up there
I do not know, for they are as shy as my aunt
about entering a canoe. I wondered that she
did not run up a tree on the way; but perhaps she was bewildered by the very crowd
of opportunities.

Twenty or thirty lumberers, Yankee and
Canadian, were coming and going, — Aleck
among the rest, — and from time to time an
Indian touched here. In the winter there are
sometimes a hundred men lodged here at once.
The most interesting piece of news that circulated
among them appeared to be, that four horses
belonging to Smith, worth seven hundred dollars, had passed by farther into the woods a
week before.

The white-pine-tree was at the bottom or
farther end of all this. It is a war against the
pines, the only real Aroostook or Penobscot war.

I have no doubt that they lived pretty much the same sort of life in the Homeric age, for men have always thought more of eating than of fighting; then, as now, their minds ran chiefly on the " hot bread and sweet cakes"; and the fur and lumber trade is an old story to Asia and Europe.   I doubt if men ever made a trade of heroism.   In the days of Achilles, even, they delighted in big barns, and perchance in pressed hay, and he who possessed the most valuable team was the best fellow.

We had designed to go on at evening up the Caucomgomoc, whose mouth was a mile or two distant, to the lake of the same name, about ten miles off; but some Indians of Joe's acquaintance, who were making canoes on the Caucomgomoc, came over from that side, and gave so poor an account of the moose-hunting, so many had been killed there lately, that my companions concluded not to go there.   Joe spent this Sunday and the night with his acquaintances.   The lumberers told me that there were many moose hereabouts, but no caribou or deer.   A man from Oldtown had killed ten or twelve moose, within a year, so near the house that they heard all his guns.   His name may have been Hercules, for aught I know, though I should rather have expected to hear the rattling of his club; but, no doubt, he keeps pace with the improvements of the age, and uses a Sharpe's rifle now; probably he gets all his armor made and repaired at Smith's shop. One moose had been killed and another shot at within sight of the house within two years. I do not know whether Smith has yet got a poet to look after the cattle, which, on account of the early breaking up of the ice, are compelled to summer in the woods, but I would suggest this office to such of my acquaintances as love to write verses and go a-gunning.

After a dinner, at which apple-sauce was the greatest luxury to me, but our moose-meat was oftenest called for by the lumberers, I walked across the clearing into the forest, southward, returning along the shore. For my dessert, I helped myself to a large slice of the Chesuncook woods, and took a hearty draught of its waters with all my senses. The woods were as fresh and full of vegetable life as a lichen in wet weather, and contained many interesting plants; but unless they are of white pine, they are treated with as little respect here as a mildew, and in the other case they are only the more quickly cut down. The shore was of coarse, flat, slate rocks, often in slabs, with the surf beating on it. The rocks and bleached drift-logs, extending some way into the shaggy woods, showed a rise and fall of six or eight feet, caused partly by the dam at the outlet. They said that in winter the snow was three feet deep on a level here, and sometimes four or five, — that the ice on the lake was two feet thick, clear, and four feet including the snow-ice. Ice had already formed in vessels.

We lodged here this Sunday night in a comfortable bedroom, apparently the best one; and all that I noticed unusual in the night — for I still kept taking notes, like a spy in the camp — was the creaking of the thin split boards, when any of our neighbors stirred.

Such were the first rude beginnings of a town. They spoke of the practicability of a winter-road to the Moosehead carry, which would not cost much, and would connect them with steam and staging and all the busy world. I almost doubted if the lake would be there, — the self-same lake, — preserve its form and identity, when the shores should be cleared and settled; as if these lakes and streams which explorers report never awaited the advent of the citizen.

The sight of one of these frontier-houses, built of these great logs, whose inhabitants have unflinchingly maintained their ground many summers and winters in the wilderness, reminds me of famous forts, like Ticonderoga or Crown Point, which have sustained memorable sieges. They are especially winter-quarters, and at this season this one had a partially deserted look, as if the siege were raised a little, the snow-banks being melted from before it, and its garrison accordingly reduced. I think of their daily food as rations, — it is called "supplies"; a Bible and a great-coat are munitions of war, and a single man seen about the premises is a sentinel on duty. You expect that he will require the countersign, and will perchance take you for Ethan Allen, come to demand the surrender of his fort in the name of the Continental Congress. It is a sort of ranger service. Arnold's expedition is a daily experience with these settlers. They can prove that they were out at almost any time; and I think that all the first generation of them deserve a pension more than any that went to the Mexican war.

Early the next morning we started on our return up the Penobscot, my companion wishing to go about twenty-five miles above the Moose-head carry to a camp near the junction of the two forks, and look for moose there. Our host allowed us something for the quarter of the moose which we had brought, and which he was glad to get. Two explorers from Chamberlain Lake started at the same time that we did. Red-flannel shirts should be worn in the woods, if only for the fine contrast which this color makes with the evergreens and the water. Thus I thought when I saw the forms of the explorers in their birch, poling up the rapids before us, far off against the forest. It is the surveyor's color also, most distinctly seen under all circumstances. We stopped to dine at Ragmuff, as before. My companion it was who wandered

up the stream to look for moose this time, while
Joe went to sleep on the bank, so that we felt
sure of him; and I improved the opportunity to
botanize and bathe. Soon after starting again,
while Joe was gone back in the canoe for the
frying-pan, which had been left, we picked a
couple of quarts of tree-cranberries for a sauce.

I was surprised by Joe's asking me how far
it was to the Moosehorn. He was pretty well
acquainted with this stream, but he had noticed
that I was curious about distances, and had
several maps. He, and Indians generally, with
whom I have talked, are not able to describe
dimensions or distances in our measures with
any accuracy. He could tell, perhaps, at what
time we should arrive, but not how far it was.
We saw a few wood-ducks, sheldrakes, and black
ducks, but they were not so numerous there
at that season as on our river at home. We
scared the same family of wood-ducks before us,
going and returning. We also heard the note
of one fish-hawk, somewhat like that of a pigeon-
woodpecker, and soon after saw him perched
near the top of a dead white-pine against the
island where we had first camped, while a company of peetweets were twittering and teetering
about over the carcass of a moose on a low sandy
spit just beneath. We drove the fish-hawk from
perch to perch, each time eliciting a scream or
whistle, for many miles before us. Our course

being up-stream, we were obliged to work much harder than before, and had frequent use for a pole. Sometimes all three of us paddled together, standing up, small and heavily laden as the canoe was. About six miles from Moosehead, we began to see the mountains east of the north end of the lake, and at four o'clock we reached the carry.

The Indians were still encamped here. There were three, including the St. Francis Indian who had come in the steamer with us. One of the others was called Sabattis. Joe and the St. Francis Indian were plainly clear Indian, the other two apparently mixed Indian and white; but the difference was confined to their features and complexions, for all that I could see. We here cooked the tongue of the moose for supper, — having left the nose, which is esteemed the choicest part, at Chesuncook, boiling, it being a good deal of trouble to prepare it. We also stewed our tree-cranberries, (*Viburnum opulus,*) sweetening them with sugar. The lumberers sometimes cook them with molasses. They were used in Arnold's expedition. This sauce was very grateful to us who had been confined to hard bread, pork, and moose-meat, and, notwithstanding their seeds, we all three pronounced them equal to the common cranberry; but perhaps some allowance is to be made for our forest appetites. It would be worth the while to cultivate them, both for beauty and for food. I afterward saw them in a garden in Bangor. Joe said that they were called *ebeemenar*.

While we were getting supper, Joe commenced curing the moose-hide, on which I had sat a good part of the voyage, he having already cut most of the hair off with his knife at the Caucomgomoc. He set up two stout forked poles on the bank, seven or eight feet high, and as much asunder east and west, and having cut slits eight or ten inches long, and the same distance apart, close to the edge, on the sides of the hide, he threaded poles through them, and then, placing one of the poles on the forked stakes, tied the other down tightly at the bottom. The two ends also were tied with cedar-bark, their usual string, to the upright poles, through small holes at short intervals. The hide, thus stretched, and slanted a little to the north, to expose its flesh side to the sun, measured, in the extreme, eight feet long by six high. Where any flesh still adhered, Joe boldly scored it with his knife to lay it open to the sun. It now appeared somewhat spotted and injured by the duck shot. You may see the old frames on which hides have been stretched at many camping-places in these woods.

For some reason or other, the going to the forks of the Penobscot was given up, and we decided to stop here, my companion intending to hunt down the stream at night. The Indians invited us to lodge with them, but my companion inclined to go to the log-camp on the carry. This camp was close and dirty, and had an ill smell, and I preferred to accept the Indians' offer, if we did not make a camp for ourselves; for, though they were dirty, too, they were more in the open air, and were much more agreeable, and even refined, company, than the lumberers. The most interesting question entertained at the lumberers' camp was, which man could "handle" any other on the carry; and, for the most part, they possessed no qualities which you could not lay hands on. So we went to the Indians' camp or wigwam.

It was rather windy, and therefore Joe concluded to hunt after midnight, if the wind went down, which the other Indians thought it would not do, because it was from the south. The two mixed-bloods, however, went off up the river for moose at dark, before we arrived at their camp. This Indian camp was a slight, patched-up affair, which had stood there several weeks, built shed-fashion, open to the fire on the west. If the wind changed, they could turn it round. It was formed by two forked stakes and a cross-bar, with rafters slanted from this to the ground. The covering was partly an old sail, partly birch-bark, quite imperfect, but securely tied on, and coming down to the ground on the sides. A large log was rolled up at the back side for a head-board, and two or three moose-hides were spread on the ground with the hair up. Various articles of their wardrobe were tucked around the sides and corners, or under the roof. They were smoking moose-meat on just such a crate as is represented by With, in De Bry's "Collectio Peregrinationum," published in 1588, and which the natives of Brazil called *boucan*, (whence buccaneer,) on which were frequently shown pieces of human flesh drying along with the rest. It was erected in front of the camp over the usual large fire, in the form of an oblong square. Two stout forked stakes, four or five feet apart and five feet high, were driven into the ground at each end, and then two poles ten feet long were stretched across over the fire, and smaller ones laid transversely on these a foot apart. On the last hung large, thin slices of moose-meat smoking and drying, a space being left open over the centre of the fire. There was the whole heart, black as a thirty-two pound ball, hanging at one corner. They said, that it took three or four days to cure this meat, and it would keep a year or more. Refuse pieces lay about on the ground in different stages of decay, and some pieces also in the fire, half buried and sizzling in the ashes, as black and dirty as an old shoe. These last I at first thought were thrown away, but

afterwards found that they were being cooked.
Also a tremendous rib-piece was roasting before
the fire, being impaled on an upright stake
forced in and out between the ribs. There was
a moose-hide stretched and curing on poles like
ours, and quite a pile of cured skins close by.
They had killed twenty-two moose within two
months, but, as they could use but very little of
the meat, they left the carcasses on the ground.
Altogether it was about as savage a sight as was
ever witnessed, and I was carried back at once
three hundred years. There were many torches
of birch-bark, shaped like straight tin horns,
lying ready for use on a stump outside.

For fear of dirt, we spread our blankets over
their hides, so as not to touch them anywhere.
The St. Francis Indian and Joe alone were
there at first, and we lay on our backs talking
with them till midnight. They were very sociable, and, when they did not talk with us, kept
up a steady chatting in their own language. We
heard a small bird just after dark, which, Joe
said, sang at a certain hour in the night, — at
ten o'clock, he believed. We also heard the
hylodes and tree-toads, and the lumberers singing in their camp a quarter of a mile off. I
told them that I had seen pictured in old books
pieces of human flesh drying on these crates;
whereupon they repeated some tradition about
the Mohawks eating human flesh, what parts

they preferred, etc., and also of a battle with the
Mohawks near Moosehead, in which many of
the latter were killed; but I found that they
knew but little of the history of their race, and
could be entertained by stories about their ancestors as readily as any way. At first I was
nearly roasted out, for I lay against one side of
the camp, and felt the heat reflected not only from
the birch-bark above, but from the side; and
again I remembered the sufferings of the Jesuit
missionaries, and what extremes of heat and cold
the Indians were said to endure. I struggled
long between my desire to remain and talk with
them, and my impulse to rush out and stretch
myself on the cool grass; and when I was about
to take the last step, Joe, hearing my murmurs,
or else being uncomfortable himself, got up and
partially dispersed the fire. I suppose that that
is Indian manners, — to defend yourself.

While lying there listening to the Indians, I
amused myself by trying to guess at their subject
by their gestures, or some proper name introduced. There can be no more startling evidence of their being a distinct and comparatively
aboriginal race, than to hear this unaltered
Indian language, which the white man cannot
speak nor understand. We may suspect change
and deterioration in almost every other particular but the language which is so wholly
unintelligible to us. It took me by surprise,

though I had found so many arrow-heads, and convinced me that the Indian was not the invention of historians and poets. It was a purely wild and primitive American sound, as much as the barking of a *chickaree*, and I could not understand a syllable of it; but Paugus, had he been there, would have understood it. These Abenakis gossiped, laughed, and jested, in the language in which Eliot's Indian Bible is written, the language which has been spoken in New England who shall say how long? These were the sounds that issued from the wig-wams of this country before Columbus was born; they have not yet died away; and, with remark-ably few exceptions, the language of their fore-fathers is still copious enough for them. I felt that I stood, or rather lay, as near to the primi-tive man of America, that night, as any of its discoverers ever did.

In the midst of their conversation, Joe sud-denly appealed to me to know how long Moose-head Lake was.

Meanwhile, as we lay there, Joe was making and trying his horn, to be ready for hunting after midnight. The St. Francis Indian also amused himself with sounding it, or rather calling through it; for the sound is made with the voice, and not by blowing through the horn. The latter appeared to be a speculator in moose-hides. He bought my companion's for two dollars and a quarter, green. Joe said that it was worth two and a half at Oldtown. Its chief use is for moccasins. One or two of these Indians wore them. I was told, that, by a recent law of Maine, foreigners are not allowed to kill moose there at any season; white Americans can kill them only at a particular season, but the Indians of Maine at all seasons. The St. Francis Indian accordingly asked my companion for a *wighiggin*, or bill, to show, since he was a foreigner. He lived near Sorel. I found that he could write his name very well, *Tahmunt Swasen*. One Ellis, an old white man of Guilford, a town through which we passed, not far from the south end of Moosehead, was the most celebrated moose-hunter of those parts. Indians and whites spoke with equal respect of him. Tahmunt said that there were more moose here than in the Adirondack country in New York, where he had hunted; that three years before there were a great many about, and there were a great many now in the woods, but they did not come out to the water. It was of no use to hunt them at midnight, — they would not come out then. I asked Sabattis, after he came home, if the moose never attacked him. He answered, that you must not fire many times so as to mad him. "I fire once and hit him in the right place, and in the morning I find him. He won't go far. But if you keep firing, you mad him. I fired once five bullets, every one through the heart, and he did not mind 'em at all; it only made him more mad." I asked him if they did not hunt them with dogs. He said, that they did so in winter, but never in the summer, for then it was of no use; they would run right off straight and swiftly a hundred miles.

Another Indian said, that the moose, once scared, would run all day. A dog will hang to their lips, and be carried along till he is swung against a tree and drops off. They cannot run on a "glaze," though they can run in snow four feet deep; but the caribou can run on ice. They commonly find two or three moose together. They cover themselves with water, all but their noses, to escape flies. He had the horns of what he called "the black moose that goes in low lands." These spread three or four feet. The "red moose" was another kind, "running on mountains," and had horns which spread six feet. Such were his distinctions. Both can move their horns. The broad flat blades are covered with hair, and are so soft, when the animal is alive, that you can run a knife through them. They regard it as a good or bad sign, if the horns turn this way or that. His caribou horns had been gnawed by mice in his wigwam, but he thought that the horns neither of the moose nor of the caribou were ever gnawed while the creature was alive, as some have asserted. An Indian, whom I met after this at Oldtown, who had carried about a bear and other animals of Maine to exhibit, told me that thirty years ago there were not so many moose in Maine as now; also, that the moose were very easily tamed, and would come back when once fed, and so would deer, but not caribou. The Indians of this neighborhood are about as familiar with the moose as we are with the ox, having associated with them for so many generations. Father Rasles, in his dictionary of the Abenaki Language, gives not only a word for the male moose, (*aianbé*,) and another for the female, (*hérar*,) but for the bone which is in the middle of the heart of the moose (!), and for his left hind-leg.

There were none of the small deer up there; they are more common about the settlements. One ran into the city of Bangor two years before, and jumped through a window of costly plate glass, and then into a mirror, where it thought it recognized one of its kind, and out again, and so on, leaping over the heads of the crowd, until it was captured. This the inhabitants speak of as the deer that went a-shopping. The last-mentioned Indian spoke of the *lunxus* or Indian devil, (which I take to be the cougar, and not the *Gulo luscus*,) as the only animal in Maine which man need fear; it would follow a man, and did not mind a fire. He also said,

that beavers were getting to be pretty numerous
again, where we went, but their skins brought
so little now that it was not profitable to hunt
them.

I had put the ears of our moose, which were
ten inches long, to dry along with the moose-
meat over the fire, wishing to preserve them;
but Sabattis told me that I must skin and cure
them, else the hair would all come off. He
observed, that they made tobacco-pouches of
the skins of their ears, putting the two together
inside to inside. I asked him how he got fire;
and he produced a little cylindrical box of
friction-matches. He also had flints and steel,
and some punk, which was not dry; I think it
was from the yellow birch. "But suppose you
upset, and all these and your powder get wet."
"Then," said he, "we wait till we get to where
there is some fire." I produced from my pocket
a little vial, containing matches, stoppled water-
tight, and told him, that, though we were upset,
we should still have some dry matches; at
which he stared without saying a word.

We lay awake thus a long while talking, and
they gave us the meaning of many Indian
names of lakes and streams in the vicinity, —
especially Tahmunt. I asked the Indian name
of Moosehead Lake. Joe answered, *Sebamook;*
Tahmunt pronounced it *Sebemook.* When I
asked what it meant, they answered, Moose-

head Lake. At length, getting my meaning, they alternately repeated the word over to themselves, as a philologist might, — *Sebamook*, — *Sebamook*, — now and then comparing notes in Indian; for there was a slight difference in their dialects; and finally Tahmunt said, "Ugh! I know," — and he rose up partly on the moosehide, — "like as here is a place, and there is a place," pointing to different parts of the hide, "and you take water from there and fill this, and it stays here; that is *Sebamook*." I understood him to mean that it was a reservoir of water which did not run away, the river coming in on one side and passing out again near the same place, leaving a permanent bay. Another Indian said, that it meant Large-Bay Lake, and that *Sebago* and *Sebec*, the names of other lakes, were kindred words, meaning large open water. Joe said that *Seboois* meant Little River. I observed their inability, often described, to convey an abstract idea. Having got the idea, though indistinctly, they groped about in vain for words with which to express it. Tahmunt thought that the whites called it Moosehead Lake, because Mount Kineo, which commands it, is shaped like a moose's head, and that Moose River was so called "because the mountain points right across the lake to its mouth." John Josselyn, writing about 1673, says, "Twelve miles from Casco Bay, and passable for men and

horses, is a lake, called by the Indians Sebug.
On the brink thereof, at one end, is the famous
rock, shaped like a moose deer or helk, diaphanous, and called the Moose Rock." He appears
to have confounded Sebamook with Sebago,
which is nearer, but has no "diaphanous" rock
on its shore.

I give more of their definitions, for what they
are worth, — partly *because* they differ sometimes from the commonly received ones. They
never analyzed these words before. After long
deliberation and repeating of the word, for it
gave much trouble, Tahmunt said that *Chesuncook* meant a place where many streams emptied
in (?), and he enumerated them, — Penobscot,
Umbazookskus, Cusabexex, Red Brook, etc.
— "*Caucomgomoc*, — what does that mean?"
"What are those large white birds?" he asked.
"Gulls," said I. "Ugh! Gull Lake." — *Pammadumcook*, Joe thought, meant the Lake
with Gravelly Bottom or Bed. — *Kenduskeag*,
Tahmunt concluded at last, after asking if
birches went up it, for he said that he was not
much acquainted with it, meant something like
this: "You go up Penobscot till you come to
Kenduskeag, and you go by, you don't turn
up there. That is *Kenduskeag*." (?) Another
Indian, however, who knew the river better,
told us afterward that it meant Little Eel River.
— *Mattawamkeag* was a place where two rivers

meet. (?) — *Penobscot* was Rocky River. One
writer says, that this was "originally the name
of only a section of the main channel, from the
head of the tide-water to a short distance above
Oldtown."

A very intelligent Indian, whom we afterward met, son-in-law of Neptune, gave us
also these other definitions: — *Umbazookskus*,
Meadow Stream; *Millinoket*, Place of Islands;
Aboljacarmegus, Smooth-Ledge Falls (and Dead-
Water); *Aboljacarmeguscook*, the stream emptying in; (the last was the word he gave when I
asked about *Aboljacknagesic*, which he did not
recognize;) *Mattahumkeag*, Sand-Creek Pond;
Piscataquis, Branch of a River.

I asked our hosts what *Musketaquid*, the Indian name of Concord, Massachusetts, meant;
but they changed it to *Musketicook*, and repeated
that, and Tahmunt said that it meant Dead
Stream, which is probably true. *Cook* appears
to mean stream, and perhaps *quid* signifies the
place or ground. When I asked the meaning
of the names of two of our hills, they answered
that they were another language. As Tahmunt
said that he traded at Quebec, my companion
inquired the meaning of the word *Quebec*, about
which there has been so much question. He
did not know, but began to conjecture. He
asked what those great ships were called that
carried soldiers. "Men-of-war," we answered.

"Well," he said, "when the English ships came
up the river, they could not go any farther, it
was so narrow there; they must go back, — go-
back, — that's Que-bec." I mention this to show
the value of his authority in the other cases.

Late at night the other two Indians came
home from moose-hunting, not having been
successful, aroused the fire again, lighted their
pipes, smoked awhile, took something strong to
drink, and ate some moose-meat, and, finding
what room they could, lay down on the moose-
hides; and thus we passed the night, two white
men and four Indians, side by side.

When I awoke in the morning the weather was
drizzling. One of the Indians was lying outside, rolled in his blanket, on the opposite side
of the fire, for want of room. Joe had neglected
to awake my companion, and he had done no
hunting that night. Tahmunt was making a
cross-bar for his canoe with a singularly shaped
knife, such as I have since seen other Indians
using. The blade was thin, about three quarters of an inch wide, and eight or nine inches
long, but curved out of its plane into a hook,
which he said made it more convenient to shave
with. As the Indians very far north and northwest use the same kind of knife, I suspect that
it was made according to an aboriginal pattern,
though some white artisans may use a similar
one. The Indians baked a loaf of flour bread

in a spider on its edge before the fire for their breakfast; and while my companion was making tea, I caught a dozen sizable fishes in the Penobscot, two kinds of sucker and one trout. After we had breakfasted by ourselves, one of our bedfellows, who had also breakfasted, came along, and, being invited, took a cup of tea, and finally, taking up the common platter, licked it clean. But he was nothing to a white fellow, a lumberer, who was continually stuffing himself with the Indians' moose-meat, and was the butt of his companions accordingly. He seems to have thought that it was a feast "to eat all." It is commonly said that the white man finally surpasses the Indian on his own ground, and it was proved true in this case. I cannot swear to his employment during the hours of darkness, but I saw him at it again as soon as it was light, though he came a quarter of a mile to his work.

The rain prevented our continuing any longer in the woods; so giving some of our provisions and utensils to the Indians, we took leave of them. This being the steamer's day, I set out for the lake at once.

I walked over the carry alone and waited at the head of the lake. An eagle, or some other large bird, flew screaming away from its perch by the shore at my approach. For an hour after I reached the shore there was not a human being to be seen, and I had all that wide prospect

to myself. I thought that I heard the sound of
the steamer before she came in sight on the open
lake. I noticed at the landing, when the steamer
came in, one of our bedfellows, who had been
a-moose-hunting the night before, now very
sprucely dressed in a clean white shirt and fine
black pants, a true Indian dandy, who had evidently come over the carry to show himself to any
arrivers on the north shore of Moosehead Lake,
just as New York dandies take a turn up Broadway and stand on the steps of a hotel.

Midway the lake we took on board two manly-
looking middle-aged men, with their *batteau,*
who had been exploring for six weeks as far as
the Canada line, and had let their beards grow.
They had the skin of a beaver, which they had
recently caught, stretched on an oval hoop,
though the fur was not good at that season. I
talked with one of them, telling him that I had
come all this distance partly to see where the
white-pine, the Eastern stuff of which our houses
are built, grew, but that on this and a previous
excursion into another part of Maine I had
found it a scarce tree; and I asked him where I
must look for it. With a smile, he answered,
that he could hardly tell me. However, he said
that he had found enough to employ two teams
the next winter in a place where there was
thought to be none left. What was considered
a "tip-top" tree now was not looked at twenty

years ago, when he first went into the business; but they succeeded very well now with what was considered quite inferior timber then. The explorer used to cut into a tree higher and higher up, to see if it was false hearted, and, if there was a rotten heart as big as his arm, he let it alone; but now they cut such a tree, and sawed it all around the rot, and it made the very best of boards, for in such a case they were never shaky.

One connected with lumbering operations at Bangor told me that the largest pine belonging to his firm, cut the previous winter, "scaled" in the woods four thousand five hundred feet, and was worth ninety dollars in the log at the Bangor boom in Oldtown. They cut a road three and a half miles long for this tree alone. He thought that the principal locality for the white-pine that came down the Penobscot now was at the head of the East Branch and the Allegash, about Webster Stream and Eagle and Chamberlain Lakes. Much timber has been stolen from the public lands. (Pray, what kind of forest-warden is the Public itself?) I heard of one man who, having discovered some particularly fine trees just within the boundaries of the public lands, and not daring to employ an accomplice, cut them down, and by means of block and tackle, without cattle, tumbled them into a stream, and so succeeded in getting off with them without the least assistance. Surely, stealing pine-trees in this way is not so mean as robbing hen-roosts.

We reached Monson that night, and the next day rode to Bangor, all the way in the rain again, varying our route a little. Some of the taverns on this road, which were particularly dirty, were plainly in a transition state from the camp to the house.

The next forenoon we went to Oldtown. One slender old Indian on the Oldtown shore, who recognized my companion, was full of mirth and gestures, like a Frenchman. A Catholic priest crossed to the island in the same *batteau* with us. The Indian houses are framed, mostly of one story, and in rows one behind another, at the south end of the island, with a few scattered ones. I counted about forty, not including the church and what my companion called the council-house. The last, which I suppose is their town-house, was regularly framed and shingled like the rest. There were several of two stories, quite neat, with front-yards enclosed, and one at least had green blinds. Here and there were moose-hides stretched and drying about them. There were no cart-paths, nor tracks of horses, but foot-paths; very little land cultivated, but an abundance of weeds, indigenous and naturalized; more introduced weeds than useful vegetables, as the Indian is said to cultivate the vices rather than the virtues of the white man. Yet this village was cleaner than I expected, far cleaner than such Irish villages as I have seen. The children were not particularly ragged nor dirty. The little boys met us with bow in hand and arrow on string, and cried, "Put up a cent." Verily, the Indian has but a feeble hold on his bow now; but the curiosity of the white man is insatiable, and from the first he has been eager to witness this forest accomplishment. That elastic piece of wood with its feathered dart, so sure to be unstrung by contact with civilization, will serve for the type, the coat-of-arms of the savage. Alas for the Hunter Race! the white man has driven off their game, and substituted a cent in its place. I saw an Indian woman washing at the water's edge. She stood on a rock, and, after dipping the clothes in the stream, laid them on the rock, and beat them with a short club. In the graveyard, which was crowded with graves, and overrun with weeds, I noticed an inscription in Indian, painted on a wooden grave-board. There was a large wooden cross on the island.

Since my companion knew him, we called on Governor Neptune, who lived in a little "ten-footer," one of the humblest of them all. Personalities are allowable in speaking of public men, therefore I will give the particulars of our visit. He was abed. When we entered the room, which was one half of the house, he was sitting on the side of the bed. There was a clock hanging in one corner. He had on a black frock-coat, and black pants, much worn, white cotton shirt, socks, a red silk handkerchief about his neck, and a straw hat. His black hair was only slightly grayed. He had very broad cheeks, and his features were decidedly and refreshingly different from those of any of the upstart Native American party whom I have seen. He was no darker than many old white men. He told me that he was eighty-nine; but he was going a-moose-hunting that fall, as he had been the previous one. Probably his companions did the hunting. We saw various squaws dodging about. One sat on the bed by his side and helped him out with his stories. They were remarkably corpulent, with smooth, round faces, apparently full of good-humor. Certainly our much-abused climate had not dried up their adipose substance. While we were there, — for we stayed a good while, — one went over to Oldtown, returned and cut out a dress, which she had bought, on another bed in the room. The Governor said, that "he could remember when the moose were much larger; that they did not use to be in the woods, but came out of the water, as all deer did. Moose was whale once. Away down Merrimack way, a whale came ashore in a shallow bay. Sea went out and left him, and he came up on land a moose. What made them know he was a whale was, that at first, before he began to run in bushes, he had no bowels inside, but" — and then the squaw who sat on the bed by his side, as the Governor's aid, and had been putting in a word now and then and confirming the story, asked me what we called that soft thing we find along the seashore. "Jelly-fish," I suggested. "Yes," said he, "no bowels, but jelly-fish."

There may be some truth in what he said about the moose growing larger formerly; for the quaint John Josselyn, a physican who spent many years in this very district of Maine in the seventeenth century, says, that the tips of their horns "are sometimes found to be two fathoms asunder," — and he is particular to tell us that a fathom is six feet, — "and [they are] in height, from the toe of the fore foot to the pitch of the shoulder, twelve foot, both which hath been taken by some of my sceptique readers to be monstrous lies;" and he adds, "There are certain tran-scendentia in every creature, which are the in-delible character of God, and which discover God." This is a greater dilemma to be caught in than is presented by the cranium of the young Bechuana ox, apparently another of the *tran-scendentia*, in the collection of Thomas Steel, Upper Brook Street, London, whose "entire length of horn, from tip to tip, along the curve, is 13 ft. 5 in.; distance (straight) between the tips of the horns, 8 ft. 8½ in." However, the size of both of the moose and the cougar, as I have found, is generally rather underrated than overrated, and I should be inclined to add to the popular estimate a part of what I subtracted from Josselyn's.

But we talked mostly with the Governor's son-in-law, a very sensible Indian; and the Governor, being so old and deaf, permitted himself to be ignored, while we asked questions about him. The former said, that there were two political parties among them, — one in favor of schools, and the other opposed to them, or rather they did not wish to resist the priest, who was opposed to them. The first had just prevailed at the election and sent their man to the legislature. Neptune and Aitteon and he himself were in favor of schools. He said, "if Indians got learning, they would keep their money." When we asked where Joe's father, Aitteon, was, he knew that he must be at Lincoln, though he was about going a-moose-hunting, for a messenger had just gone to him there to get his signature to some papers. I asked Neptune if they had any of the old breed of dogs yet. He answered, "Yes." "But that," said I, pointing to one that had just come in, "is a Yankee dog." He assented. I said that he did not look like a good one. "O yes!" he said, and he told, with much gusto, how, the year before, he had caught and held by the throat a wolf. A very small black puppy rushed into the room and made at the Governor's feet, as he sat in his stockings with his legs dangling from the bedside. The Governor rubbed his hands and dared him to come on, entering into the sport with spirit. Nothing more that was significant transpired, to my knowledge, during this interview. This was the first time that I ever called on a governor, but, as I did not ask for an office, I can speak of it with the more freedom.

An Indian who was making canoes behind a house, looking up pleasantly from his work, — for he knew my companion, — said that his name was Old John Pennyweight. I had heard of him long before, and I inquired after one of his contemporaries, Joe Fourpence-ha'penny; but, alas! he no longer circulates. I made a faithful study of canoe-building, and I thought that I should like to serve an apprenticeship at that trade for one season, going into the woods for bark with my "boss," making the canoe there, and returning in it at last.

While the *batteau* was coming over to take us off, I picked up some fragments of arrow-heads on the shore, and one broken stone chisel, which were greater novelties to the Indians than to me.

After this, on Old Fort Hill, at the bend of the Penobscot, three miles above Bangor, looking for the site of an Indian town which some think stood thereabouts, I found more arrow-heads, and two little dark and crumbling fragments of Indian earthenware, in the ashes of their fires. The Indians on the Island appeared to live quite happily and to be well treated by the inhabitants of Oldtown.

We visited Veazie's mills, just below the Island, where were sixteen sets of saws, — some gang saws, sixteen in a gang, not to mention circular saws. On one side, they were hauling the logs up an inclined plane by water-power; on the other, passing out the boards, planks, and sawed timber, and forming them into rafts. The trees were literally drawn and quartered there. In forming the rafts, they use the lower three feet of hard-wood saplings, which have a crooked and knobbed butt-end, for bolts, passing them up through holes bored in the corners and sides of the rafts, and keying them. In another apartment they were making fence-slats, such as stand all over New England, out of odds and ends, — and it may be that I saw where the picket-fence behind which I dwell at home came from. I was surprised to find a boy collecting the long edgings of boards as fast as cut off, and thrusting them down a hopper, where they were *ground up* beneath the mill, that they might be out of the way; otherwise they accumulate in vast piles by the side of the building, increasing the danger from fire, or, floating off, they obstruct the river. This was not only a saw-mill, but a grist-mill, then. The inhabitants of Oldtown, Stillwater, and Bangor cannot suffer for want of kindling stuff, surely. Some get their living exclusively by picking up the drift-wood and selling it by the cord in the winter. In one place I saw where an Irishman, who keeps a team and a man for the purpose, had covered the shore for a long distance with regular piles, and I was told that he had sold twelve hundred dollars' worth in a year. Another, who lived by the shore, told me that he got all the material of his out-buildings and fences from the river; and in that neighborhood I perceived that this refuse wood was frequently used instead of sand to fill hollows with, being apparently cheaper than dirt.

I got my first clear view of Ktaadn, on this excursion, from a hill about two miles north-west of Bangor, whither I went for this purpose. After this I was ready to return to Massachusetts.

Humboldt has written an interesting chapter on the primitive forest, but no one has yet described for me the difference between that wild forest which once occupied our oldest town-ships, and the tame one which I find there to-day. It is a difference which would be

worth attending to. The civilized man not only
clears the land permanently to a great extent,
and cultivates open fields, but he tames and
cultivates to a certain extent the forest itself.
By his mere presence, almost, he changes the
nature of the trees as no other creature does.
The sun and air, and perhaps fire, have been
introduced, and grain raised where it stands.
It has lost its wild, damp, and shaggy look, the
countless fallen and decaying trees are gone, and
consequently that thick coat of moss which lived
on them is gone too. The earth is comparatively
bare and smooth and dry. The most primitive
places left with us are the swamps, where the
spruce still grows shaggy with usnea. The surface of the ground in the Maine woods is everywhere spongy and saturated with moisture. I
noticed that the plants which cover the forest
floor there are such as are commonly confined to
swamps with us, — the *Clintonia borealis*, orchises, creeping snowberry, and others; and the
prevailing aster there is the *Aster acuminatus*,
which with us grows in damp and shady woods.
The asters *cordifolius* and *macrophyllus* also
are common, asters of little or no color, and
sometimes without petals. I saw no soft, spreading second-growth white-pines, with smooth bark,
acknowledging the presence of the wood-chopper,
but even the young white-pines were all tall and
slender rough-barked trees.

Those Maine woods differ essentially from ours. There you are never reminded that the wilderness which you are threading is, after all, some villager's familiar wood-lot, some widow's thirds, from which her ancestors have sledded fuel for generations, minutely described in some old deed which is recorded, of which the owner has got a plan too, and old bound-marks may be found every forty rods, if you will search. 'T is true, the map may inform you that you stand on land granted by the State to some academy, or on Bingham's purchase; but these names do not impose on you, for you see nothing to remind you of the academy or of Bingham. What were the "forests" of England to these? One writer relates of the Isle of Wight, that in Charles the Second's time "there were woods in the island so complete and extensive, that it is said a squirrel might have travelled in several parts many leagues together on the top of the trees." If it were not for the rivers, (and he might go round their heads,) a squirrel could here travel thus the whole breadth of the country.

We have as yet had no adequate account of a primitive pine-forest. I have noticed that in a physical atlas lately published in Massachusetts, and used in our schools, the "wood land" of North America is limited almost solely to the valleys of the Ohio and some of the Great Lakes, and the great pine-forests of the globe are not represented. In our vicinity, for instance, New Brunswick and Maine are exhibited as bare as Greenland. It may be that the children of Greenville, at the foot of Moosehead Lake, who surely are not likely to be scared by an owl, are referred to the valley of the Ohio to get an idea of a forest; but they would not know what to do with their moose, bear, caribou, beaver, etc., there. Shall we leave it to an Englishman to inform us, that "in North America, both in the United States and Canada, are the most extensive pine-forests in the world"? The greater part of New Brunswick, the northern half of Maine, and adjacent parts of Canada, not to mention the northeastern part of New York and other tracts farther off, are still covered with an almost unbroken pine-forest.

But Maine, perhaps, will soon be where Massachusetts is. A good part of her territory is already as bare and commonplace as much of our neighborhood, and her villages generally are not so well shaded as ours. We seem to think that the earth must go through the ordeal of sheep-pasturage before it is habitable by man. Consider Nahant, the resort of all the fashion of Boston, — which peninsula I saw but indistinctly in the twilight, when I steamed by it, and thought that it was unchanged since the discovery. John Smith described it in 1614 as "the Mattahunts, two pleasant isles of groves,

gardens, and cornfields"; and others tell us that
it was once well wooded, and even furnished timber to build the wharves of Boston. Now it is
difficult to make a tree grow there, and the
visitor comes away with a vision of Mr. Tudor's
ugly fences, a rod high, designed to protect a
few pear-shrubs. And what are we coming to
in our Middlesex towns? — a bald, staring town-
house, or meeting-house, and a bare liberty-pole,
as leafless as it is fruitless, for all I can see. We
shall be obliged to import the timber for the
last, hereafter, or splice such sticks as we have;
— and our ideas of liberty are equally mean
with these. The very willow-rows lopped every
three years for fuel or powder, — and every
sizable pine and oak, or other forest tree, cut
down within the memory of man! As if individual speculators were to be allowed to export
the clouds out of the sky, or the stars out of the
firmament, one by one. We shall be reduced to
gnaw the very crust of the earth for nutriment.

They have even descended to smaller game.
They have lately, as I hear, invented a machine
for chopping up huckleberry-bushes fine, and
so converting them into fuel! — bushes which,
for fruit alone, are worth all the pear-trees in
the country many times over. (I can give you
a list of the three best kinds, if you want it.)
At this rate, we shall all be obliged to let our
beards grow at least, if only to hide the naked-

ness of the land and make a sylvan appearance.
The farmer sometimes talks of "brushing up,"
simply as if bare ground looked better than
clothed ground, than that which wears its
natural vesture, — as if the wild hedges, which,
perhaps, are more to his children than his
whole farm beside, were *dirt.* I know of one
who deserves to be called the Tree-hater, and,
perhaps, to leave this for a new patronymic to
his children. You would think that he had
been warned by an oracle that he would be
killed by the fall of a tree, and so was resolved
to anticipate them. The journalists think that
they cannot say too much in favor of such
"improvements" in husbandry; it is a safe
theme, like piety; but as for the beauty of one of
these "model farms," I would as lief see a
patent churn and a man turning it. They are,
commonly, places merely where somebody is
making money, it may be counterfeiting. The
virtue of making two blades of grass grow where
only one grew before does not begin to be super-
human.

Nevertheless, it was a relief to get back to
our smooth, but still varied landscape. For a
permanent residence, it seemed to me that there
could be no comparison between this and the
wilderness, necessary as the latter is for a re-
source and a background, the raw material of
all our civilization. The wilderness is simple,

almost to barrenness. The partially cultivated country it is which chiefly has inspired, and will continue to inspire, the strains of poets, such as compose the mass of any literature. Our woods are sylvan, and their inhabitants wood-men and rustics, — that is, *selvaggia*, and the inhabitants are *salvages*. A civilized man, using the word in the ordinary sense, with his ideas and associations, must at length pine there, like a cultivated plant, which clasps its fibres about a crude and undissolved mass of peat. At the extreme North, the voyagers are obliged to dance and act plays for employment. Perhaps our own woods and fields, — in the best wooded towns, where we need not quarrel about the huckleberries, — with the primitive swamps scat-tered here and there in their midst, but not pre-vailing over them, are the perfection of parks and groves, gardens, arbors, paths, vistas, and landscapes. They are the natural consequence of what art and refinement we as a people have, — the common which each village possesses, its true paradise, in comparison with which all elaborately and wilfully wealth-constructed parks and gardens are paltry imitations. Or, I would rather say, such *were* our groves twenty years ago. The poet's, commonly, is not a logger's path, but a woodman's. The logger and pioneer have preceded him, like John the Baptist; eaten the wild honey, it may be, but the locusts also; banished decaying wood and the spongy mosses which feed on it, and built hearths and humanized Nature for him.

But there are spirits of a yet more liberal culture, to whom no simplicity is barren. There are not only stately pines, but fragile flowers, like the orchises, commonly described as too delicate for cultivation, which derive their nu-triment from the crudest mass of peat. These remind us, that, not only for strength, but for beauty, the poet must, from time to time, travel the logger's path and the Indian's trail, to drink at some new and more bracing fountain of the Muses, far in the recesses of the wilderness.

The kings of England formerly had their forests "to hold the king's game," for sport or food, sometimes destroying villages to create or extend them; and I think that they were impelled by a true instinct. Why should not we, who have renounced the king's authority, have our national preserves, where no villages need be destroyed, in which the bear and panther, and some even of the hunter race, may still exist, and not be "civilized off the face of the earth," — our forests, not to hold the king's game merely, but to hold and preserve the king him-self also, the lord of creation, — not for idle sport or food, but for inspiration and our own true rec-reation ? or shall we, like villains, grub them all up poaching on our own national domains ?

THE ALLEGASH AND EAST BRANCH

I STARTED on my third excursion to the Maine woods Monday, July 20th, 1857, with one companion, arriving at Bangor the next day at noon. We had hardly left the steamer, when we passed Molly Molasses in the street. As long as she lives the Penobscots may be considered extant as a tribe. The succeeding morning, a relative of mine, who is well acquainted with the Penobscot Indians, and who had been my companion in my two previous excursions into the Maine woods, took me in his wagon to Oldtown, to assist me in obtaining an Indian for this expedition. We were ferried across to the Indian Island in a batteau. The ferryman's boy had got the key to it, but the father, who was a blacksmith, after a little hesitation, cut the chain with a cold-chisel on the rock. He told me that the Indians were nearly all gone to the seaboard and to Massachusetts, partly on account of the small-pox, of which they are very much afraid, having broken out in Oldtown, and it was doubtful whether we should find a suitable one at home. The old chief Neptune, however, was there still. The first man we saw on the island was an Indian named Joseph Polis, whom my relative had known from a boy, and now addressed familiarly as "Joe." He was dressing a deerskin in his yard. The skin was spread over a slanting log, and he was scraping it with a stick, held by both hands. He was stoutly built, perhaps a little above the middle height, with a broad face, and, as others said, perfect Indian features and complexion. His house was a two-story white one with blinds, the best looking that I noticed there, and as good as an average one on a New England village street. It was surrounded by a garden and fruit-trees, single cornstalks standing thinly amid the beans. We asked him if he knew any good Indian who would like to go into the woods with us, that is, to the Allegash Lakes, by way of Moosehead, and return by the East Branch of the Penobscot, or vary from this as we pleased. To which he answered, out of that strange remoteness in which the Indian ever dwells to the white man, "Me like to go myself; me want to get some moose;" and kept on scraping the skin. His brother had been into the woods with my relative only a year or two before, and the Indian now inquired what the latter had done to him, that he did not come back, for he had not seen or heard from him since.

At length we got round to the more interesting topic again. The ferryman had told us that all the best Indians were gone except Polis, who was one of the aristocracy. He to be sure would be the best man we could have, but if he went at all would want a great price; so we did not expect to get him. Polis asked at first two dollars a day, but agreed to go for a dollar and a half, and fifty cents a week for his canoe. He would come to Bangor with his canoe by the seven o'clock train that evening, — we might depend on him. We thought ourselves lucky to secure the services of this man, who was known to be particularly steady and trustworthy.

I spent the afternoon with my companion, who had remained in Bangor, in preparing for our expedition, purchasing provisions, hard bread, pork, coffee, sugar, etc., and some India-rubber clothing.

We had at first thought of exploring the St. John from its source to its mouth, or else to go up the Penobscot by its East Branch to the lakes of the St. John, and return by way of Chesuncook and Moosehead. We had finally inclined to the last route, only reversing the order of it, going by way of Moosehead, and returning by the Penobscot, otherwise it would have been all the way up stream and taken twice as long.

At evening the Indian arrived in the cars, and I led the way while he followed me three quarters of a mile to my friend's house, with the canoe on his head. I did not know the exact route myself, but steered by the lay of the land, as I do

in Boston, and I tried to enter into conversation
with him, but as he was puffing under the weight
of his canoe, not having the usual apparatus for
carrying it, but, above all, was an Indian, I
might as well have been thumping on the bottom
of his birch the while. In answer to the various
observations which I made by way of breaking
the ice, he only grunted vaguely from beneath his
canoe once or twice, so that I knew he was there.

Early the next morning (July 23d) the stage
called for us, the Indian having breakfasted with
us, and already placed the baggage in the canoe
to see how it would go. My companion and I
had each a large knapsack as full as it would
hold, and we had two large India-rubber bags
which held our provision and utensils. As for
the Indian, all the baggage he had, beside his
axe and gun, was a blanket, which he brought
loose in his hand. However, he had laid in a
store of tobacco and a new pipe for the excursion.
The canoe was securely lashed diagonally across
the top of the stage, with bits of carpet tucked
under the edge to prevent its chafing. The
very accommodating driver appeared as much
accustomed to carrying canoes in this way as
bandboxes.

At the Bangor House we took in four men
bound on a hunting excursion, one of the men
going as cook. They had a dog, a middling-
sized brindled cur, which ran by the side of the

stage, his master showing his head and whistling from time to time; but after we had gone about three miles the dog was suddenly missing, and two of the party went back for him, while the stage, which was full of passengers, waited. I suggested that he had taken the back track for the Bangor House. At length one man came back, while the other kept on. This whole party of hunters declared their intention to stop till the dog was found; but the very obliging driver was ready to wait a spell longer. He was evidently unwilling to lose so many passengers, who would have taken a private conveyance, or perhaps the other line of stages, the next day. Such progress did we make with a journey of over sixty miles, to be accomplished that day, and a rain-storm just setting in. We discussed the subject of dogs and their instincts till it was threadbare, while we waited there, and the scenery of the suburbs of Bangor is still distinctly impressed on my memory. After full half an hour the man returned, leading the dog by a rope. He had overtaken him just as he was entering the Bangor House. He was then tied on the top of the stage, but being wet and cold, several times in the course of the journey he jumped off, and I saw him dangling by his neck. This dog was depended on to stop bears with. He had already stopped one somewhere in New Hampshire, and I can testify that he stopped a stage

in Maine. This party of four probably paid
nothing for the dog's ride, nor for his run, while
our party of three paid two dollars, and were
charged four for the light canoe which lay still
on the top.

It soon began to rain, and grew more and
more stormy as the day advanced. This was
the third time that I had passed over this route,
and it rained steadily each time all day. We
accordingly saw but little of the country. The
stage was crowded all the way, and I attended
the more to my fellow-travellers. If you had
looked inside this coach you would have thought
that we were prepared to run the gantlet of a
band of robbers, for there were four or five guns
on the front seat, the Indian's included, and one
or two on the back one, each man holding his
darling in his arms. One had a gun which
carried twelve to a pound. It appeared that
this party of hunters was going our way, but
much farther down the Allegash and St. John,
and thence up some other stream, and across
to the Pistigouche and the Bay of Chaleur, to
be gone six weeks. They had canoes, axes, and
supplies deposited some distance along the route.
They carried flour, and were to have new bread
made every day. Their leader was a handsome man about thirty years old, of good height,
but not apparently robust, of gentlemanly address and faultless toilet; such a one as you

might expect to meet on Broadway. In fact, in the popular sense of the word, he was the most "gentlemanly" appearing man in the stage, or that we saw on the road. He had a fair white complexion, as if he had always lived in the shade, and an intellectual face, and with his quiet manners might have passed for a divinity student who had seen something of the world. I was surprised to find, on talking with him in the course of the day's journey, that he was a hunter at all, — for his gun was not much exposed, — and yet more to find that he was probably the chief white hunter of Maine, and was known all along the road. He had also hunted in some of the States farther south and west. I afterwards heard him spoken of as one who could endure a great deal of exposure and fatigue without showing the effect of it; and he could not only use guns, but make them, being himself a gunsmith. In the spring, he had saved a stage-driver and two passengers from drowning in the backwater of the Piscataquis in Foxcroft on this road, having swum ashore in the freezing water and made a raft and got them off, — though the horses were drowned, — at great risk to himself, while the only other man who could swim withdrew to the nearest house to prevent freezing. He could now ride over this road for nothing. He knew our man, and remarked that we had a good Indian there, a good hunter; adding that he was said to be worth $6,000. The Indian also knew him, and said to me, "the great hunter."

The former told me that he practised a kind of still hunting, new or uncommon in those parts, that the caribou, for instance, fed round and round the same meadow, returning on the same path, and he lay in wait for them.

The Indian sat on the front seat, saying nothing to anybody, with a stolid expression of face, as if barely awake to what was going on. Again I was struck by the peculiar vagueness of his replies when addressed in the stage, or at the taverns. He really never said anything on such occasions. He was merely stirred up, like a wild beast, and passively muttered some insignificant response. His answer, in such cases, was never the consequence of a positive mental energy, but vague as a puff of smoke, suggesting no *responsibility*, and if you considered it, you would find that you had got nothing out of him. This was instead of the conventional palaver and smartness of the white man, and equally profitable. Most get no more than this out of the Indian, and pronounce him stolid accordingly. I was surprised to see what a foolish and impertinent style a Maine man, a passenger, used in addressing him, as if he were a child, which only made his eyes glisten a little. A tipsy Canadian asked him at a tavern, in a drawling tone, if he smoked, to which he answered with an indefinite "yes." "Won't you lend me your pipe a little while?" asked the other. He replied, looking straight by the man's head, with a face singularly vacant to all neighboring interests, "Me got no pipe;" yet I had seen him put a new one, with a supply of tobacco, into his pocket that morning.

Our little canoe, so neat and strong, drew a favorable criticism from all the wiseacres among the tavern loungers along the road. By the roadside, close to the wheels, I noticed a splendid great purple-fringed orchis with a spike as big as an epilobium, which I would fain have stopped the stage to pluck, but as this had never been known to stop a bear, like the cur on the stage, the driver would probably have thought it a waste of time.

When we reached the lake, about half past eight in the evening, it was still steadily raining, and harder than before; and, in that fresh, cool atmosphere, the hylodes were peeping and the toads singing about the lake universally, as in the spring with us. It was as if the season had revolved backward two or three months, or I had arrived at the abode of perpetual spring.

We had expected to go upon the lake at once, and after paddling up two or three miles, to camp on one of its islands; but on account of the steady and increasing rain, we decided to go

to one of the taverns for the night, though, for
my own part, I should have preferred to camp
out.

About four o'clock the next morning, (July
24th,) though it was quite cloudy, accompanied
by the landlord to the water's edge, in the
twilight, we launched our canoe from a rock on
the Moosehead Lake. When I was there four
years before we had a rather small canoe for
three persons, and I had thought that this time
I would get a larger one, but the present one was
even smaller than that. It was 18¼ feet long by
2 feet 6½ inches wide in the middle, and one foot
deep within, as I found by measurement, and I
judged that it would weigh not far from eighty
pounds. The Indian had recently made it himself, and its smallness was partly compensated
for by its newness, as well as stanchness and
solidity, it being made of very thick bark and
ribs. Our baggage weighed about 166 pounds,
so that the canoe carried about 600 pounds in
all, or the weight of four men. The principal
part of the baggage was, as usual, placed in the
middle of the broadest part, while we stowed
ourselves in the chinks and crannies that were
left before and behind it, where there was no
room to extend our legs, the loose articles being
tucked into the ends. The canoe was thus as
closely packed as a market-basket, and might
possibly have been upset without spilling any of

its contents. The Indian sat on a cross-bar in the stern, but we flat on the bottom, with a splint or chip behind our backs, to protect them from the cross-bar, and one of us commonly paddled with the Indian. He foresaw that we should not want a pole till we reached the Umbazookskus River, it being either dead-water or down stream so far, and he was prepared to make a sail of his blanket in the bows, if the wind should be fair; but we never used it.

It had rained more or less the four previous days, so that we thought we might count on some fair weather. The wind was at first southwesterly.

Paddling along the eastern side of the lake in the still of the morning, we soon saw a few shel-drakes, which the Indian called *Shecorways*, and some peetweets *Naramekechus*, on the rocky shore; we also saw and heard loons, *Medawisla*, which he said was a sign of wind. It was in-spiriting to hear the regular dip of the paddles, as if they were our fins or flippers, and to realize that we were at length fairly embarked. We who had felt strangely as stage-passengers and tavern-lodgers were suddenly naturalized there and presented with the freedom of the lakes and the woods. Having passed the small rocky isles within two or three miles of the foot of the lake, we had a short consultation respecting our course, and inclined to the western shore for the sake of its lee; for otherwise, if the wind should rise, it would be impossible for us to reach Mount Kineo, which is about midway up the lake on the east side, but at its narrowest part, where probably we could recross if we took the western side. The wind is the chief obstacle to crossing the lakes, especially in so small a canoe. The Indian remarked several times that he did not like to cross the lakes "in littlum canoe," but nevertheless, "just as we say, it made no odds to him." He sometimes took a straight course up the middle of the lake between Sugar and Deer Islands, when there was no wind.

Measured on the map, Moosehead Lake is twelve miles wide at the widest place, and thirty miles long in a direct line, but longer as it lies. The captain of the steamer called it thirty-eight miles as he steered. We should probably go about forty. The Indian said that it was called "*Mspame*, because large water." Squaw Mountain rose darkly on our left, near the outlet of the Kennebec, and what the Indian called Spencer Bay Mountain, on the east, and already we saw Mount Kineo before us in the north.

Paddling near the shore, we frequently heard the *pe-pe* of the olive-sided fly-catcher, also the wood-pewee, and the kingfisher, thus early in the morning. The Indian reminding us that he could not work without eating, we stopped to breakfast on the main shore, southwest of Deer

Island, at a spot where the *Mimulus ringens*
grew abundantly. We took out our bags, and
the Indian made a fire under a very large
bleached log, using white-pine bark from a
stump, though he said that hemlock was better,
and kindling with canoe-birch bark. Our table
was a large piece of freshly peeled birch-bark,
laid wrong-side-up, and our breakfast consisted
of hard bread, fried pork, and strong coffee,
well sweetened, in which we did not miss the
milk.

While we were getting breakfast a brood of
twelve black dippers, half grown, came paddling
by within three or four rods, not at all alarmed;
and they loitered about as long as we stayed,
now huddled close together, within a circle of
eighteen inches in diameter, now moving off in
a long line, very cunningly. Yet they bore a
certain proportion to the great Moosehead Lake
on whose bosom they floated, and I felt as if
they were under its protection.

Looking northward from this place it appeared
as if we were entering a large bay, and we did
not know whether we should be obliged to diverge
from our course and keep outside a point which
we saw, or should find a passage between this
and the mainland. I consulted my map and
used my glass, and the Indian did the same, but
we could not find our place exactly on the map,
nor could we detect any break in the shore.

When I asked the Indian the way, he answered "I don't know," which I thought remarkable, since he had said that he was familiar with the lake; but it appeared that he had never been up this side. It was misty dog-day weather, and we had already penetrated a smaller bay of the same kind, and knocked the bottom out of it, though we had been obliged to pass over a small bar, between an island and the shore, where there was but just breadth and depth enough to float the canoe, and the Indian had observed, "Very easy makum bridge here," but now it seemed that, if we held on, we should be fairly embayed. Presently, however, though we had not stirred, the mist lifted somewhat, and revealed a break in the shore northward, showing that the point was a portion of Deer Island, and that our course lay westward of it. Where it had seemed a continuous shore even through a glass, one portion was now seen by the naked eye to be much more distant than the other which overlapped it, merely by the greater thickness of the mist which still rested on it, while the nearer or island portion was comparatively bare and green. The line of separation was very distinct, and the Indian immediately remarked, "I guess you and I go there, — I guess there's room for my canoe there." This was his common expression instead of saying we. He never addressed us by our names, though curious to know how they were spelled and what they meant, while we called him Polis. He had already guessed very accurately at our ages, and said that he was forty-eight.

After breakfast I emptied the melted pork that was left into the lake, making what sailors call a "slick," and watching to see how much it spread over and smoothed the agitated surface. The Indian looked at it a moment and said, "That make hard paddlum thro'; hold 'em canoe. So say old times."

We hastily reloaded, putting the dishes loose in the bows, that they might be at hand when wanted, and set out again. The western shore, near which we paddled along, rose gently to a considerable height, and was everywhere densely covered with the forest, in which was a large proportion of hard wood to enliven and relieve the fir and spruce.

The Indian said that the usnea lichen which we saw hanging from the trees was called *chor-chorque*. We asked him the names of several small birds which we heard this morning. The wood-thrush, which was quite common, and whose note he imitated, he said was called *Adelungquamooktum;* but sometimes he could not tell the name of some small bird which I heard and knew, but he said, "I tell all the birds about here, — this country; can't tell littlum noise, but I see 'em, then I can tell."

I observed that I should like to go to school to him to learn his language, living on the Indian island the while; could not that be done? "O, yer," he replied, "good many do so." I asked how long he thought it would take. He said one week. I told him that in this voyage I would tell him all I knew, and he should tell me all he knew, to which he readily agreed.

The birds sang quite as in our woods, — the red-eye, red-start, veery, wood-pewee, etc., but we saw no bluebirds in all our journey, and several told me in Bangor that they had not the bluebird there. Mount Kineo, which was generally visible, though occasionally concealed by islands or the mainland in front, had a level bar of cloud concealing its summit, and all the mountain-tops about the lake were cut off at the same height. Ducks of various kinds — sheldrake, summer ducks, etc. — were quite common, and ran over the water before us as fast as a horse trots. Thus they were soon out of sight.

The Indian asked the meaning of *reality*, as near as I could make out the word, which he said one of us had used; also of "*interrent*," that is, intelligent. I observed that he could rarely sound the letter *r*, but used *l*, as also *r* for *l* sometimes; as *load* for road, *pickelel* for pickerel, *Soogle* Island for Sugar Island, *lock* for rock, etc. Yet he trilled the *r* pretty well after me.

He generally added the syllable *um* to his words when he could, — as paddl*um*, etc. I have once heard a Chippewa lecture, who made his audience laugh unintentionally by putting *ne* after the word *too*, which word he brought in continually and unnecessarily, accenting and prolonging this sound into *m ar* sonorously as if it were necessary to bring in so much of his vernacular as a relief to his organs, a compensation for twisting his jaws about, and putting his tongue into every corner of his mouth, as he complained that he was obliged to do when he spoke English. There was so much of the Indian accent resounding through his English, so much of the "bow-arrow tang" as my neighbor calls it, and I have no doubt that word seemed to him the best pronounced. It was a wild and refreshing sound, like that of the wind among the pines, or the booming of the surf on the shore.

I asked him the meaning of the word *Musketi-cook*, the Indian name of Concord River. He nounced it *Muskéeticook*, emphasizing the second syllable with a peculiar guttural sound, and said that it meant "Dead-water," which it is, and in this definition he agreed exactly with the St. Francis Indian with whom I talked in 1853.

On a point on the mainland some miles southwest of Sand-bar Island, where we landed to stretch our legs and look at the vegetation, going inland a few steps, I discovered a fire still glowing beneath its ashes, where somebody had breakfasted, and a bed of twigs prepared for the following night. So I knew not only that they had just left, but that they designed to return, and by the breadth of the bed that there was more than one in the party. You might have gone within six feet of these signs without seeing them. There grew the beaked hazel, the only hazel which I saw on this journey, the *Diervilla*, rue seven feet high, which was very abundant on all the lake and river shores, and *Cornus stolonifera*, or red osier, whose bark, the Indian said, was good to smoke, and was called *maquoxigill*, "tobacco before white people came to this country, Indian tobacco."

The Indian was always very careful in approaching the shore, lest he should injure his canoe on the rocks, letting it swing round slowly sidewise, and was still more particular that we should not step into it on shore, nor till it floated free, and then should step gently lest we should open its seams, or make a hole in the bottom. He said that he would tell us when to jump.

Soon after leaving this point we passed the mouth of the Kennebec, and heard and saw the falls at the dam there, for even Moosehead Lake is dammed. After passing Deer Island, we saw the little steamer from Greenville, far east in the middle of the lake, she appeared nearly stationary. Sometimes we could hardly tell her from an island which had a few trees on it. Here we were exposed to the wind from over the whole breadth of the lake, and ran a little risk of being swamped. While I had my eye fixed on the spot where a large fish had leaped, we took in a gallon or two of water, which filled my lap; but we soon reached the shore and took the canoe over the bar, at Sand-bar Island, a few feet wide only, and so saved a considerable distance. One landed first at a more sheltered place, and walking round caught the canoe by the prow, to prevent it being injured against the shore.

Again we crossed a broad bay opposite the mouth of Moose River, before reaching the narrow strait at Mount Kineo, made what the voyageurs call a *traverse*, and found the water quite rough. A very little wind on these broad lakes raises a sea which will swamp a canoe. Looking off from a lee shore, the surface may appear to be very little agitated, almost smooth, a mile distant, or if you see a few white crests they appear nearly level with the rest of the lake; but when you get out so far, you may find quite a sea running, and erelong, before you think of it, a wave will gently creep up the side of the canoe and fill your lap, like a monster deliberately covering you with its slime before it swallows you, or it will strike the canoe violently and break into it. The same thing may happen when the wind rises suddenly, though it were perfectly calm and smooth there a few minutes before; so that nothing can save you, unless you can swim ashore, for it is impossible to get into a canoe again when it is upset. Since you sit flat on the bottom, though the danger should not be imminent, a little water is a great inconvenience, not to mention the wetting of your provisions. We rarely crossed even a bay directly, from point to point, when there was wind, but made a slight curve corresponding somewhat to the shore, that we might the sooner reach it if the wind increased.

When the wind is aft, and not too strong, the Indian makes a spritsail of his blanket. He thus easily skims over the whole length of this lake in a day.

The Indian paddled on one side, and one of us on the other, to keep the canoe steady, and when he wanted to change hands he would say "t'other side." He asserted, in answer to our questions, that he had never upset a canoe himself, though he may have been upset by others.

Think of our little egg-shell of a canoe tossing across that great lake, a mere black speck to the eagle soaring above it.

My companion trailed for trout as we paddled along, but the Indian warning him that a big fish might upset us, for there are some very large ones there, he agreed to pass the line quickly to him in the stern if he had a bite. Beside trout, I heard of cusk, white-fish, etc., as found in this lake.

While we were crossing this bay, where Mount Kineo rose dark before us, within two or three miles, the Indian repeated the tradition respecting this mountain's having anciently been a cow moose, — how a mighty Indian hunter, whose name I forget, succeeding in killing this queen of the moose tribe with great difficulty, while her calf was killed somewhere among the islands in Penobscot Bay, and, to his eyes, this mountain had still the form of the moose in a reclining posture, its precipitous side presenting the outline of her head. He told this at some length, though it did not amount to much, and with apparent good faith, and asked us how we supposed the hunter could have killed such a mighty moose as that, — how we could do it. Whereupon a man-of-war to fire broadsides into her was suggested, etc. An Indian tells such a story as if he thought it deserved to have a good deal said about it, only he has not got it to say, and so he makes up for the deficiency by a drawling tone, long-windedness, and a dumb wonder which he hopes will be contagious.

We approached the land again through pretty rough water, and then steered directly across the lake, at its narrowest part, to the eastern side, and were soon partly under the lee of the mountain, about a mile north of the Kineo House, having paddled about twenty miles. It was now about noon.

We designed to stop there that afternoon and night, and spent half an hour looking along the shore northward for a suitable place to camp. We took out all our baggage at one place in vain, it being too rocky and uneven, and while engaged in this search we made our first acquaintance with the moose-fly. At length, half a mile farther north, by going half a dozen rods into the dense spruce and fir wood on the side of the mountain, almost as dark as a cellar, we found a place sufficiently clear and level to lie down on, after cutting away a few bushes. We required a space only seven feet by six for our bed, the fire being four or five feet in front, though it made no odds how rough the hearth was; but it was not always easy to find this in those woods. The Indian first cleared a path to it from the shore with his axe, and we then carried up all our baggage, pitched our tent, and made our bed, in order to be ready for foul weather, which then threatened us, and for the night. He gathered a large armful of fir twigs, breaking them off, which he said were the best for our bed, partly, I thought, because they were the largest and could be most rapidly collected. It had been raining more or less for four or five days, and the wood was even damper than usual, but he got dry bark for the fire from the under-side of a dead leaning hemlock, which he said he could always do.

This noon his mind was occupied with a law question, and I referred him to my companion, who was a lawyer.   It appeared that he had been buying land lately, (I think it was a hundred acres,) but there was probably an incumbrance to it, somebody else claiming to have bought some grass on it for this year.   He wished to know to whom the grass belonged, and was told that if the other man could prove that he bought the grass before he, Polis, bought the land, the former could take it, whether the latter knew it or not.   To which he only answered, "Strange!" He went over this several times, fairly sat down to it, with his back to a tree, as if he meant to confine us to this topic henceforth; but as he made no headway, only reached the jumping-off place of his wonder at white men's institutions after each explanation, we let the subject die.

He said that he had fifty acres of grass, potatoes, etc., somewhere above Oldtown, be-side some about his house; that he hired a good deal of his work, hoeing, etc., and preferred white men to Indians, because "they keep steady, and know how."

After dinner we returned southward along the shore, in the canoe, on account of the difficulty of climbing over the rocks and fallen trees, and

began to ascend the mountain along the edge
of the precipice. But a smart shower coming
up just then, the Indian crept under his canoe,
while we, being protected by our rubber coats,
proceeded to botanize. So we sent him back to
the camp for shelter, agreeing that he should
come there for us with his canoe toward night.
It had rained a little in the forenoon, and we
trusted that this would be the clearing-up shower,
which it proved; but our feet and legs were
thoroughly wet by the bushes. The clouds
breaking away a little, we had a glorious wild
view, as we ascended, of the broad lake with
its fluctuating surface and numerous forest-
clad islands, extending beyond our sight both
north and south, and the boundless forest un-
dulating away from its shores on every side, as
densely packed as a rye-field, and enveloping
nameless mountains in succession; but above
all, looking westward over a large island was
visible a very distant part of the lake, though we
did not then suspect it to be Moosehead, — at
first a mere broken white line seen through the
tops of the island trees, like hay-caps, but spreading to a lake when we got higher. Beyond this
we saw what appears to be called Bald Mountain
on the map, some twenty-five miles distant, near
the sources of the Penobscot. It was a perfect
lake of the woods. But this was only a tran-
sient gleam, for the rain was not quite over.

Looking southward, the heavens were completely overcast, the mountains capped with clouds, and the lake generally wore a dark and stormy appearance, but from its surface just north of Sugar Island, six or eight miles distant, there was reflected upward to us through the misty air a bright blue tinge from the distant unseen sky of another latitude beyond. They probably had a clear sky then at Greenville, the south end of the lake. Standing on a mountain in the midst of a lake, where would you look for the first sign of approaching fair weather? Not into the heavens, it seems, but into the lake.

Again we mistook a little rocky islet seen through the "drisk," with some taller bare trunks or stumps on it, for the steamer with its smoke-pipes, but as it had not changed its position after half an hour, we were undeceived. So much do the works of man resemble the works of nature. A moose might mistake a steamer for a floating isle, and not be scared till he heard its puffing or its whistle.

If I wished to see a mountain or other scenery under the most favorable auspices, I would go to it in foul weather, so as to be there when it cleared up; we are then in the most suitable mood, and nature is most fresh and inspiring. There is no serenity so fair as that which is just established in a tearful eye.

Jackson, in his Report on the Geology of

Maine, in 1838, says of this mountain: "Horn-stone, which will answer for flints, occurs in various parts of the State, where trap-rocks have acted upon silicious slate. The largest mass of this stone known in the world is Mount Kineo, upon Moosehead Lake, which appears to be entirely composed of it, and rises seven hundred feet above the lake level. This variety of hornstone I have seen in every part of New England in the form of Indian arrow-heads, hatchets, chisels, etc., which were probably obtained from this mountain by the aboriginal inhabitants of the country." I have myself found hundreds of arrow-heads made of the same material. It is generally slate-colored, with white specks, becoming a uniform white where exposed to the light and air, and it breaks with a conchoidal fracture, producing a ragged cutting edge. I noticed some conchoidal hollows more than a foot in diameter. I picked up a small thin piece which had so sharp an edge that I used it as a dull knife, and to see what I could do, fairly cut off an aspen one inch thick with it, by bending it and making many cuts; though I cut my fingers badly with the back of it in the meanwhile.

From the summit of the precipice which forms the southern and eastern sides of this mountain peninsula, and is its most remarkable feature, being described as five or six hundred feet high, we looked, and probably might have jumped down to the water, or to the seemingly dwarfish trees on the narrow neck of land which connects it with the main. It is a dangerous place to try the steadiness of your nerves. Hodge says that these cliffs descend "perpendicularly ninety feet" below the surface of the water.

The plants which chiefly attracted our attention on this mountain were the mountain cinquefoil (*Potentilla tridentata*), abundant and in bloom still at the very base, by the water-side, though it is usually confined to the summits of mountains in our latitude; very beautiful harebells overhanging the precipice; bear-berry; the Canada blueberry (*Vaccinium Canadense*), similar to (the *V. Pennsylvanicum*) our earliest one, but entire leaved and with a downy stem and leaf; I have not seen it in Massachusetts; *Diervilla trifida; Microstylis ophioglossoides*, an orchidaceous plant new to us; wild holly (*Nemopanthes Canadensis*); the great round-leaved orchis (*Platanthera orbiculata*), not long in bloom; *Spiranthes cernua*, at the top; bunch-berry, reddening as we ascended, green at the base of the mountain, red at the top; and the small fern, *Woodsia ilvensis*, growing in tufts, now in fruit. I have also received *Liparis liliifolia*, or twayblade, from this spot. Having explored the wonders of the mountain, and the weather being now entirely cleared up, we commenced the descent. We met the Indian, puffing and panting, about one third of the way up, but thinking that he must be near the top, and saying that it took his breath away. I thought that superstition had something to do with his fatigue. Perhaps he believed that he was climbing over the back of a tremendous moose. He said that he had never ascended Kineo. On reaching the canoe we found that he had caught a lake trout weighing about three pounds, at the depth of twenty-five or thirty feet, while we were on the mountain.

When we got to the camp, the canoe was taken out and turned over, and a log laid across it to prevent its being blown away. The Indian cut some large logs of damp and rotten hard wood to smoulder and keep fire through the night. The trout was fried for supper. Our tent was of thin cotton cloth and quite small, forming with the ground a triangular prism closed at the rear end, six feet long, seven wide, and four high, so that we could barely sit up in the middle. It required two forked stakes, a smooth ridge-pole, and a dozen or more pins to pitch it. It kept off dew and wind, and an ordinary rain, and answered our purpose well enough. We reclined within it till bedtime, each with his baggage at his head, or else sat about the fire, having hung our wet clothes on a pole before the fire for the night.

As we sat there, just before night, looking out through the dusky wood, the Indian heard a noise which he said was made by a snake. He imitated it at my request, making a low whistling note, — *pheet* — *pheet*, — two or three times repeated, somewhat like the peep of the hylodes, but not so loud. In answer to my inquiries, he said that he had never seen them while making it, but going to the spot he finds the snake. This, he said on another occasion, was a sign of rain. When I had selected this place for our camp, he had remarked that there were snakes there, — he saw them. But they won't do any hurt, I said. "O no," he answered, "just as you say, it makes no difference to me."

He lay on the right side of the tent, because, as he said, he was partly deaf in one ear, and he wanted to lie with his good ear up. As we lay there, he inquired if I ever heard "Indian sing." I replied that I had not often, and asked him if he would not favor us with a song. He readily assented, and lying on his back, with his blanket wrapped around him, he commenced a slow, somewhat nasal, yet musical chant, in his own language, which probably was taught his tribe long ago by the Catholic missionaries. He translated it to us, sentence by sentence, afterward, wishing to see if we could remember it. It proved to be a very simple religious exercise or hymn, the burden of which was, that there was only one God who ruled all the world. This was hammered (or sung) out very thin, so that some stanzas wellnigh meant nothing at all, merely keeping up the idea. He then said that he would sing us a Latin song; but we did not detect any Latin, only one or two Greek words in it, — the rest may have been Latin with the Indian pronunciation.

His singing carried me back to the period of the discovery of America, to San Salvador and the Incas, when Europeans first encountered the simple faith of the Indian. There was, indeed, a beautiful simplicity about it; nothing of the dark and savage, only the mild and infantile. The sentiments of humility and reverence chiefly were expressed.

It was a dense and damp spruce and fir wood in which we lay, and, except for our fire, perfectly dark; and when I awoke in the night, I either heard an owl from deeper in the forest behind us, or a loon from a distance over the lake. Getting up some time after midnight to collect the scattered brands together, while my companions were sound asleep, I observed, partly in the fire, which had ceased to blaze, a perfectly regular elliptical ring of light, about five inches in its shortest diameter, six or seven in its longer, and from one eighth to one quarter of an inch wide. It was fully as bright as the fire, but not reddish or scarlet like a coal, but a white and slumbering light, like the glowworm's. I could tell it from the fire only by its whiteness. I saw at once that it must be phosphorescent wood, which I had so often heard of, but never chanced to see. Putting my finger on it, with a little hesitation, I found that it was a piece of dead moose-wood (*Acer striatum*) which the Indian had cut off in a slanting direction the evening before. Using my knife, I discovered that the light proceeded from that portion of the sap-wood immediately under the bark, and thus presented a regular ring at the end, which, indeed, appeared raised above the level of the wood, and when I pared off the bark and cut into the sap, it was all aglow along the log. I was surprised to find the wood quite hard and apparently sound, though probably decay had commenced in the sap, and I cut out some little triangular chips, and placing them in the hollow of my hand, carried them into the camp, waked my companion, and showed them to him. They lit up the inside of my hand, revealing the lines and wrinkles, and appearing exactly like coals of fire raised to a white heat, and I saw at once how, probably, the Indian jugglers had imposed on their people and on travellers, pretending to hold coals of fire in their mouths.

I also noticed that part of a decayed stump within four or five feet of the fire, an inch wide and six inches long, soft and shaking wood, shone with equal brightness.

I neglected to ascertain whether our fire had anything to do with this, but the previous day's rain and long-continued wet weather undoubtedly had.

I was exceedingly interested by this phenomenon, and already felt paid for my journey. It could hardly have thrilled me more if it had taken the form of letters, or of the human face. If I had met with this ring of light while groping in this forest alone, away from any fire, I should have been still more surprised. I little thought that there was such a light shining in the darkness of the wilderness for me.

The next day the Indian told me their name for this light, — *Artoosoqu'*, — and on my inquiring concerning the will-o'-the-wisp, and the like phenomena, he said that his "folks" sometimes saw fires passing along at various heights, even as high as the trees, and making a noise. I was prepared after this to hear of the most startling and unimagined phenomena witnessed by "his folks," they are abroad at all hours and seasons in scenes so unfrequented by white men. Nature must have made a thousand revelations to them which are still secrets to us.

I did not regret my not having seen this before, since I now saw it under circumstances so favorable. I was in just the frame of mind to see something wonderful, and this was a phenomenon adequate to my circumstances and expectation,

and it put me on the alert to see more like it.
I exulted like "a pagan suckled in a creed"
that had never been worn at all, but was bran
new, and adequate to the occasion. I let science
slide, and rejoiced in that light as if it had been
a fellow-creature. I saw that it was excellent,
and was very glad to know that it was so cheap.
A scientific *explanation*, as it is called, would
have been altogether out of place there. That
is for pale daylight. Science with its retorts
would have put me to sleep; it was the opportunity to be ignorant that I improved. It suggested to me that there was something to be
seen if one had eyes. It made a believer of me
more than before. I believed that the woods
were not tenantless, but chokefull of honest
spirits as good as myself any day, — not an
empty chamber, in which chemistry was left to
work alone, but an inhabited house, — and for
a few moments I enjoyed fellowship with them.
Your so-called wise man goes trying to persuade
himself that there is no entity there but himself
and his traps, but it is a great deal easier to believe the truth. It suggested, too, that the same
experience always gives birth to the same sort
of belief or religion. One revelation has been
made to the Indian, another to the white man.
I have much to learn of the Indian, nothing of
the missionary. I am not sure but all that would
tempt me to teach the Indian my religion would

be his promise to teach me *his*. Long enough I had heard of irrelevant things; now at length I was glad to make acquaintance with the light that dwells in rotten wood. Where is all your knowledge gone to? It evaporates completely, for it has no depth.

I kept those little chips and wet them again the next night, but they emitted no light.

SATURDAY, July 25.

At breakfast this Saturday morning, the Indian, evidently curious to know what would be expected of him the next day, whether we should go along or not, asked me how I spent the Sunday when at home. I told him that I commonly sat in my chamber reading, etc., in the forenoon, and went to walk in the afternoon. At which he shook his head and said, "Er, that is ver bad." "How do you spend it?" I asked. He said that he did no work, that he went to church at Oldtown when he was at home; in short, he did as he had been taught by the whites. This led to a discussion in which I found myself in the minority. He stated that he was a Protestant, and asked me if I was. I did not at first know what to say, but I thought that I could answer with truth that I was.

When we were washing the dishes in the lake, many fishes, apparently chivin, came close up to us to get the particles of grease.

The weather seemed to be more settled this morning, and we set out early in order to finish our voyage up the lake before the wind arose. Soon after starting the Indian directed our attention to the Northeast Carry, which we could plainly see, about thirteen miles distant in that direction as measured on the map, though it is called much farther. This carry is a rude wooden railroad, running north and south about two miles, perfectly straight, from the lake to the Penobscot, through a low tract, with a clearing three or four rods wide; but low as it is, it passes over the height of land there. This opening appeared as a clear bright or light point in the horizon, resting on the edge of the lake, whose breadth a hair could have covered at a considerable distance from the eye, and of no appreciable height. We should not have suspected it to be visible if the Indian had not drawn our attention to it. It was a remarkable kind of light to steer for, — daylight seen through a vista in the forest, — but visible as far as an ordinary beacon by night.

We crossed a deep and wide bay which makes eastward north of Kineo, leaving an island on our left, and keeping up the eastern side of the lake. This way or that led to some Tomhegan or *Socatarian* stream, up which the Indian had hunted, and whither I longed to go. The last name, however, had a bogus sound, too much like sectarian for me, as if a missionary had tampered with it; but I know that the Indians were very liberal. I think I should have inclined to the Tomhegan first.

We then crossed another broad bay, which, as we could no longer observe the shore particularly, afforded ample time for conversation. The Indian said that he had got his money by hunting, mostly high up the west branch of the Penobscot, and toward the head of the St. John; he had hunted there from a boy, and knew all about that region. His game had been beaver, otter, black cat (or fisher), sable, moose, etc. Loup cervier (or Canada lynx) were plenty yet in burnt grounds. For food in the woods, he uses partridges, ducks, dried moose-meat, hedgehog, etc. Loons, too, were good, only "bile 'em good." He told us at some length how he had suffered from starvation when a mere lad, being overtaken by winter when hunting with two grown Indians in the northern part of Maine, and obliged to leave their canoe on account of ice.

Pointing into the bay, he said that it was the way to various lakes which he knew. Only solemn bear-haunted mountains, with their great wooded slopes were visible; where, as man is not, we suppose some other power to be. My imagination personified the slopes themselves, as if by their very length they would waylay you and compel you to camp again on them before night. Some invisible glutton would seem to drop from the trees and gnaw at the heart of the solitary hunter who threaded those woods; and yet I was tempted to walk there. The Indian said that he had been along there several times.

I asked him how he guided himself in the woods. "O," said he, "I can tell good many ways." When I pressed him further, he answered, "Sometimes I lookum side-hill," and he glanced toward a high hill or mountain on the eastern shore, "great difference between the north and south, see where the sun has shone most. So trees, — the large limbs bend toward south. Sometimes I lookum locks" (rocks). I asked what he saw on the rocks, but he did not describe anything in particular, answering vaguely in a mysterious or drawling tone, "Bare locks on lake shore, — great difference between N. S. E. W. side — can tell what the sun has shone on." "Suppose," said I, "that I should take you in a dark night, right up here into the middle of the woods a hundred miles, set you down, and turn you round quickly twenty times, could you steer straight to Oldtown?" "O yer," said he, "have done pretty much same thing. I will tell you. Some years ago I met an old white hunter at Millinocket; very good hunter. He said he could go anywhere in the woods. He wanted to hunt with me that day, so we start.

We chase a moose all the forenoon, round and round, till middle of afternoon, when we kill him. Then I said to him, now you go straight to camp. Don't go round and round where we've been, but go straight. He said, I can't do that, I don't know where I am. Where you think camp? I asked. He pointed so. Then I laugh at him. I take the lead and go right off the other way, cross our tracks many times, straight camp." "How do you do that?" asked I. "O, I can't tell *you*," he replied. "Great difference between me and white man."

It appeared as if the sources of information were so various that he did not give a distinct, conscious attention to any one, and so could not readily refer to any when questioned about it, but he found his way very much as an animal does. Perhaps what is commonly called instinct in the animal, in this case is merely a sharpened and educated sense. Often, when an Indian says, "I don't know," in regard to the route he is to take, he does not mean what a white man would by those words, for his Indian instinct may tell him still as much as the most confident white man knows. He does not carry things in his head, nor remember the route exactly like a white man, but relies on himself at the moment. Not having experienced the need of the other sort of knowledge, all labelled and arranged, he has not acquired it.

The white hunter with whom I talked in the stage knew some of the resources of the Indian. He said that he steered by the wind, or by the limbs of the hemlocks, which were largest on the south side; also, sometimes when he knew that there was a lake near, by firing his gun and listening to hear the direction and distance of the echo from over it.

The course we took over this lake, and others afterward, was rarely direct, but a succession of curves from point to point, digressing considerably into each of the bays; and this was not merely on account of the wind, for the Indian, looking toward the middle of the lake, said it was hard to go there, easier to keep near the shore, because he thus got over it by successive reaches and saw by the shore how he got along.

The following will suffice for a common experience in crossing lakes in a canoe. As the forenoon advanced the wind increased. The last bay which we crossed before reaching the desolate pier at the northeast carry, was two or three miles over, and the wind was southwesterly. After going a third of the way, the waves had increased so as occasionally to wash into the canoe, and we saw that it was worse and worse ahead. At first we might have turned about, but were not willing to. It would have been of no use to follow the course of the shore, for not only the distance would have been

much greater, but the waves ran still higher
there on account of the greater sweep the wind
had. At any rate it would have been dangerous now to alter our course, because the waves
would have struck us at an advantage. It will
not do to meet them at right angles, for then
they will wash in both sides, but you must take
them quartering. So the Indian stood up in the
canoe, and exerted all his skill and strength for
a mile or two, while I paddled right along in
order to give him more steerage-way. For more
than a mile he did not allow a single wave to
strike the canoe as it would, but turned it
quickly from this side to that, so that it would
always be on or near the crest of a wave when it
broke, where all its force was spent, and we
merely settled down with it. At length I jumped
out on to the end of the pier, against which the
waves were dashing violently, in order to lighten
the canoe, and catch it at the landing, which
was not much sheltered; but just as I jumped
we took in two or three gallons of water. I
remarked to the Indian, "You managed that
well," to which he replied, "Ver few men do
that. Great many waves; when I look out for
one, another come quick."

While the Indian went to get cedar-bark, etc.,
to carry his canoe with, we cooked the dinner
on the shore, at this end of the carry, in the
midst of a sprinkling rain.

He prepared his canoe for carrying in this wise. He took a cedar shingle or splint eighteen inches long and four or five wide, rounded at one end, that the corners might not be in the way, and tied it with cedar-bark by two holes made midway, near the edge on each side, to the middle cross-bar of the canoe. When the canoe was lifted upon his head bottom up, this shingle, with its rounded end uppermost, distributed the weight over his shoulders and head, while a band of cedar-bark, tied to the cross-bar on each side of the shingle, passed round his breast, and another longer one, outside of the last, round his forehead; also a hand on each side rail served to steer the canoe and keep it from rocking. He thus carried it with his shoulders, head, breast, forehead, and both hands, as if the upper part of his body were all one hand to clasp and hold it. If you know of a better way, I should like to hear of it. A cedar-tree furnished all the gear in this case, as it had the woodwork of the canoe. One of the paddles rested on the cross-bars in the bows. I took the canoe upon my head and found that I could carry it with ease, though the straps were not fitted to my shoulders; but I let him carry it, not caring to establish a different precedent, though he said that if I would carry the canoe, he would take all the rest of the baggage, except my companion's. This shingle remained tied to the cross-bar throughout the voyage, was always ready for the carries, and also served to protect the back of one passenger.

We were obliged to go over this carry twice, our load was so great. But the carries were an agreeable variety, and we improved the opportunity to gather the rare plants which we had seen, when we returned empty-handed.

We reached the Penobscot about four o'clock, and found there some St. Francis Indians encamped on the bank, in the same place where I camped with four Indians four years before. They were making a canoe, and, as then, drying moose-meat. The meat looked very suitable to make a *black* broth at least. Our Indian said it was not good. Their camp was covered with spruce-bark. They had got a young moose, taken in the river a fortnight before, confined in a sort of cage of logs piled up cob-fashion, seven or eight feet high. It was quite tame, about four feet high, and covered with moose-flies. There was a large quantity of cornel (*C. stolonifera*), red maple, and also willow and aspen boughs, stuck through between the logs on all sides, butt-ends out, and on their leaves it was browsing. It looked at first as if it were in a bower rather than a pen.

Our Indian said that *he* used *black* spruce-roots to sew canoes with, obtaining it from high lands or mountains. The St. Francis Indian thought that *white* spruce-roots might be best. But the former said, "No good, break, can't split 'em;" also that they were hard to get, deep in ground, but the black were near the surface, on higher land, as well as tougher. He said that the white spruce was *subekoondark*, black, *skusk*. I told him I thought that I could make a canoe, but he expressed great doubt of it; at any rate, he thought that my work would not be "neat" the first time. An Indian at Greenville had told me that the winter bark, that is, bark taken off before the sap flows in May, was harder and much better than summer bark.

Having reloaded, he paddled down the Penobscot, which, as the Indian remarked, and even I detected, remembering how it looked before, was uncommonly full. We soon after saw a splendid yellow lily (*Lilium Canadense*) by the shore, which I plucked. It was six feet high, and had twelve flowers, in two whorls, forming a pyramid, such as I have seen in Concord. We afterward saw many more thus tall along the stream, and also still more numerous on the East Branch, and, on the latter, one which I thought approached yet nearer to the *Lilium superbum*. The Indian asked what we called it, and said that the "loots" (roots) were good for soup, that is, to cook with meat, to thicken it, taking the place of flour. They get them in the fall. I dug some, and found a mass of bulbs pretty deep in the earth, two inches in diameter, looking, and even tasting, somewhat like raw green corn on the ear.

When we had gone about three miles down the Penobscot, we saw through the tree-tops a thunder-shower coming up in the west, and we looked out a camping-place in good season, about five o'clock, on the west side, not far below the mouth of what Joe Aitteon, in '53, called Lobster Stream, coming from Lobster Pond. Our present Indian, however, did not admit this name, nor even that of *Matahum-keag*, which is on the map, but called the lake *Beskabekuk*.

I will describe, once for all, the routine of camping at this season. We generally told the Indian that we would stop at the first suitable place, so that he might be on the lookout for it. Having observed a clear, hard, and flat beach to land on, free from mud, and from stones which would injure the canoe, one would run up the bank to see if there were open and level space enough for the camp between the trees, of if it could be easily cleared, preferring at the same time a cool place, on account of insects. Sometimes we paddled a mile or more before finding one to our minds, for where the shore was suit-ble, the bank would often be too steep, or else too low and grassy, and therefore mosquitoey. We then took out the baggage and drew up the canoe, sometimes turning it over on shore for safety. The Indian cut a path to the spot we had selected, which was usually within two or three rods of the water, and we carried up our baggage. One, perhaps, takes canoe-birch bark, always at hand, and dead dry-wood or bark, and kindles a fire five or six feet in front of where we intend to lie. It matters not, commonly, on which side this is, because there is little or no wind in so dense a wood at that season; and then he gets a kettle of water from the river, and takes out the pork, bread, coffee, etc., from their several packages.

Another, meanwhile, having the axe, cuts down the nearest dead rock-maple or other dry hard wood, collecting several large logs to last through the night, also a green stake, with a notch or fork to it, which is slanted over the fire, perhaps resting on a rock, or forked stake, to hang the kettle on, and two forked stakes and a pole for the tent.

The third man pitches the tent, cuts a dozen or more pins with his knife, usually of moose-wood, the common underwood, to fasten it down with, and then collects an armful or two of fir-twigs,[1] arbor-vitæ, spruce, or hemlock, which-ever is at hand, and makes the bed, beginning at either end, and laying the twigs wrong-side up, in regular rows, covering the stub-ends of

[1] These twigs are called in Rasle's Dictionary, *Sediak*.

the last row; first, however, filling the hollows, if there are any, with coarser material. Wrangel says that his guides in Siberia first strewed a quantity of dry brushwood on the ground, and then cedar twigs on that.

Commonly, by the time the bed is made, or within fifteen or twenty minutes, the water boils, the pork is fried, and supper is ready. We eat this sitting on the ground, or a stump, if there is any, around a large piece of birch-bark for a table, each holding a dipper in one hand and a piece of ship-bread or fried pork in the other, frequently making a pass with his hand, or thrusting his head into the smoke, to avoid the mosquitoes.

Next, pipes are lit by those who smoke, and veils are donned by those who have them, and we hastily examine and dry our plants, anoint our faces and hands, and go to bed, — and — the mosquitoes.

Though you have nothing to do but see the country, there's rarely any time to spare, hardly enough to examine a plant, before the night or drowsiness is upon you.

Such was the ordinary experience, but this evening we had camped earlier on account of the rain, and had more time.

We found that our camp to-night was on an old, and now more than usually indistinct, supply-road, running along the river. What is

called a road there shows no ruts or trace of
wheels, for they are not used; nor, indeed, of
runners, since they are used only in the winter,
when the snow is several feet deep. It is only
an indistinct vista through the wood, which it
takes an experienced eye to detect.

We had no sooner pitched our tent than the
thunder-shower burst on us, and we hastily
crept under it, drawing our bags after us, curious
to see how much of a shelter our thin cotton
roof was going to be in this excursion. Though
the violence of the rain forced a fine shower
through the cloth before it was fairly wetted and
shrunk, with which we were well bedewed, we
managed to keep pretty dry, only a box of
matches having been left out and spoiled, and
before we were aware of it the shower was over,
and only the dripping trees imprisoned us.

Wishing to see what fishes there were in the
river there, we cast our lines over the wet bushes
on the shore, but they were repeatedly swept
down the swift stream in vain. So, leaving the
Indian, we took the canoe just before dark, and
dropped down the river a few rods to fish at
the mouth of a sluggish brook on the opposite
side. We pushed up this a rod or two, where,
perhaps, only a canoe had been before. But
though there were a few small fishes, mostly
chivin, there, we were soon driven off by the
mosquitoes. While there we heard the Indian

fire his gun twice in such rapid succession that
we thought it must be double-barrelled, though
we observed afterward that it was single. His
object was to clean out and dry it after the rain,
and he then loaded it with ball, being now on
ground where he expected to meet with large
game. This sudden, loud, crashing noise in
the still aisles of the forest, affected me like an
insult to nature, or ill manners at any rate,
as if you were to fire a gun in a hall or temple.
It was not heard far, however, except along
the river, the sound being rapidly hushed up
or absorbed by the damp trees and mossy
ground.

The Indian made a little smothered fire of
damp leaves close to the back of the camp, that
the smoke might drive through and keep out the
mosquitoes; but just before we fell asleep this
suddenly blazed up, and came near setting fire
to the tent. We were considerably molested by
mosquitoes at this camp.

SUNDAY, July 26.

The note of the white-throated sparrow, a
very inspiriting but almost wiry sound, was the
first heard in the morning, and with this all the
woods rang. This was the prevailing bird in
the northern part of Maine. The forest generally was all alive with them at this season, and
they were proportionally numerous and musical

about Bangor. They evidently breed in that State. Wilson did not know where they bred, and says, "Their only note is a kind of chip." Though commonly unseen, their simple *ah*, *te-te-te*, *te-te-te*, *te-te-te*, so sharp and piercing, was as distinct to the ear as the passage of a spark of fire shot into the darkest of the forest would be to the eye. I thought that they commonly uttered it as they flew. I hear this note for a few days only in the spring, as they go through Concord, and in the fall see them again going southward, but then they are mute. We were commonly aroused by their lively strain very early. What a glorious time they must have in that wilderness, far from mankind and election day !

I told the Indian that we would go to church to Chesuncook this (Sunday) morning, some fifteen miles. It was settled weather at last. A few swallows flitted over the water, we heard the white throats along the shore, the phebe notes of the chicadee, and, I believe, red-starts, and moose-flies of large size pursued us in mid-stream.

The Indian thought that we should lie by on Sunday. Said he, "We come here lookum things, look all round; but come Sunday, lock up all that, and then Monday look again." He spoke of an Indian of his acquaintance who had been with some ministers to Ktaadn, and had told him how they conducted. This he described in a low and solemn voice. "They make a long prayer every morning and night, and at every meal. Come Sunday," said he, "they stop 'em, no go at all that day, — keep still, — preach all day, — first one then another, just like church. O, ver good men." "One day," said he, "going along a river, they came to the body of a man in the water, drowned good while, all ready fall to pieces. They go right ashore, — stop there, go no farther that day, — they have meeting there, preach and pray just like Sunday. Then they get poles and lift up the body, and they go back and carry the body with them. O, they ver good men."

I judged from this account that their every camp was a camp-meeting, and they had mistaken their route, — they should have gone to Eastham; that they wanted an opportunity to preach somewhere more than to see Ktaadn. I read of another similar party that seem to have spent their time there singing the songs of Zion. I was glad that I did not go to that mountain with such slow coaches.

However, the Indian added, plying the paddle all the while, that if we would go along, he must go with us, he our man, and he suppose that if he no takum pay for what he do Sunday, then there's no harm, but if he takum pay, then wrong. I told him that he was stricter than

white men. Nevertheless, I noticed that he did
not forget to reckon in the Sundays at last.

He appeared to be a very religious man, and
said his prayers in a loud voice, in Indian,
kneeling before the camp, morning and evening,
— sometimes scrambling up again in haste when
he had forgotten this, and saying them with
great rapidity. In the course of the day, he
remarked, not very originally, "Poor man remem-
berum God more than rich."

We soon passed the island where I had camped
four years before, and I recognized the very
spot. The dead water, a mile or two below it,
the Indian called, *Beska bekukskishtuk*, from
the lake *Beskabekuk*, which empties in above.
This dead water, he said, was "a great place for
moose always." We saw the grass bent where
a moose came out the night before, and the Indian said that he could smell one as far as he
could see him; but, he added, that if he should
see five or six to-day close by canoe, he no shoot
'em. Accordingly, as he was the only one of
the party who had a gun, or had come a-hunting,
the moose were safe.

Just below this, a cat-owl flew heavily over the
stream, and he, asking if I knew what it was,
imitated very well the common *hoo, hoo, hoo,
hoorer, hoo,* of our woods; making a hard, guttural sound, "Ugh, ugh, ugh, — ugh, ugh."
When we passed the Moose-horn, he said that

it had no name. What Joe Aitteon had called Ragmuff, he called *Pay tay te quick*, and said that it meant Burnt Ground Stream. We stopped there, where I had stopped before, and I bathed in this tributary. It was shallow but cold, apparently too cold for the Indian, who stood looking on. As we were pushing away again, a white-beaked eagle sailed over our heads. A reach some miles above Pine Stream, where there were several islands, the Indian said was *Nonglangyis*, dead-water. Pine Stream he called Black River, and said that its Indian name was *Karsaootuk*. He could go to Caribou Lake that way.

We carried a part of the baggage about Pine Stream Falls, while the Indian went down in the canoe. A Bangor merchant had told us that two men in his employ were drowned some time ago while passing these falls in a batteau, and a third clung to a rock all night, and was taken off in the morning. There were magnificent great purple-fringed orchises on this carry and the neighboring shores. I measured the largest canoe birch which I saw in this journey near the end of the carry. It was 14½ feet in circumference at two feet from the ground, but at five feet divided into three parts. The canoe-birches thereabouts were commonly marked by conspicuous dark spiral ridges, with a groove between, so that I thought at first that they had been struck by lightning, but, as the Indian said, it was evidently caused by the grain of the tree. He cut a small, woody knob, as big as a filbert, from the trunk of a fir, apparently an old balsam vesicle filled with wood, which he said was good medicine.

After we had embarked and gone half a mile, my companion remembered that he had left his knife, and we paddled back to get it, against the strong and swift current. This taught us the difference between going up and down the stream, for while we were working our way back a quarter of a mile, we should have gone down a mile and a half at least. So we landed, and while he and the Indian were gone back for it, I watched the motions of the foam, a kind of white water-fowl near the shore, forty or fifty rods below. It alternately appeared and disappeared behind the rock, being carried round by an eddy. Even this semblance of life was interesting on that lonely river.

Immediately below these falls was the Chesuncook dead-water, caused by the flowing back of the lake. As we paddled slowly over this, the Indian told us a story of his hunting thereabouts, and something more interesting about himself. It appeared that he had represented his tribe at Augusta, and also once at Washington, where he had met some Western chiefs. He had been consulted at Augusta, and gave advice, which he said was followed, respecting the eastern boundary of Maine, as determined by highlands and streams, at the time of the difficulties on that side. He was employed with the surveyors on the line. Also he had called on Daniel Webster in Boston, at the time of his Bunker Hill oration.

I was surprised to hear him say that he liked to go to Boston, New York, Philadelphia, etc., etc.; that he would like to live there. But then, as if relenting a little, when he thought what a poor figure he would make there, he added, "I suppose, I live in New York, I be poorest hunter, I expect." He understood very well both his superiority and his inferiority to the whites. He criticised the people of the United States as compared with other nations, but the only distinct idea with which he labored was, that they were "very strong," but, like some individuals, "too fast." He must have the credit of saying this just before the general breaking down of railroads and banks. He had a great idea of education, and would occasionally break out into such expressions as this, "Kademy — a-cad-e-my — good thing — I suppose they usum Fifth Reader there. . . . You been college?"

From this dead-water the outlines of the mountains about Ktaadn were visible. The top of Ktaadn was concealed by a cloud, but the

Souneunk Mountains were nearer and quite visible. We steered across the northwest end of the lake, from which we looked down south-southeast, the whole length to Joe Merry Mountain, seen over its extremity. It is an agreeable change to cross a lake, after you have been shut up in the woods, not only on account of the greater expanse of water, but also of sky. It is one of the surprises which Nature has in store for the traveller in the forest. To look down, in this case, over eighteen miles of water, was liberating and civilizing even. No doubt, the short distance to which you can see in the woods, and the general twilight, would at length react on the inhabitants, and make them *salvages*. The lakes also reveal the mountains, and give ample scope and range to our thought. The very gulls which we saw sitting on the rocks, like white specks, or circling about, reminded me of custom-house officers. Already there were half a dozen log-huts about this end of the lake, though so far from a road. I perceive that in these woods the earliest settlements are, for various reasons, clustering about the lakes, but partly, I think, for the sake of the neighborhood as the oldest clearings. They are forest schools already established, — great centres of light. Water is a pioneer which the settler follows, taking advantage of its improvements.

Thus far only I had been before. About noon

we turned northward, up a broad kind of estuary, and at its northeast corner found the Caucomgomoc River, and after going about a mile from the lake, reached the Umbazookskus, which comes in on the right at a point where the former river, coming from the west, turns short to the south. Our course was up the Umbazookskus, but as the Indian knew of a good camping-place, that is, a cool place where there were few mosquitoes, about half a mile farther up the Caucomgomoc, we went thither. The latter river, judging from the map, is the longer and principal stream, and, therefore, its name must prevail below the junction. So quickly we changed the civilizing sky of Chesuncook for the dark wood of the Caucomgomoc. On reaching the Indian's camping-ground, in the south side, where the bank was about a dozen feet high, I read on the trunk of a fir-tree blazed by an axe an inscription in charcoal which had been left by him. It was surmounted by a drawing of a bear paddling a canoe, which he said was the sign which had been used by his family always. The drawing, though rude, could not be mistaken for anything but a bear, and he doubted my ability to copy it. The inscription ran thus, *verbatim et literatim.* I interline the English of his Indian as he gave it to me.

[The figure of a bear in a boat.]

July 26,
1853.

––––––––––

Niasoseb.

We alone	Joseph.
Polis	*clioi*
Polis	start
sia	*olta*
for	Oldtown
ouke	*ni*
right	away.
quambi.	

––––––––––

July 15,
1855.
Niasoseb.

He added now below : —

1857,
July 26.
Io. Polis.

This was one of his homes. I saw where he
had sometimes stretched his moose-hides on the
opposite or sunny north side of the river, where
there was a narrow meadow.

After we had selected a place for our camp,
and kindled our fire, almost exactly on the site
of the Indian's last camp here, he, looking up,
observed, "That tree danger." It was a dead
part, more than a foot in diameter, of a large

canoe-birch, which branched at the ground. This branch, rising thirty feet or more, slanted directly over the spot which we had chosen for our bed. I told him to try it with his axe; but he could not shake it perceptibly, and, therefore, seemed inclined to disregard it, and my companion expressed his willingness to run the risk. But it seemed to me that we should be fools to lie under it, for though the lower part was firm the top, for aught we knew, might be just ready to fall, and we should at any rate be very uneasy if the wind arose in the night. It is a common accident for men camping in the woods to be killed by a falling tree. So the camp was moved to the other side of the fire.

It was, as usual, a damp and shaggy forest, that Caucomgomoc one, and the most you knew about it was that on this side it stretched toward the settlements, and on that to still more unfrequented regions. You carried so much topography in your mind always, — and sometimes it seemed to make a considerable difference whether you sat or lay nearer the settlements, or farther off, than your companions, — were the rear or frontier man of the camp. But there is really the same difference between our positions wherever we may be camped, and some are nearer the frontiers on feather-beds in the towns than others on fir-twigs in the backwoods.

The Indian said that the Umbazookskus,

being a dead stream with broad meadows, was a good place for moose, and he frequently came a-hunting here, being out alone three weeks or more from Oldtown. He sometimes, also, went a-hunting to the Seboois Lakes, taking the stage, with his gun and ammunition, axe and blankets, hard bread and pork, perhaps for a hundred miles of the way, and jumped off at the wildest place on the road, where he was at once at home, and every rod was a tavern-site for him. Then, after a short journey through the woods, he would build a spruce-bark canoe in one day, putting but few ribs into it, that it might be light, and after doing his hunting with it on the lakes, would return with his furs the same way he had come. Thus you have an Indian availing himself cunningly of the advantages of civil-ization, without losing any of his woodcraft, but proving himself the more successful hunter for it.

This man was very clever and quick to learn anything in his line. Our tent was of a kind new to him; but when he had once seen it pitched it was surprising how quickly he would find and prepare the pole and forked stakes to pitch it with, cutting and placing them right the first time, though I am sure that the majority of white men would have blundered several times.

This river came from Caucomgomoc Lake,

about ten miles farther up. Though it was sluggish here, there were falls not far above us, and we saw the foam from them go by from time to time. The Indian said that *Caucomgomoc* meant Big-gull Lake, (i.e. Herring-gull, I suppose,) *gomoc* meaning lake. Hence this was *Caucomgomoctook*, or the river from that lake. This was the Penobscot *Caucomgomoc-took!* there was another St. John one not far north. He finds the eggs of this gull, sometimes twenty together, as big as hen's eggs, on rocky ledges on the west side of Millinocket River, for instance, and eats them.

Now I thought I would observe how he spent his Sunday. While I and my companion were looking about at the trees and river, he went to sleep. Indeed, he improved every opportunity to get a nap, whatever the day.

Rambling about the woods at this camp, I noticed that they consisted chiefly of firs, black spruce, and some white, red maple, canoe-birch, and, along the river, the hoary alder, *Alnus incana*. I name them in the order of their abundance. The *Viburnum nudum* was a common shrub, and of smaller plants there were the dwarf-cornel, great round-leaved orchis, abundant and in bloom (a greenish-white flower growing in little communities), *Uvularia grandiflora*, whose stem tasted like a cucumber, *Pyrola secunda*, apparently the commonest Pyrola in those woods, now out of bloom, *Pyrola elliptica*, and *Chiogenes hispidula*. The *Clintonia borealis*, with ripe berries, was very abundant, and perfectly at home there. Its leaves, disposed commonly in triangles about its stem, were just as handsomely formed and green, and its berries as blue and glossy, as if it grew by some botanist's favorite path.

I could trace the outlines of large birches that had fallen long ago, collapsed and rotted and turned to soil, by faint yellowish-green lines of feather-like moss, eighteen inches wide and twenty or thirty feet long, crossed by other similar lines.

I heard a Maryland yellow-throat's midnight strain, wood-thrush, kingfisher (tweezer bird), or parti-colored warbler, and a night-hawk. I also heard and saw red squirrels, and heard a bull-frog. The Indian said that he heard a snake.

Wild as it was, it was hard for me to get rid of the associations of the settlements. Any steady and monotonous sound, to which I did not distinctly attend, passed for a sound of human industry. The water-falls which I heard were not without their dams and mills to my imagination, — and several times I found that I had been regarding the steady rushing sound of the wind from over the woods beyond the rivers as that of a train of cars, — the cars at Quebec. Our minds anywhere, when left to themselves, are always thus busily drawing conclusions from false premises.

I asked the Indian to make us a sugar-bowl of birch-bark, which he did, using the great knife which dangled in a sheath from his belt; but the bark broke at the corners when he bent it up, and he said it was not good; that there was a great difference in this respect between the bark of one canoe-birch and that of another, i.e. one cracked more easily than another. I used some thin and delicate sheets of this bark which he split and cut, in my flower book; thinking it would be good to separate the dried specimens from the green.

My companion, wishing to distinguish between the black and white spruce, asked Polis to show him a twig of the latter, which he did at once, together with the black; indeed, he could distinguish them about as far as he could see them; but as the two twigs appeared very much alike, my companion asked the Indian to point out the difference; whereupon the latter, taking the twigs, instantly remarked, as he passed his hand over them successively in a stroking manner, that the white was rough (i.e. the needles stood up nearly perpendicular), but the black smooth (i.e. as if bent or combed down). This was an obvious difference, both to sight and touch. However, if I remember rightly, this would not

serve to distinguish the white spruce from the
light-colored variety of the black.

I asked him to let me see him get some black
spruce root, and make some thread. Whereupon, without looking up at the trees overhead,
he began to grub in the ground, instantly distinguishing the black spruce roots, and cutting
off a slender one, three or four feet long, and as
big as a pipe-stem, he split the end with his
knife, and taking a half between the thumb and
forefinger of each hand, rapidly separated its
whole length into two equal semi-cylindrical
halves; then giving me another root, he said,
"You try." But in my hands it immediately
ran off one side, and I got only a very short
piece. In short, though it looked very easy,
I found that there was a great art in splitting
these roots. The split is skilfully humored by
bending short with this hand or that, and so kept
in the middle. He then took off the bark, from
each half, pressing a short piece of cedar bark
against the convex side with both hands, while
he drew the root upward with his teeth. An
Indian's teeth are strong, and I noticed that he
used his often where we should have used a
hand. They amounted to a third hand. He
thus obtained, in a moment, a very neat, tough,
and flexible string, which he could tie into a
knot, or make into a fish-line even. It is said
that in Norway and Sweden the roots of the

Norway spruce (*Abies excelsa*) are used in the same way for the same purpose. He said that you would be obliged to give half a dollar for spruce root enough for a canoe, thus prepared. He had hired the sewing of his own canoe, though he made all the rest. The root in his canoe was of a pale slate color, probably acquired by exposure to the weather, or perhaps from being boiled in water first.

He had discovered the day before that his canoe leaked a little, and said that it was owing to stepping into it violently, which forced the water under the edge of the horizontal seams on the side. I asked him where he would get pitch to mend it with, for they commonly use hard-pitch, obtained of the whites at Oldtown. He said that he could make something very similar, and equally good, not of spruce gum, or the like, but of material which we had with us; and he wished me to guess what. But I could not, and he would not tell me, though he showed me a ball of it when made, as big as a pea, and like black pitch, saying, at last, that there were some things which a man did not tell even his wife. It may have been his own discovery. In Arnold's expedition the pioneers used for their canoe "the turpentine of the pine, and the scrapings of the pork-bag."

Being curious to see what kind of fishes there were in this dark, deep, sluggish river, I cast in my line just before night, and caught several small somewhat yellowish sucker-like fishes, which the Indian at once rejected, saying that they were *Michigan* fish (i.e. *soft* and *stinking* fish) and good for nothing. Also, he would not touch a pout, which I caught, and said that neither Indians nor whites thereabouts ever ate them, which I thought was singular, since they are esteemed in Massachusetts, and he had told me that he ate hedgehogs, loons, etc. But he said that some small silvery fishes, which I called white chivin, which were similar in size and form to the first, were the best fish in the Penobscot waters, and if I would toss them up the bank to him, he would cook them for me. After cleaning them, not very carefully, leaving the heads on, he laid them on the coals and so broiled them.

Returning from a short walk, he brought a vine in his hand, and asked me if I knew what it was, saying that it made the best tea of anything in the woods. It was the Creeping Snowberry (*Chiogenes hispidula*), which was quite common there, its berries just grown. He called it *cowosnebagosar*, which name implies that it grows where old prostrate trunks have collapsed and rotted. So we determined to have some tea made of this to-night. It had a slight checkerberry flavor, and we both agreed that it was really better than the black tea which we had

brought. We thought it quite a discovery, and
that it might well be dried, and sold in the shops.
I, for one, however, am not an old tea-drinker,
and cannot speak with authority to others. It
would have been particularly good to carry along
for a cold drink during the day, the water thereabouts being invariably warm. The Indian
said that they also used for tea a certain herb
which grew in low ground, which he did not
find there, and *Ledum*, or Labrador tea, which
I have since found and tried in Concord; also
hemlock leaves, the last especially in the winter,
when the other plants were covered with snow;
and various other things; but he did not approve
of *arbor-vitæ*, which I said I had drunk in those
woods. We could have had a new kind of tea
every night.

Just before night we saw a *musquash*, (he did
not say muskrat,) the only one we saw in this
voyage, swimming downward on the opposite
side of the stream. The Indian, wishing to get
one to eat, hushed us, saying, "Stop, me call
'em;" and sitting flat on the bank, he began to
make a curious squeaking, wiry sound with his
lips, exerting himself considerably. I was greatly
surprised, — thought that I had at last got into
the wilderness, and that he was a wild man indeed, to be talking to a musquash! I did not
know which of the two was the strangest to me.
He seemed suddenly to have quite forsaken hu-

manity, and gone over to the musquash side. The musquash, however, as near as I could see, did not turn aside, though he may have hesitated a little, and the Indian said that he saw our fire; but it was evident that he was in the habit of calling the musquash to him, as he said. An acquaintance of mine who was hunting moose in those woods a month after this, tells me that his Indian in this way repeatedly called the musquash within reach of his paddle in the moonlight, and struck at them.

The Indian said a particularly long prayer this Sunday evening, as if to atone for working in the morning.

MONDAY, July 27.

Having rapidly loaded the canoe, which the Indian always carefully attended to, that it might be well trimmed, and each having taken a look, as usual, to see that nothing was left, we set out again, descending the Caucomgomoc, and turning northeasterly up the *Umbazookskus*. This name, the Indian said, meant *Much Meadow River*. We found it a very meadowy stream, and dead-water, and now very wide on account of the rains, though, he said, it was sometimes quite narrow. The space between the woods, chiefly bare meadow, was from fifty to two hundred rods in breadth, and is a rare place for moose. It reminded me of the Concord; and what increased the resemblance, was one old musquash house almost afloat.

In the water on the meadows grew sedges, wool-grass, the common blue-flag abundantly, its flower just showing itself above the high water, as if it were a blue water-lily, and higher in the meadows a great many clumps of a peculiar narrow-leaved willow (*Salix petiolaris*), which is common in our river meadows. It was the prevailing one here, and the Indian said that the musquash ate much of it; and here also grew the red osier (*Cornus stolonifera*), its large fruit now whitish.

Though it was still early in the morning, we saw nighthawks circling over the meadow, and as usual heard the *Pepe* (*Muscicapa Cooperi*), which is one of the prevailing birds in these woods, and the robin.

It was unusual for the woods to be so distant from the shore, and there was quite an echo from them, but when I was shouting in order to awake it, the Indian reminded me that I should scare the moose, which he was looking out for, and which we all wanted to see. The word for echo was *Pockadunkquaywayle*.

A broad belt of dead larch-trees along the distant edge of the meadow, against the forest on each side, increased the usual wildness of the scenery. The Indian called these juniper, and said that they had been killed by the back water caused by the dam at the outlet of Chesuncook Lake, some twenty miles distant. I plucked at the water's edge the *Asclepias incarnata*, with quite handsome flowers, a brighter red than our variety (the *pulchra*). It was the only form of it which I saw there.

Having paddled several miles up the Um-bazookskus, it suddenly contracted to a mere brook, narrow and swift, the larches and other trees approaching the bank and leaving no open meadow, and we landed to get a black-spruce pole for pushing against the stream. This was the first occasion for one. The one selected was quite slender, cut about ten feet long, merely whittled to a point, and the bark shaved off. The stream, though narrow and swift, was still deep, with a muddy bottom, as I proved by div-ing to it. Beside the plants which I have men-tioned, I observed on the bank here the *Salix cordata* and *rostrata*, *Ranunculus recurvatus*, and *Rubus triflorus* with ripe fruit.

While we were thus employed, two Indians in a canoe hove in sight round the bushes, coming down stream. Our Indian knew one of them, an old man, and fell into conversation with him in Indian. He belonged at the foot of Moose-head. The other was of another tribe. They were returning from hunting. I asked the younger if they had seen any moose, to which he said no; but I, seeing the moose-hides sticking

out from a great bundle made with their blankets
in the middle of the canoe, added, "Only their
hides." As he was a foreigner, he may have
wished to deceive me, for it is against the law for
white men and foreigners to kill moose in Maine
at this season. But, perhaps, he need not have
been alarmed, for the moose-wardens are not
very particular. I heard quite directly of one,
who being asked by a white man going into the
woods what he would say if he killed a moose,
answered, "If you bring me a quarter of it, I
guess you won't be troubled," his duty being, as
he said, only to prevent the "indiscriminate"
slaughter of them for their hides. I suppose
that he would consider it an *indiscriminate*
slaughter when a quarter was not reserved for
himself. Such are the perquisites of this office.

We continued along through the most extensive larch wood which I had seen, — tall and
slender trees with fantastic branches. But
though this was the prevailing tree here, I do
not remember that we saw any afterward. You
do not find straggling trees of this species here
and there throughout the wood, but rather a
little forest of them. The same is the case with
the white and red pines, and some other trees,
greatly to the convenience of the lumberer.
They are of a social habit, growing in "veins,"
"clumps," "groups," or "communities," as
the explorers call them, distinguishing them far

away, from the top of a hill or a tree, the white pines towering above the surrounding forest, or else they form extensive forests by themselves. I would have liked to come across a large community of pines, which had never been invaded by the lumbering army.

We saw some fresh moose tracks along the shore, but the Indian said that the moose were not driven out of the woods by the flies, as usual this season, on account of the abundance of water everywhere. The stream was only from one and one-half to three rods wide, quite winding, with occasional small islands, meadows, and some very swift and shallow places. When we came to an island, the Indian never hesitated which side to take, as if the current told him which was the shortest and deepest. It was lucky for us that the water was so high. We had to walk but once on this stream, carrying a part of the load, at a swift and shallow reach while he got up with the canoe, not being obliged to take out, though he said it was very strong water. Once or twice we passed the red wreck of a batteau which had been stove some spring.

While making this portage I saw many splendid specimens of the great purple-fringed orchis, three feet high. It is remarkable that such delicate flowers should here adorn these wilderness paths.

Having resumed our seats in the canoe, I felt

the Indian wiping my back, which he had accidentally spat upon. He said it was a sign that I
was going to be married.

The Umbazookskus River is called ten miles
long. Having pulled up the narrowest point
some three or four miles, the next opening in the
sky was over Umbazookskus Lake, which we
suddenly entered about eleven o'clock in the
forenoon. It stretches northwesterly four or
five miles, with what the Indian called the Caucomgomoc Mountain seen far beyond it. It
was an agreeable change.

This lake was very shallow a long distance
from the shore, and I saw stone heaps on the
bottom, like those in the Assabet at home. The
canoe ran into one. The Indian thought that
they were made by an eel. Joe Aitteon in 1853
thought that they were made by chub. We
crossed the southeast end of the lake to the carry
into Mud Pond.

Umbazookskus Lake is the head of the Penobscot in this direction, and Mud Pond is the nearest bend of the Allegash, one of the chief sources
of the St. John. Hodge, who went through this
way to the St. Lawrence in the service of the
State, calls the portage here a mile and three
quarters long, and states that Mud Pond has
been found to be fourteen feet higher than Umbazookskus Lake. As the west branch of the
Penobscot at the Moosehead carry is considered

about twenty-five feet lower than Moosehead Lake, it appears that the Penobscot in the upper part of its course runs in a broad and shallow valley, between the Kennebec and St. John, and lower than either of them, though, judging from the map, you might expect it to be the highest.

Mud Pond is about half-way from Umbazook-skus to Chamberlain Lake, into which it empties, and to which we were bound. The Indian said that this was the wettest carry in the State, and as the season was a very wet one, we anticipated an unpleasant walk. As usual he made one large bundle of the pork-keg, cooking utensils, and other loose traps, by tying them up in his blanket. We should be obliged to go over the carry twice, and our method was to carry one half part way, and then go back for the rest.

Our path ran close by the door of a log-hut in a clearing at this end of the carry, which the Indian, who alone entered it, found to be occupied by a Canadian and his family, and that the man had been blind for a year. He seemed peculiarly unfortunate to be taken blind there, where there were so few eyes to see for him. He could not even be led out of that country by a dog, but must be taken down the rapids as passively as a barrel of flour. This was the first house above Chesuncook, and the last on the Penobscot waters, and was built here, no doubt, because it was the route of the lumberers in the winter and spring.

After a slight ascent from the lake through the springy soil of the Canadian's clearing, we entered on a level and very wet and rocky path through the universal dense evergreen forest, a loosely paved gutter merely, where we went leaping from rock to rock and from side to side, in the vain attempt to keep out of the water and mud. We concluded that it was yet Penobscot water, though there was no flow to it. It was on this carry that the white hunter whom I met in the stage, as he told me, had shot two bears a few months before. They stood directly in the path, and did not turn out for him. They might be excused for not turning out there, or only taking the right as the law directs. He said that at this season bears were found on the mountains and hillsides, in search of berries, and were apt to be saucy, — that we might come across them up Trout Stream; and he added, what I hardly credited, that many Indians slept in their canoes, not daring to sleep on land, on account of them.

Here commences what was called, twenty years ago, the best timber land in the State. This very spot was described as "covered with the greatest abundance of pine," but now this appeared to me, comparatively, an uncommon tree there, — and yet you did not see where any more

could have stood, amid the dense growth of
cedar, fir, etc. It was then proposed to cut a
canal from lake to lake here, but the outlet was
finally made farther east, at Telos Lake, as we
shall see.

The Indian with his canoe soon disappeared
before us; but erelong he came back and told
us to take a path which turned off westward, it
being better walking, and, at my suggestion, he
agreed to leave a bough in the regular carry at
that place, that we might not pass it by mistake.
Thereafter, he said, we were to keep the main
path, and he added, "You see 'em my tracks."
But I had not much faith that we could distinguish his tracks, since others had passed over
the carry within a few days.

We turned off at the right place, but were soon
confused by numerous logging-paths, coming
into the one we were on, by which lumberers
had been to pick out those pines which I have
mentioned. However, we kept what we considered the main path, though it was a winding
one, and in this, at long intervals, we distinguished a faint trace of a footstep. This, though
comparatively unworn, was at first a better, or,
at least, a drier road, than the regular carry which
we had left. It led through an arbor-vitæ wilderness of the grimmest character. The great
fallen and rotting trees had been cut through and
rolled aside, and their huge trunks abutted on the

path on each side, while others still lay across it two or three feet high. It was impossible for us to discern the Indian's trail in the elastic moss, which, like a thick carpet, covered every rock and fallen tree, as well as the earth. Nevertheless, I did occasionally detect the track of a man, and I gave myself some credit for it. I carried my whole load at once, a heavy knapsack, and a large India-rubber bag, containing our bread and a blanket, swung on a paddle; in all, about sixty pounds; but my companion preferred to make two journeys, by short stages, while I waited for him. We could not be sure that we were not depositing our loads each time farther off from the true path.

As I sat waiting for my companion, he would seem to be gone a long time, and I had ample opportunity to make observations on the forest. I now first began to be seriously molested by the black-fly, a very small but perfectly formed fly of that color, about one-tenth of an inch long, which I first felt, and then saw, in swarms about me, as I sat by a wider and more than usually doubtful fork in this dark forest-path. The hunters tell bloody stories about them, — how they settle in a ring about your neck, before you know it, and are wiped off in great numbers with your blood. But remembering that I had a wash in my knapsack, prepared by a thoughtful hand in Bangor, I made haste to apply it to my

face and hands, and was glad to find it effectual,
as long as it was fresh, or for twenty minutes,
not only against black-flies, but all the insects
that molested us. They would not alight on the
part thus defended. It was composed of sweet-
oil and oil of turpentine, with a little oil of
spearmint and camphor. However, I finally
concluded that the remedy was worse than the
disease. It was so disagreeable and inconven-
ient to have your face and hands covered with
such a mixture.

Three large slate-colored birds of the jay
genus (*Garrulus Canadensis*), the Canada-jay,
moose-bird, meat-bird, or what not, came flitting silently and by degrees toward me, and
hopped down the limbs inquisitively to within
seven or eight feet. They were more clumsy and
not nearly so handsome as the blue-jay. Fish-
hawks, from the lake, uttered their sharp whistling notes low over the top of the forest near me,
as if they were anxious about a nest there.

After I had sat there some time, I noticed at
this fork in the path a tree which had been blazed,
and the letters "Chamb. L." written on it with
red chalk. This I knew to mean Chamberlain
Lake. So I concluded that on the whole we were
on the right course, though as we had come nearly
two miles, and saw no signs of Mud Pond, I did
harbor the suspicion that we might be on a
direct course to Chamberlain Lake, leaving out

Mud Pond. This I found by my map would be about five miles northeasterly, and I then took the bearing by my compass.

My companion having returned with his bag, and also defended his face and hands with the insect-wash, we set forward again. The walking rapidly grew worse, and the path more indistinct, and at length, after passing through a patch of *calla palustris*, still abundantly in bloom, we found ourselves in a more open and regular swamp, made less passable than ordinary by the unusual wetness of the season. We sank a foot deep in water and mud at every step, and sometimes up to our knees, and the trail was almost obliterated, being no more than that a musquash leaves in similar places, when he parts the floating sedge. In fact, it probably was a musquash trail in some places. We concluded that if Mud Pond was as muddy as the approach to it was wet, it certainly deserved its name. It would have been amusing to behold the dogged and deliberate pace at which we entered that swamp, without interchanging a word, as if determined to go through it, though it should come up to our necks. Having penetrated a considerable distance into this, and found a tussock on which we could deposit our loads, though there was no place to sit, my companion went back for the rest of his pack. I had thought to observe on this carry when we crossed the dividing line between the Penobscot and St. John, but as my feet had hardly been out of water the whole distance, and it was all level and stagnant, I began to despair of finding it. I remembered hearing a good deal about the "highlands" dividing the waters of the Penobscot from those of the St. John, as well as the St. Lawrence, at the time of the northeast boundary dispute, and I observed by my map, that the line claimed by Great Britain as the boundary prior to 1842 passed between Umbazookskus Lake and Mud Pond, so that we had either crossed or were then on it. These, then, according to *her* interpretation of the treaty of '83, were the "highlands which divide those rivers that empty themselves into the St. Lawrence from those which fall into the Atlantic Ocean." Truly an interesting spot to stand on, — if that were it, — though you could not sit down there. I thought that if the commissioners themselves, and the king of Holland with them, had spent a few days here, with their packs upon their backs, looking for that "highland," they would have had an interesting time, and perhaps it would have modified their views of the question somewhat. The king of Holland would have been in his element. Such were my meditations while my companion was gone back for his bag.

It was a cedar swamp, through which the peculiar note of the white-throated sparrow rang loud and clear. There grew the side-saddle flower, Labrador tea, *Kalmia glauca*, and, what was new to me, the Low Birch (*Betula pumila*), a little round-leaved shrub, two or three feet high only. We thought to name this swamp after the latter.

After a long while my companion came back, and the Indian with him. We had taken the wrong road, and the Indian had lost us. He had very wisely gone back to the Canadian's camp, and asked him which way we had probably gone, since he could better understand the ways of white men, and he told him correctly that we had undoubtedly taken the supply road to Chamberlain Lake (slender supplies they would get over such a road at this season). The Indian was greatly surprised that we should have taken what he called a "tow" (i. e. tote or toting or supply) road, instead of a carry path, — that we had not followed his tracks, — said it was "strange," and evidently thought little of our woodcraft.

Having held a consultation, and eaten a mouthful of bread, we concluded that it would, perhaps, be nearer for us two now to keep on to Chamberlain Lake, omitting Mud Pond, than to go back and start anew for the last place, though the Indian had never been through this way, and knew nothing about it. In the meanwhile he would go back and finish carrying over his canoe and bundle to Mud Pond, cross that, and go down its outlet and up Chamberlain Lake, and trust to meet us there before night. It was now a little after noon. He supposed that the water in which we stood had flowed back from Mud Pond, which could not be far off eastward, but was unapproachable through the dense cedar swamp.

Keeping on, we were erelong agreeably disappointed by reaching firmer ground, and we crossed a ridge where the path was more distinct, but there was never any outlook over the forest. While descending the last, I saw many specimens of the great round-leaved orchis, of large size; one which I measured had leaves, as usual, flat on the ground, nine and a half inches long, and nine wide, and was two feet high. The dark, damp wilderness is favorable to some of these orchidaceous plants, though they are too delicate for cultivation. I also saw the swamp gooseberry (*Ribes lacustre*), with green fruit, and in all the low ground, where it was not too wet, the *Rubus triflorus* in fruit. At one place I heard a very clear and piercing note from a small hawk, like a single note from a white-throated sparrow, only very much louder, as he dashed through the tree-tops over my head. I wondered that he allowed himself to be disturbed by our presence, since it seemed as if he could not easily find his nest again himself in that wilderness. We also saw and heard several times the red squirrel, and often, as before observed, the bluish scales of the fir cones which it had left on a rock or fallen tree. This, according to the Indian, is the only squirrel found in those woods, except a very few striped ones. It must have a solitary time in that dark evergreen forest, where there is so little life, seventy-five miles from a road as we had come. I wondered how he could call any particular tree there his home; and yet he would run up the stem of one out of the myriads, as if it were an old road to him. How can a hawk ever find him there? I fancied that he must be glad to see us, though he did seem to chide us. One of those sombre fir and spruce woods is not complete unless you hear from out its cavernous mossy and twiggy recesses his fine alarm, — his spruce voice, like the working of the sap through some crack in the tree, — the working of the spruce beer. Such an impertinent fellow would occasionally try to alarm the wood about me. "O," said I, "I am well acquainted with your family, I know your cousins in Concord very well. Guess the mail's irregular in these parts, and you'd like to hear from 'em." But my overtures were vain, for he would withdraw by his aerial turnpikes into a more distant cedar-top, and spring his rattle again.

We then entered another swamp, at a neces-

sarily slow pace, where the walking was worse
than ever, not only on account of the water,
but the fallen timber, which often obliterated the
indistinct trail entirely. The fallen trees were
so numerous, that for long distances the route
was through a succession of small yards, where
we climbed over fences as high as our heads,
down into water often up to our knees, and then
over another fence into a second yard, and so
on; and going back for his bag my companion
once lost his way and came back without it.
In many places the canoe would have run if it
had not been for the fallen timber. Again it
would be more open, but equally wet, too wet
for trees to grow, and no place to sit down. It
was a mossy swamp, which it required the long
legs of a moose to traverse, and it is very likely
that we scared some of them in our transit,
though we saw none. It was ready to echo
the growl of a bear, the howl of a wolf, or the
scream of a panther; but when you get fairly
into the middle of one of these grim forests,
you are surprised to find that the larger inhabitants are not at home commonly, but have left
only a puny red squirrel to bark at you. Generally speaking, a howling wilderness does not
howl: it is the imagination of the traveller that
does the howling. I did, however, see one dead
porcupine; perhaps he had succumbed to the
difficulties of the way. These bristly fellows

are a very suitable small fruit of such unkempt wildernesses.

Making a logging-road in the Maine woods is called "swamping it," and they who do the work are called "swampers." I now perceived the fitness of the term. This was the most perfectly swamped of all the roads I ever saw. Nature must have co-operated with art here. However, I suppose they would tell you that this name took its origin from the fact that the chief work of roadmakers in those woods is to make the swamps passable. We came to a stream where the bridge, which had been made of logs tied together with cedar bark, had been broken up, and we got over as we could. This probably emptied into Mud Pond, and perhaps the Indian might have come up it and taken us in there if he had known it. Such as it was, this ruined bridge was the chief evidence that we were on a path of any kind.

We then crossed another low rising ground, and I, who wore shoes, had an opportunity to wring out my stockings, but my companion, who used boots, had found that this was not a safe experiment for him, for he might not be able to get his wet boots on again. He went over the whole ground, or water, three times, for which reason our progress was very slow; beside that the water softened our feet, and to some extent unfitted them for walking. As I sat waiting for him, it would naturally seem an unaccountable time that he was gone. Therefore, as I could see through the woods that the sun was getting low, and it was uncertain how far the lake might be, even if we were on the right course, and in what part of the world we should find ourselves at nightfall, I proposed that I should push through with what speed I could, leaving boughs to mark my path, and find the lake and the Indian, if possible, before night, and send the latter back to carry my companion's bag.

Having gone about a mile, and got into low ground again, I heard a noise like the note of an owl, which I soon discovered to be made by the Indian, and answering him, we soon came together. He had reached the lake, after crossing Mud Pond and running some rapids below it, and had come up about a mile and a half on our path. If he had not come back to meet us, we probably should not have found him that night, for the path branched once or twice before reaching this particular part of the lake. So he went back for my companion and his bag, while I kept on. Having waded through another stream where the bridge of logs had been broken up and half floated away, — and this was not altogether worse than our ordinary walking, since it was less muddy, — we continued on, through alternate mud and water, to the shore of Apmoojenegamook Lake, which we reached in season for a late supper, instead of dining there, as we had expected, having gone without our dinner. It was at least five miles by the way we had come, and as my companion had gone over most of it three times, he had walked full a dozen miles, bad as it was. In the winter, when the water is frozen, and the snow is four feet deep, it is no doubt a tolerable path to a footman. As it was, I would not have missed that walk for a good deal. If you want an exact recipe for making such a road, take one part Mud Pond, and dilute it with equal parts of Umbazookskus and Apmoojenegamook; then send a family of musquash through to locate it, look after the grades and culverts, and finish it to their minds, and let a hurricane follow to do the fencing.

We had come out on a point extending into Apmoojenegamook, or Chamberlain Lake, west of the outlet of Mud Pond, where there was a broad, gravelly, and rocky shore, encumbered with bleached logs and trees. We were rejoiced to see such dry things in that part of the world. But at first we did not attend to dryness so much as to mud and wetness. We all three walked into the lake up to our middle to wash our clothes.

This was another noble lake, called twelve miles long, east and west; if you add Tebos Lake, which, since the dam was built, has

been connected with it by dead-water, it will be
twenty; and it is apparently from a mile and a
half to two miles wide. We were about midway
its length, on the south side. We could see the
only clearing in these parts, called the "Chamberlain Farm," with two or three log buildings
close together, on the opposite shore, some two
and a half miles distant. The smoke of our
fire on the shore brought over two men in a
canoe from the farm, that being a common
signal agreed on when one wishes to cross. It
took them about half an hour to come over,
and they had their labor for their pains this
time. Even the English name of the lake had
a wild, woodland sound, reminding me of that
Chamberlain who killed Paugus at Lovewell's
fight.

After putting on such dry clothes as we had,
and hanging the others to dry on the pole, which
the Indian arranged over the fire, we ate our
supper, and lay down on the pebbly shore with
our feet to the fire, without pitching our tent,
making a thin bed of grass to cover the stones.

Here first I was molested by the little midge
called the No-see-em (*Simulium nocivum*, the
latter word is not the Latin for no-see-em),
especially over the sand at the water's edge, for
it is a kind of sand-fly. You would not observe
them but for their light-colored wings. They
are said to get under your clothes, and produce

a feverish heat, which I suppose was what I felt that night.

Our insect foes in this excursion, to sum them up, were, first, mosquitoes, the chief ones, but only troublesome at night, or when we sat still on shore by day; second, black flies (*Simulium molestum*), which molested us more or less on the carries by day, as I have before described, and sometimes in narrower parts of the stream. Harris mistakes when he says that they are not seen after June. Third, moose-flies. The big ones, Polis said, were called *Bososquasis*. It is a stout brown fly, much like a horse-fly, about eleven sixteenths of an inch long, commonly rusty colored beneath, with unspotted wings. They can bite smartly, according to Polis, but are easily avoided or killed. Fourth, the No-see-ems above mentioned. Of all these, the mosquitoes are the only ones that troubled me seriously; but, as I was provided with a wash, and a veil, they have not made any deep impression.

The Indian would not use our wash to protect his face and hands, for fear that it would hurt his skin, nor had he any veil; he, therefore, suffered from insects now, and throughout this journey, more than either of us. I think that he suffered more than I did, when neither of us was protected. He regularly tied up his face in his handkerchief, and buried it in his blanket, and he now finally lay down on the sand between us and the fire for the sake of the smoke, which he tried to make enter his blanket about his face, and for the same purpose he lit his pipe and breathed the smoke into his blanket.

As we lay thus on the shore, with nothing between us and the stars, I inquired what stars he was acquainted with, or had names for. They were the Great Bear, which he called by this name, the Seven Stars, which he had no English name for, "the morning star," and "the north star."

In the middle of the night, as indeed each time that we lay on the shore of a lake, we heard the voice of the loon, loud and distinct, from far over the lake. It is a very wild sound, quite in keeping with the place and the circumstances of the traveller, and very unlike the voice of a bird. I could lie awake for hours listening to it, it is so thrilling. When camping in such a wilderness as this, you are prepared to hear sounds from some of its inhabitants which will give voice to its wildness. Some idea of bears, wolves, or panthers runs in your head naturally, and when this note is first heard very far off at midnight, as you lie with your ear to the ground, — the forest being perfectly still about you, you take it for granted that it is the voice of a wolf or some other wild beast, for only the last part is heard when at a distance, — you conclude that it is a pack of wolves baying the moon, or, perchance, cantering after a moose. Strange as it may seem, the "mooing" of a cow on a mountain-side comes nearest to my idea of the voice of a bear; and this bird's note resembled that. It was the unfailing and characteristic sound of those lakes. We were not so lucky as to hear wolves howl, though that is an occasional serenade. Some friends of mine, who two years ago went up the Caucomgomoc River, were serenaded by wolves while moose-hunting by moonlight. It was a sudden burst, as if a hundred demons had broke loose, — a startling sound enough, which, if any, would make your hair stand on end, and all was still again. It lasted but a moment, and you'd have thought there were twenty of them, when probably there were only two or three. They heard it twice only, and they said that it gave expression to the wilderness which it lacked before. I heard of some men who, while skinning a moose lately in those woods, were driven off from the carcass by a pack of wolves, which ate it up.

This of the loon — I do not mean its laugh, but its looning — is a long-drawn call, as it were, sometimes singularly human to my ear, — *hoo-hoo-ooooo*, like the hallooing of a man on a very high key, having thrown his voice into his head. I have heard a sound exactly like it when breathing heavily through my own nostrils, half awake at ten at night, suggesting my affinity to the loon; as if its language were but a dialect of my own, after all. Formerly, when lying awake at midnight in those woods, I had listened to hear some words or syllables of their language, but it chanced that I listened in vain until I heard the cry of the loon. I have heard it occasionally on the ponds of my native town, but there its wildness is not enhanced by the surrounding scenery.

I was awakened at midnight by some heavy, low-flying bird, probably a loon, flapping by close over my head, along the shore. So, turning the other side of my half-clad body to the fire, I sought slumber again.

TUESDAY, July 28.

When we awoke we found a heavy dew on our blankets. I lay awake very early, and listened to the clear, shrill *ah-tette-tette-te*, of the white-throated sparrow, repeated at short intervals, without the least variation, for half an hour, as if it could not enough express its happiness. Whether my companions heard it or not, I know not, but it was a kind of matins to me, and the event of that forenoon.

It was a pleasant sunrise, and we had a view of the mountains in the southeast. Ktaadn appeared about southeast by south. A double-topped mountain about southeast by east, and another portion of the same, east-southeast.

The last the Indian called Nerlumskeechticook, and said that it was at the head of the East Branch, and we should pass near it on our return that way.

We did some more washing in the lake this morning, and with our clothes hung about on the dead trees and rocks, the shore looked like washing-day at home. The Indian, taking the hint, borrowed the soap, and walking into the lake, washed his only cotton shirt on his person, then put on his pants and let it dry on him.

I observed that he wore a cotton shirt, originally white, a greenish flannel one over it, but no waistcoat, flannel drawers, and strong linen or duck pants, which also had been white, blue woollen stockings, cowhide boots, and a Kossuth hat. He carried no change of clothing, but putting on a stout, thick jacket, which he laid aside in the canoe, and seizing a full-sized axe, his gun and ammunition, and a blanket, which would do for a sail or knapsack, if wanted, and strapping on his belt, which contained a large sheath-knife, he walked off at once, ready to be gone all summer. This looked very independent; a few simple and effective tools, and no India-rubber clothing. He was always the first ready to start in the morning, and if it had not held some of our property would not have been obliged to roll up his blanket. Instead of carrying a large bundle of his own extra cloth-

ing, etc., he brought back the great-coats of
moose tied up in his blanket. I found that his
outfit was the result of a long experience, and
in the main hardly to be improved on, unless by
washing and an extra shirt. Wanting a button
here, he walked off to a place where some Indians
had recently encamped, and searched for one,
but I believe in vain.

Having softened our stiffened boots and shoes
with the pork fat, the usual disposition of what
was left at breakfast, we crossed the lake early,
steering in a diagonal direction northeasterly
about four miles, to the outlet, which was not
to be discovered till we were close to it. The
Indian name, Apmoojenegamook, means lake
that is crossed, because the usual course lies
across, and not along it. This is the largest of
the Allegash lakes, and was the first St. John's
water that we floated on. It is shaped in the
main like Chesuncook. There are no mountains
or high hills very near it. At Bangor we had
been told of a township many miles farther
northwest; it was indicated to us as containing
the highest land thereabouts, where, by climbing
a particular tree in the forest, we could get a
general idea of the country. I have no doubt
that the last was good advice, but we did not go
there. We did not intend to go far down the
Allegash, but merely to get a view of the great
lakes which are its source, and then return this

way to the East Branch of the Penobscot. The
water now, by good rights, flowed northward,
if it could be said to flow at all.

After reaching the middle of the lake, we found
the waves as usual pretty high, and the Indian
warned my companion, who was nodding, that he
must not allow himself to fall asleep in the canoe,
lest he should upset us; adding, that when Indians want to sleep in a canoe, they lie down
straight on the bottom. But in this crowded one
that was impossible. However, he said that he
would nudge him if he saw him nodding.

A belt of dead trees stood all around the lake,
some far out in the water, with others prostrate
behind them, and they made the shore, for the
most part, almost inaccessible. This is the effect
of the dam at the outlet. Thus the natural
sandy or rocky shore, with its green fringe, was
concealed and destroyed. We coasted westward along the north side, searching for the outlet, about one quarter of a mile distant from
this savage-looking shore, on which the waves
were breaking violently, knowing that it might
easily be concealed amid this rubbish, or by
the overlapping of the shore. It is remarkable
how little these important gates to a lake are
blazoned. There is no triumphal arch over the
modest inlet or outlet, but at some undistin-
guished point it trickles in or out through the
uninterrupted forest, almost as through a sponge.

We reached the outlet in about an hour, and carried over the dam there, which is quite a solid structure, and about one quarter of a mile farther there was a second dam. The reader will perceive that the result of this particular damming about Chamberlain Lake is, that the head-waters of the St. John are made to flow by Bangor. They have thus dammed all the larger lakes, raising their broad surfaces many feet; Moosehead, for instance, some forty miles long, with its steamer on it; thus turning the forces of nature against herself, that they might float their spoils out of the country. They rapidly run out of these immense forests all the finer and more accessible pine timber, and then leave the bears to watch the decaying dams, not clearing nor cultivating the land, nor making roads, nor building houses, but leaving it a wilderness, as they found it. In many parts, only these dams remain, like deserted beaver-dams. Think how much land they have flowed, without asking Nature's leave! When the State wishes to endow an academy or university, it grants it a tract of forest land: one saw represents an academy; a gang, a university.

The wilderness experiences a sudden rise of all her streams and lakes, she feels ten thousand vermin gnawing at the base of her noblest trees, many combining, drag them off, jarring over the roots of the survivors, and tumble them into the nearest stream, till the fairest having fallen, they scamper off to ransack some new wilderness, and all is still again. It is as when a migrating army of mice girdles a forest of pines. The chopper fells trees from the same motive that the mouse gnaws them, — to get his living. You tell me that he has a more interesting family than the mouse. That is as it happens. He speaks of a "berth" of timber, a good place for him to get into, just as a worm might. When the chopper would praise a pine, he will commonly tell you that the one he cut was so big that a yoke of oxen stood on its stump; as if that were what the pine had grown for, to become the footstool of oxen. In my mind's eye, I can see these unwieldy tame deer, with a yoke binding them together, and brazen-tipped horns betraying their servitude, taking their stand on the stump of each giant pine in succession throughout this whole forest, and chewing their cud there, until it is nothing but an ox-pasture, and run out at that. As if it were good for the oxen, and some terebinthine or other medicinal quality ascended into their nostrils. Or is their elevated position intended merely as a symbol of the fact that the pastoral comes next in order to the sylvan or hunter life?

The character of the logger's admiration is betrayed by his very mode of expressing it. If he told all that was in his mind, he would say, it was so big that I cut it down and then a yoke of oxen could stand on its stump. He admires the log, the carcass or corpse, more than the tree. Why, my dear sir, the tree might have stood on its own stump, and a great deal more comfortably and firmly than a yoke of oxen can, if you had not cut it down. What right have you to celebrate the virtues of the man you murdered?

The Anglo-American can indeed cut down, and grub up all this waving forest, and make a stump speech, and vote for Buchanan on its ruins, but he cannot converse with the spirit of the tree he fells, he cannot read the poetry and mythology which retire as he advances. He ignorantly erases mythological tablets in order to print his handbills and town-meeting warrants on them. Before he has learned his a b c in the beautiful but mystic lore of the wilderness which Spenser and Dante had just begun to read, he cuts it down, coins a *pine-tree* shilling, (as if to signify the pine's value to him,) puts up a *dee*strict school-house, and introduces Webster's spelling-book.

Below the last dam, the river being swift and shallow though broad enough, we two walked about half a mile to lighten the canoe. I made it a rule to carry my knapsack when I walked, and also to keep it tied to a cross-bar when in the canoe, that it might be found with the canoe if we should upset.

I heard the dog-day locust here, and afterward on the carries, a sound which I had associated only with more open, if not settled countries. The area for locusts must be small in the Maine woods.

We were now fairly on the Allegash River, which name our Indian said meant hemlock bark. These waters flow northward about 100 miles, at first very feebly, then southeasterly 250 more to the Bay of Fundy. After perhaps two miles of river, we entered Heron Lake, called on the map *Pongokwahem*, scaring up forty or fifty young *shecorways*, sheldrakes, at the entrance, which ran over the water with great rapidity, as usual in a long line.

This was the fourth great lake, lying northwest and southeast, like Chesuncook, and most of the long lakes in that neighborhood, and, judging from the map, it is about ten miles long. We had entered it on the southwest side, and saw a dark mountain northeast over the lake, not very far off nor high, which the Indian said was called *Peaked Mountain*, and used by explorers to look for timber from. There was also some other high land more easterly. The shores were in the same ragged and unsightly condition, encumbered with dead timber, both fallen and standing, as in the last lake, owing to the dam on the Allegash below. Some low points or islands were almost drowned.

I saw something white a mile off on the water, which turned out to be a great gull on a rock in the middle, which the Indian would have been glad to kill and eat, but it flew away long before we were near; and also a flock of summer ducks, that were about the rock with it. I asking him about herons, since this was Heron Lake, he said that he found the blue heron's nests in the hard-wood trees. I thought that I saw a light-colored object move along the opposite or northern shore, four or five miles distant. He did not know what it could be, unless it were a moose, though he had never seen a white one; but he said that he could distinguish a moose "anywhere on shore, clear across the lake."

Rounding a point, we stood across a bay for a mile and a half or two miles, toward a large island, three or four miles down the lake. We met with ephemeræ (shad-fly) midway, about a mile from the shore, and they evidently fly over the whole lake. On Moosehead I had seen a large devil's-needle half a mile from the shore, coming from the middle of the lake, where it was three or four miles wide at least. It had probably crossed. But at last, of course, you come to lakes, so large that an insect cannot fly across them; and this, perhaps, will serve to distinguish a large lake from a small one.

We landed on the southeast side of the island, which was rather elevated, and densely wooded,

with a rocky shore, in season for an early dinner.
Somebody had camped there not long before,
and left the frame on which they stretched a
moose-hide, which our Indian criticised severely,
thinking it showed but little woodcraft. Here
were plenty of the shells of crayfish, or fresh-
water lobsters, which had been washed ashore,
such as have given a name to some ponds and
streams. They are commonly four or five
inches long. The Indian proceeded at once to
cut a canoe-birch, slanted it up against another
tree on the shore, tying it with a withe, and lay
down to sleep in its shade.

When we were on the Caucomgomoc, he recommended to us a new way home, the very one
which we had first thought of, by the St. John.
He even said that it was easier, and would take
but little more time than the other, by the east
branch of the Penobscot, though very much
farther round; and taking the map, he showed
where we should be each night, for he was
familiar with the route. According to his calculation, we should reach the French settlements
the next night after this, by keeping northward
down the Allegash, and when we got into the
main St. John the banks would be more or less
settled all the way; as if that were a recom-
mendation. There would be but one or two
falls, with short carrying-places, and we should
go down the stream very fast, even a hundred

miles a day, if the wind allowed; and he indicated where we should carry over into Eel River to save a bend below Woodstock in New Brunswick, and so into the Schoodic Lake, and thence to the Mattawamkeag. It would be about three hundred and sixty miles to Bangor this way, though only about one hundred and sixty by the other; but in the former case we should explore the St. John from its source through two thirds of its course, as well as the Schoodic Lake and Mattawamkeag, — and we were again tempted to go that way. I feared, however, that the banks of the St. John were too much settled. When I asked him which course would take us through the wildest country, he said the route by the East Branch. Partly from this consideration, as also from its shortness, we resolved to adhere to the latter route, and perhaps ascend Ktaadn on the way. We made this island the limit of our excursion in this direction.

We had now seen the largest of the Allegash Lakes. The next dam "was about fifteen miles" farther north, down the Allegash, and it was dead-water so far. We had been told in Bangor of a man who lived alone, a sort of hermit, at that dam, to take care of it, who spent his time tossing a bullet from one hand to the other, for want of employment, — as if we might want to call on him. This sort of tit-for-tat intercourse between his two hands, bandying to and fro a leaden subject, seems to have been his symbol for society.

This island, according to the map, was about a hundred and ten miles in a straight line north-northwest from Bangor, and about ninety-nine miles east-southeast from Quebec. There was another island visible toward the north end of the lake, with an elevated clearing on it; but we learned afterward that it was not inhabited, had only been used as a pasture for cattle which summered in these woods, though our informant said that there was a hut on the mainland near the outlet of the lake. This unnaturally smooth-shaven, squarish spot, in the midst of the otherwise uninterrupted forest, only reminded us how uninhabited the country was. You would sooner expect to meet with a bear than an ox in such a clearing. At any rate, it must have been a surprise to the bears when they came across it. Such, seen far or near, you know at once to be man's work, for Nature never does it. In order to let in the light to the earth as on a lake, he clears off the forest on the hillsides and plains, and sprinkles fine grass-seed, like an enchanter, and so carpets the earth with a firm sward.

Polis had evidently more curiosity respecting the few settlers in those woods than we. If nothing was said, he took it for granted that we wanted to go straight to the next log-hut. Hav-

ing observed that we came by the log-huts at
Chesuncook, and the blind Canadian's at the
Mud Pond carry, without stopping to communicate with the inhabitants, he took occasion
now to suggest that the usual way was, when
you came near a house, to go to it, and tell the
inhabitants what you had seen or heard, and
then they tell you what they had seen; but we
laughed, and said that we had had enough of
houses for the present, and had come here partly
to avoid them.

In the mean while, the wind, increasing, blew
down the Indian's birch and created such a sea
that we found ourselves prisoners on the island,
the nearest shore, which was the western, being
perhaps a mile distant, and we took the canoe
out to prevent its drifting away. We did not
know but we should be compelled to spend the
rest of the day and the night there. At any rate,
the Indian went to sleep again, in the shade of
his birch, my companion busied himself drying
his plants, and I rambled along the shore westward, which was quite stony, and obstructed
with fallen bleached or drifted trees for four or
five rods in width. I found growing on this
broad rocky and gravelly shore the *Salix rostrata*,
discolor, and *lucida*, *Ranunculus recurvatus*,
Potentilla Norvegica, *Scutellaria lateriflora*, *Eupatorium purpureum*, *Aster Tradescanti*, *Mentha
Canadensis*, *Epilobium angustifolium*, abundant.

Lycopus minatus, Solidago lanceolata, Spiræa salicifolia, Antennaria margaraticea, Prunella, Rumex acetosella, Raspberries, Wool-grass, *Onoclea,* etc. The nearest trees were *Betula papyracea* and *excelsa,* and *Populus tremuloides.* I give these names because it was my farthest northern point.

Our Indian said that he was a doctor, and could tell me some medicinal use for every plant I could show him. I immediately tried him. He said that the inner bark of the aspen (*Populus tremuloides*) was good for sore eyes; and so with various other plants, proving himself as good as his word. According to his account, he had acquired such knowledge in his youth from a wise old Indian with whom he associated, and he lamented that the present generation of Indians "had lost a great deal."

He said that the caribou was a "very great runner," that there was none about this lake now, though there used to be many, and pointing to the belt of dead trees caused by the dams, he added, "No likum stump, — when he sees that he scared."

Pointing southeasterly over the lake and distant forest, he observed, "Me go Oldtown in three days." I asked how he would get over the swamps and fallen trees. "O," said he, "in winter all covered, go anywhere on snow-shoes, right across lakes." When I asked how he went,

he said, "First I go Ktaadn, west side, then I go
Millinocket, then Pamadumcook, then Nickatou,
then Lincoln, then Oldtown," or else he went a
shorter way by the Piscataquis. What a wilderness walk for a man to take alone! None of your
half-mile swamps, none of your mile-wide woods
merely, as on the skirts of our towns, without
hotels, only a dark mountain or a lake for guide-
board and station, over ground much of it im-
passable in summer!

It reminded me of Prometheus Bound. Here
was travelling of the old heroic kind over the
unaltered face of nature. From the Allegash, or
Hemlock River, and Pongoquahem Lake, across
great Apmoojenegamook, and leaving the Nerlumskeechticook Mountain on his left, he takes
his way under the bear-haunted slopes of Souneunk and Ktaadn Mountains to Pamadumcook
and Millinocket's inland seas, (where often
gulls'-eggs may increase his store,) and so on to
the forks of the Nickatou, (*nia soseb* "we alone
Joseph" seeing what our folks see,) ever pushing the boughs of the fir and spruce aside, with
his load of furs, contending day and night,
night and day, with the shaggy demon vegetation, travelling through the mossy graveyard of
trees. Or he could go by "that rough tooth
of the sea," Kineo, great source of arrows and
of spears to the ancients, when weapons of stone
were used. Seeing and hearing moose, caribou,

porcupines, lynxes, wolves, and panthers. Places where he might live and die and never hear of the United States, which make such a noise in the world, — never hear of America, so called from the name of a European gentleman.

There is a lumberer's road called the Eagle Lake road, from the Seboois to the east side of this lake. It may seem strange that any road through such a wilderness should be passable, even in winter, when the snow is three or four feet deep, but at that season, wherever lumbering operations are actively carried on, teams are continually passing on the single track, and it becomes as smooth almost as a railway. I am told that in the Aroostook country, the sleds are required by law to be of one width, (four feet,) and sleighs must be altered to fit the track, so that one runner may go in one rut and the other follow the horse. Yet it is very bad turning out.

We had for some time seen a thunder-shower coming up from the west over the woods of the island, and heard the muttering of the thunder, though we were in doubt whether it would reach us; but now the darkness rapidly increasing, and a fresh breeze rustling the forest, we hastily put up the plants which we had been drying, and with one consent made a rush for the tent material and set about pitching it. A place was selected and stakes and pins cut in the shortest possible time, and we were pinning it down lest it should be blown away, when the storm suddenly burst over us.

As we lay huddled together under the tent, which leaked considerably about the sides, with our baggage at our feet, we listened to some of the grandest thunder which I ever heard, — rapid peals, round and plump, bang, bang, bang, in succession, like artillery from some fortress in the sky; and the lightning was proportionally brilliant. The Indian said, "It must be good powder." All for the benefit of the moose and us, echoing far over the concealed lakes. I thought it must be a place which the thunder loved, where the lightning practised to keep its hand in, and it would do no harm to shatter a few pines. What had become of the ephemeræ and devil's-needles then? Were they prudent enough to seek harbor before the storm? Perhaps their motions might guide the voyageur.

Looking out I perceived that the violent shower falling on the lake had almost instantaneously flattened the waves, — the commander of that fortress had smoothed it for us so, — and it clearing off, we resolved to start immediately, before the wind raised them again.

Going outside, I said that I saw clouds still in the southwest, and heard thunder there. The Indian asked if the thunder went "lound" (round), saying that if it did we should have more rain. I thought that it did. We embarked, nevertheless, and paddled rapidly back toward the dams. The white-throated sparrows on the shore were about, singing, *Ah te, e, e, te, e, e, te,* or else *ah te, e, e, te, e, e, te, e, e, te, e, e.*

At the outlet of Chamberlain Lake we were overtaken by another gusty rain-storm, which compelled us to take shelter, the Indian under his canoe on the bank, and we ran under the edge of the dam. However, we were more scared than wet. From my covert I could see the Indian peeping out from beneath his canoe to see what had become of the rain. When we had taken our respective places thus once or twice, the rain not coming down in earnest, we commenced rambling about the neighborhood, for the wind had by this time raised such waves on the lake that we could not stir, and we feared that we should be obliged to camp there. We got an early supper on the dam and tried for fish there, while waiting for the tumult to subside. The fishes were not only few, but small and worthless, and the Indian declared that there were no good fishes in the St. John's waters; that we must wait till we got to the Penobscot waters.

At length, just before sunset, we set out again. It was a wild evening when we coasted up the north side of this Apmoojenegamook Lake. One thunder-storm was just over, and the waves which it had raised still running with violence,

and another storm was now seen coming up in
the southwest, far over the lake; but it might
be worse in the morning, and we wished to get as
far as possible on our way up the lake while we
might. It blowed hard against the northern
shore about an eighth of a mile distant on our
left, and there was just as much sea as our shallow
canoe would bear, without our taking unusual
care. That which we kept off, and toward which
the waves were driving, was as dreary and har-
borless a shore as you can conceive. For half
a dozen rods in width it was a perfect maze of
submerged trees, all dead and bare and bleach-
ing, some standing half their original height,
others prostrate, and criss-across, above or
beneath the surface, and mingled with them were
loose trees and limbs and stumps, beating about.
Imagine the wharves of the largest city in the
world, decayed, and the earth and planking
washed away, leaving the spiles standing in
loose order, but often of twice the ordinary
height, and mingled with and beating against
them the wreck of ten thousand navies, all
their spars and timbers, while there rises from
the water's edge the densest and grimmest wilderness, ready to supply more material when the
former fails, and you may get a faint idea of that
coast. We could not have landed if we would,
without the greatest danger of being swamped;
so, blow as it might, we must depend on coasting

by it. It was twilight, too, and that stormy cloud was advancing rapidly in our rear. It was a pleasant excitement, yet we were glad to reach, at length, in the dusk, the cleared shore of the Chamberlain Farm.

We landed on a low and thinly wooded point there, and while my companions were pitching the tent, I ran up to the house to get some sugar, our six pounds being gone; — it was no wonder they were, for Polis had a sweet tooth. He would first fill his dipper nearly a third full of sugar, and then add the coffee to it. Here was a clearing extending back from the lake to a hill-top, with some dark-colored log buildings and a storehouse in it, and half a dozen men standing in front of the principal hut, greedy for news. Among them was the man who tended the dam on the Allegash and tossed the bullet. He having charge of the dams, and learning that we were going to Webster Stream the next day, told me that some of their men, who were haying at Telos Lake, had shut the dam at the canal there in order to catch trout, and if we wanted more water to take us through the canal we might raise the gate, for he would like to have it raised. The Chamberlain Farm is no doubt a cheerful opening in the woods, but such was the lateness of the hour that it has left but a dusky impression on my mind. As I have said, the influx of light merely is civilizing, yet I fancied that they

walked about on Sundays in their clearing somewhat as in a prison-yard.

They were unwilling to spare more than four
pounds of brown sugar, — unlocking the store-
house to get it, — since they only kept a little
for such cases as this, and they charged twenty
cents a pound for it, which certainly it was
worth to get it up there.

When I returned to the shore it was quite
dark, but we had a rousing fire to warm and dry
us by, and a snug apartment behind it. The
Indian went up to the house to inquire after a
brother who had been absent hunting a year or
two, and while another shower was beginning,
I groped about cutting spruce and arbor-vitæ
twigs for a bed. I preferred the arbor-vitæ on
account of its fragrance, and spread it particularly thick about the shoulders. It is remarkable with what pure satisfaction the traveller
in these woods will reach his camping-ground on
the eve of a tempestuous night like this, as if he
had got to his inn, and, rolling himself in his
blanket, stretch himself on his six feet by two
bed of dripping fir-twigs, with a thin sheet of
cotton for roof, snug as a meadow-mouse in its
nest. Invariably our best nights were those
when it rained, for then we were not troubled
with mosquitoes.

You soon come to disregard rain on such excursions, at least in the summer, it is so easy to

dry yourself, supposing a dry change of clothing is not to be had. You can much sooner dry you by such a fire as you can make in the woods than in anybody's kitchen, the fireplace is so much larger, and wood so much more abundant. A shed-shaped tent will catch and reflect the heat like a Yankee-baker, and you may be drying while you are sleeping.

Some who have leaky roofs in the towns may have been kept awake, but we were soon lulled asleep by a steady, soaking rain, which lasted all night. To-night, the rain not coming at once with violence, the twigs were soon dried by the reflected heat.

WEDNESDAY, July 29.

When we awoke it had done raining, though it was still cloudy. The fire was put out, and the Indian's boots, which stood under the eaves of the tent, were half full of water. He was much more improvident in such respects than either of us, and he had to thank us for keeping his powder dry. We decided to cross the lake at once, before breakfast, or while we could; and before starting I took the bearing of the shore, which we wished to strike, S. S. E. about three miles distant, lest a sudden misty rain should conceal it when we were midway. Though the bay in which we were was perfectly quiet and smooth, we found the lake already wide awake outside, but not dangerously or unpleasantly so; nevertheless, when you get out on one of those lakes in a canoe like this, you do not forget that you are completely at the mercy of the wind, and a fickle power it is. The playful waves may at any time become too rude for you in their sport, and play right on over you. We saw a few *shecorways* and a *fish-hawk* thus early, and after much steady paddling and dancing over the dark waves of Apmoojenegamook, we found ourselves in the neighborhood of the southern land, heard the waves breaking on it, and turned our thoughts wholly to that side. After coasting eastward along this shore a mile or two, we breakfasted on a rocky point, the first convenient place that offered.

It was well enough that we crossed thus early, for the waves now ran quite high, and we should have been obliged to go round somewhat, but beyond this point we had comparatively smooth water. You can commonly go along one side or the other of a lake, when you cannot cross it.

The Indian was looking at the hard-wood ridges from time to time, and said that he would like to buy a few hundred acres somewhere about this lake, asking our advice. It was to buy as near the crossing place as possible.

My companion and I having a minute's discussion on some point of ancient history, were amused by the attitude which the Indian, who

could not tell what we were talking about, assumed. He constituted himself umpire, and,
judging by our air and gesture, he very seriously
remarked from time to time, "you beat," or
"he beat."

Leaving a spacious bay, a northeasterly pro-
longation of Chamberlain Lake, on our left, we
entered through a short strait into a small lake
a couple of miles over, called on the map *Telasi-
nis*, but the Indian had no distinct name for it,
and thence into *Telos* Lake, which he called
Paytaywecomgomoc, or Burnt-Ground Lake.
This curved round toward the northeast, and
may have been three or four miles long as we
paddled. He had not been here since 1825. He
did not know what Telos meant; thought it
was not Indian. He used the word "*Spokelogan*"
(for an inlet in the shore which led nowhere),
and when I asked its meaning said that there
was "no Indian in 'em." There was a clearing,
with a house and barn, on the southwest shore,
temporarily occupied by some men who were
getting the hay, as we had been told; also a
clearing for a pasture on a hill on the west side
of the lake.

We landed on a rocky point on the northeast
side, to look at some Red Pines (*Pinus resinosa*),
the first we had noticed, and get some cones, for
our few which grow in Concord do not bear any.

The outlet from the lake into the East Branch

of the Penobscot is an artificial one, and it was not very apparent where it was exactly, but the lake ran curving far up northeasterly into two narrow valleys or ravines, as if it had for a long time been groping its way toward the Penobscot waters, or remembered when it anciently flowed there; by observing where the horizon was lowest, and following the longest of these, we at length reached the dam, having come about a dozen miles from the last camp. Somebody had left a line set for trout, and the jackknife with which the bait had been cut on the dam beside it, an evidence that man was near, and on a deserted log close by a loaf of bread baked in a Yankee-baker. These proved the property of a solitary hunter, whom we soon met, and canoe and gun and traps were not far off. He told us that it was twenty miles farther on our route to the foot of Grand Lake, where you could catch as many trout as you wanted, and that the first house below the foot of the lake, on the East Branch, was Hunt's, about forty-five miles farther; though there was one about a mile and a half up Trout Stream, some fifteen miles ahead, but it was rather a blind route to it. It turned out that, though the stream was in our favor, we did not reach the next house till the morning of the third day after this. The nearest permanently inhabited house behind us was now a dozen miles distant, so that the interval between the two nearest houses on our route was about sixty miles.

This hunter, who was a quite small, sunburnt man, having already carried his canoe over, and baked his loaf, had nothing so interesting and pressing to do as to observe our transit. He had been out a month or more alone. How much more wild and adventurous his life than that of the hunter in Concord woods, who gets back to his house and the mill-dam every night! Yet they in the towns who have wild oats to sow commonly sow them on cultivated and comparatively exhausted ground. And as for the rowdy world in the large cities, so little enterprise has it that it never adventures in this direction, but like vermin clubs together in alleys and drinking-saloons, its highest accomplishment, perchance, to run beside a fire-engine and throw brickbats. But the former is comparatively an independent and successful man, getting his living in a way that he likes, without disturbing his human neighbors. How much more respectable also is the life of the solitary pioneer or settler in these, or any woods, — having real difficulties, not of his own creation, drawing his subsistence directly from nature, — than that of the helpless multitudes in the towns who depend on gratifying the extremely artificial wants of society and are thrown out of employment by hard times!

Here for the first time we found the raspberries really plenty, — that is, on passing the height of land between the Allegash and the East Branch of the Penobscot; the same was true of the blueberries.

Telos Lake, the head of the St. John on this side, and Webster Pond, the head of the East Branch of the Penobscot, are only about a mile apart, and they are connected by a ravine, in which but little digging was required to make the water of the former, which is the highest, flow into the latter. This canal, which is something less than a mile long and about four rods wide, was made a few years before my first visit to Maine. Since then the lumber of the upper Allegash and its lakes has been run down the Penobscot, that is, up the Allegash, which here consists principally of a chain of large and stagnant lakes, whose thoroughfares, or river-links, have been made nearly equally stagnant by damming, and then down the Penobscot. The rush of the water has produced such changes in the canal that it has now the appearance of a very rapid mountain stream flowing through a ravine, and you would not suspect that any digging had been required to persuade the waters of the St. John to flow into the Penobscot here. It was so winding that one could see but little way down.

It is stated by Springer, in his "Forest Life,"

that the cause of this canal being dug was this. According to the treaty of 1842 with Great Britain, it was agreed that all the timber run down the St. John, which rises in Maine, "when within the Province of New Brunswick . . . shall be dealt with as if it were the produce of the said Province," which was thought by our side to mean that it should be free from taxation. Immediately, the Province, wishing to get something out of the Yankees, levied a duty on all the timber that passed down the St. John; but to satisfy its own subjects "made a corresponding discount on the stumpage charged those hauling timber from the crown lands." The result was that the Yankees made the St. John run the other way, or down the Penobscot, so that the Province lost both its duty and its water, while the Yankees, being greatly enriched, had reason to thank it for the suggestion.

It is wonderful how well watered this country is. As you paddle across a lake, bays will be pointed out to you, by following up which, and perhaps the tributary stream which empties in, you may, after a short portage, or possibly, at some seasons, none at all, get into another river, which empties far away from the one you are on. Generally, you may go in any direction in a canoe, by making frequent but not very long portages. You are only realizing once more what all nature distinctly remembers here, for

no doubt the waters flowed thus in a former
geological period, and instead of being a lake
country, it was an archipelago. It seems as if
the more youthful and impressible streams can
hardly resist the numerous invitations and temp-
tations to leave their native beds and run down
their neighbors' channels. Your carries are
often over half-submerged ground, on the dry
channels of a former period. In carrying from
one river to another, I did not go over such high
and rocky ground as in going about the falls of
the same river. For in the former case I was
once lost in a swamp, as I have related, and,
again, found an artificial canal which appeared
to be natural.

I remember once dreaming of pushing a canoe
up the rivers of Maine, and that, when I had got
so high that the channels were dry, I kept on
through the ravines and gorges, nearly as well
as before, by pushing a little harder, and now it
seemed to me that my dream was partially
realized.

Wherever there is a channel for water, there
is a road for the canoe. The pilot of the steamer
which ran from Oldtown up the Penobscot in
1854 told me that she drew only fourteen inches,
and would run easily in two feet of water, though
they did not like to. It is said that some Western
steamers can run on a heavy dew, whence we
can imagine what a canoe may do. Montresor,

who was sent from Quebec by the English about
1760 to explore the route to the Kennebec, over
which Arnold afterward passed, supplied the
Penobscot near its source with water by opening
the beaver-dams, and he says, "This is often
done." He afterward states that the Governor
of Canada had forbidden to molest the beaver
about the outlet of the Kennebec from Moosehead Lake, on account of the service which their
dams did by raising the water for navigation.

This canal, so called, was a considerable and
extremely rapid and rocky river. The Indian
decided that there was water enough in it without
raising the dam, which would only make it more
violent, and that he would run down it alone,
while we carried the greater part of the baggage.
Our provision being about half consumed, there
was the less left in the canoe. We had thrown
away the pork-keg, and wrapt its contents in
birch bark, which is the unequalled wrapping-
paper of the woods.

Following a moist trail through the forest, we
reached the head of Webster Pond about the
same time with the Indian, notwithstanding the
velocity with which he moved, our route being
the most direct. The Indian name of Webster
Stream, of which this pond is the source, is,
according to him, *Madunkchunk*, i. e. Height of
Land, and of the pond, *Madunkchunk-gamooc*,
or Height of Land Pond. The latter was two

or three miles long. We passed near a pine on its shore which had been splintered by lightning, perhaps the day before. This was the first proper East Branch Penobscot water that we came to.

At the outlet of Webster Lake was another dam, at which we stopped and picked raspberries, while the Indian went down the stream a half-mile through the forest, to see what he had got to contend with. There was a deserted log camp here, apparently used the previous winter, with its "hovel" or barn for cattle. In the hut was a large fir-twig bed, raised two feet from the floor, occupying a large part of the single apartment, a long narrow table against the wall, with a stout log bench before it, and above the table a small window, the only one there was, which admitted a feeble light. It was a simple and strong fort erected against the cold, and suggested what valiant trencher work had been done there. I discovered one or two curious wooden traps, which had not been used for a long time, in the woods near by. The principal part consisted of a long and slender pole.

We got our dinner on the shore, on the upper side of the dam. As we were sitting by our fire, concealed by the earth bank of the dam, a long line of sheldrake, half grown, came waddling over it from the water below, passing within about a rod of us, so that we could almost have caught them in our hands. They were very abundant on all the streams and lakes which we visited, and every two or three hours they would rush away in a long string over the water before us, twenty to fifty of them at once, rarely ever flying, but running with great rapidity up or down the stream, even in the midst of the most violent rapids, and apparently as fast up as down, or else crossing diagonally, the old, as it appeared, behind, and driving them, and flying to the front from time to time, as if to direct them. We also saw many small black dippers, which behaved in a similar manner, and, once or twice, a few black ducks.

An Indian at Oldtown had told us that we should be obliged to carry ten miles between Telos Lake on the St. John's and Second Lake on the East Branch of the Penobscot; but the lumberers whom we met assured us that there would not be more than a mile of carry. It turned out that the Indian, who had lately been over this route, was nearest right, as far as we were concerned. However, if one of us could have assisted the Indian in managing the canoe in the rapids, we might have run the greater part of the way; but as he was alone in the manage-ment of the canoe in such places, we were obliged to walk the greater part. I did not feel quite ready to try such an experiment on Webster

Stream, which has so bad a reputation. According to my observation, a batteau, properly manned, shoots rapids as a matter of course, which a single Indian with a canoe carries round.

My companion and I carried a good part of the baggage on our shoulders, while the Indian took that which would be least injured by wet in the canoe. We did not know when we should see him again, for he had not been this way since the canal was cut, nor for more than thirty years. He agreed to stop when he got to smooth water, come up and find our path if he could, and halloo for us, and after waiting a reasonable time go on and try again, — and we were to look out in like manner for him.

He commenced by running through the sluice-way and over the dam, as usual, standing up in his tossing canoe, and was soon out of sight behind a point in a wild gorge. This Webster Stream is well known to lumbermen as a difficult one. It is exceedingly rapid and rocky, and also shallow, and can hardly be considered navigable, unless that may mean that what is launched in it is sure to be carried swiftly down it, though it may be dashed to pieces by the way. It is somewhat like navigating a thunder-spout. With commonly an irresistible force urging you on, you have got to choose your own course each moment, between the rocks and shallows, and to get into it, moving forward always with the utmost possible moderation, and often holding on, if you can, that you may inspect the rapids before you.

By the Indian's direction we took an old path on the south side, which appeared to keep down the stream, though at a considerable distance from it, cutting off bends, perhaps to Second Lake, having first taken the course from the map with a compass, which was northeasterly, for safety. It was a wild wood-path, with a few tracks of oxen which had been driven over it, probably to some old camp clearing, for pasturage, mingled with the tracks of moose which had lately used it. We kept on steadily for about an hour without putting down our packs, occasionally winding around or climbing over a fallen tree, for the most part far out of sight and hearing of the river; till, after walking about three miles, we were glad to find that the path came to the river again at an old camp ground, where there was a small opening in the forest, at which we paused. Swiftly as the shallow and rocky river ran here, a continuous rapid with dancing waves, I saw, as I sat on the shore, a long string of sheldrakes, which something scared, run up the opposite side of the stream by me, with the same ease that they commonly did down it, just touching the surface of the waves, and getting an impulse from them as they flowed from under them; but they soon came back, driven by the Indian, who had fallen a little behind us, on account of the windings. He shot round a point just above, and came to land by us, with considerable water in his canoe. He had found it, as he said, "very strong water," and had been obliged to land once before to empty out what he had taken in. He complained that it strained him to paddle so hard in order to keep his canoe straight in its course, having no one in the bows to aid him, and, shallow as it was, said that it would be no joke to upset there, for the force of the water was such that he had as lief I would strike him over the head with a paddle as have that water strike him. Seeing him come out of that gap was as if you should pour water down an inclined and zig-zag trough, then drop a nutshell into it, and taking a short cut to the bottom, get there in time to see it come out, notwithstanding the rush and tumult, right side up, and only partly full of water.

After a moment's breathing space, while I held his canoe, he was soon out of sight again around another bend, and we, shouldering our packs, resumed our course.

We did not at once fall into our path again, but made our way with difficulty along the edge of the river, till at length, striking inland, through the forest, we recovered it. Before going a mile we heard the Indian calling to us. He had come up through the woods and along the path to find us, having reached sufficiently smooth water to warrant his taking us in. The shore was about one fourth of a mile distant, through a dense, dark forest, and as he led us back to it, winding rapidly about to the right and left, I had the curiosity to look down carefully, and found that he was following his steps backward. I could only occasionally perceive his trail in the moss, and yet he did not appear to look down nor hesitate an instant, but led us out exactly to his canoe. This surprised me, for without a compass, or the sight or noise of the river to guide us, we could not have kept our course many minutes, and could have retraced our steps but a short distance, with a great deal of pains and very slowly, using a laborious circum-spection. But it was evident that he could go back through the forest wherever he had been during the day.

After this rough walking in the dark woods it was an agreeable change to glide down the rapid river in the canoe once more. This river, which was about the size of our Assabet (in Concord), though still very swift, was almost perfectly smooth here, and showed a very visible declivity, a regularly inclined plane, for several miles, like a mirror set a little aslant, on which we coasted down. This very obvious regular descent, particularly plain when I regarded the water-line against the shores, made a singular impression on me, which the swiftness of our motion probably enhanced, so that we seemed to be gliding down a much steeper declivity than we were, and that we could not save ourselves from rapids and falls if we should suddenly come to them. My companion did not perceive this slope, but I have a surveyor's eyes, and I satisfied myself that it was no ocular illusion. You could tell at a glance, on approaching such a river, which way the water flowed, though you might perceive no motion. I observed the angle at which a level line would strike the surface, and calculated the amount of fall in a rod, which did not need to be remarkably great to produce this effect.

It was very exhilarating, and the perfection of travelling, quite unlike floating on our dead Concord River, and coasting down this inclined mirror, which was now and then gently winding, down a mountain, indeed, between two evergreen forests, edged with lofty dead white pines, sometimes slanted half-way over the stream, and destined soon to bridge it. I saw some monsters there, nearly destitute of branches, and scarcely diminishing in diameter for eighty or ninety feet.

As we thus swept along, our Indian repeated in a deliberate and drawling tone the words "Daniel Webster, great lawyer," apparently reminded of him by the name of the stream, and he described his calling on him once in Boston, at what he supposed was his boarding-house. He had no business with him, but merely went to pay his respects, as we should say. In answer to our questions, he described his person well enough. It was on the day after Webster delivered his Bunker Hill oration, which I believe Polis heard. The first time he called he waited till he was tired without seeing him, and then went away. The next time, he saw him go by the door of the room in which he was waiting several times, in his shirt-sleeves, without noticing him. He thought that if he had come to see Indians, they would not have treated him so. At length, after very long delay, he came in, walked toward him, and asked in a loud voice, gruffly, "What do you want?" and he, thinking at first, by the motion of his hand, that he was going to strike him, said to himself, "You'd better take care, if you try that I shall know what to do." He did not like him, and declared that all he said, "was not worth talk about a musquash." We suggested that probably Mr. Webster was very busy, and had a great many visitors just then.

Coming to falls and rapids, our easy progress was suddenly terminated. The Indian went along shore to inspect the water, while we climbed over the rocks, picking berries. The peculiar growth of blueberries on the tops of large rocks here made the impression of high land, and indeed this was the Height-of-land stream. When the Indian came back he remarked, "You got to walk; ver strong water." So, taking out his canoe, he launched it again below the falls, and was soon out of sight. At such times, he would step into the canoe, take up his paddle, and, with an air of mystery, start off, looking far down stream, and keeping his own counsel, as if absorbing all the intelligence of forest and stream into himself; but I sometimes detected a little fun in his face, which could yield to my sympathetic smile, for he was thoroughly good-humored. We meanwhile scrambled along the shore with our packs, without any path. This was the last of *our* boating for the day.

The prevailing rock here was a kind of slate, standing on its edges, and my companion, who was recently from California, thought it exactly like that in which the gold is found, and said that if he had had a pan he would have liked to wash a little of the sand here.

The Indian now got along much faster than we, and waited for us from time to time. I found here the only cool spring that I drank at anywhere on this excursion, a little water filling a hollow in the sandy bank. It was a quite memorable event, and due to the elevation of the country, for wherever else we had been the water in

the rivers and the streams emptying in was dead
and warm, compared with that of a mountainous region. It was very bad walking along the
shore over fallen and drifted trees and bushes,
and rocks, from time to time swinging ourselves
round over the water, or else taking to a gravel
bar or going inland. At one place, the Indian
being ahead, I was obliged to take off all my
clothes in order to ford a small but deep stream
emptying in, while my companion, who was
inland, found a rude bridge, high up in the woods,
and I saw no more of him for some time. I saw
there very fresh moose tracks, found a new
golden-rod to me (perhaps *Solidago thyrsoidea*),
and I passed one white-pine log, which had
lodged, in the forest near the edge of the stream,
which was quite five feet in diameter at the butt.
Probably its size detained it.

Shortly after this, I overtook the Indian at the
edge of some burnt land, which extended three
or four miles at least, beginning about three
miles above Second Lake, which we were expecting to reach that night, and which is about
ten miles from Telos Lake. This burnt region
was still more rocky than before, but, though
comparatively open, we could not yet see the
lake. Not having seen my companion for some
time, I climbed, with the Indian, a singular
high rock on the edge of the river, forming a
narrow ridge only a foot or two wide at top, in

order to look for him; and after calling many times, I at length heard him answer from a considerable distance inland, he having taken a trail which led off from the river, perhaps directly to the lake, and was now in search of the river again. Seeing a much higher rock, of the same character, about one third of a mile farther east, or down stream, I proceeded toward it, through the burnt land, in order to look for the lake from its summit, supposing that the Indian would keep down the stream in his canoe, and hallooing all the while that my companion might join me on the way. Before we came together, I noticed where a moose, which possibly I had scared by my shouting, had apparently just run along a large rotten trunk of a pine, which made a bridge, thirty or forty feet long, over a hollow, as convenient for him as for me. The tracks were as large as those of an ox, but an ox could not have crossed there. This burnt land was an exceedingly wild and desolate region. Judging by the weeds and sprouts, it appeared to have been burnt about two years before. It was covered with charred trunks, either prostrate or standing, which crocked our clothes and hands, and we could not easily have distinguished a bear there by his color. Great shells of trees, sometimes unburnt without, or burnt on one side only, but black within, stood twenty or forty feet high.

The fire had run up inside, as in a chimney, leaving the sap-wood. Sometimes we crossed a rocky ravine fifty feet wide, on a fallen trunk; and there were great fields of fire-weed (*Epilobium angustifolium*) on all sides, the most extensive that I ever saw, which presented great masses of pink. Intermixed with these were blueberry and raspberry bushes.

Having crossed a second rocky ridge, like the first, when I was beginning to ascend the third, the Indian, whom I had left on the shore some fifty rods behind, beckoned to me to come to him, but I made sign that I would first ascend the highest rock before me, whence I expected to see the lake. My companion accompanied me to the top. This was formed just like the others. Being struck with the perfect parallelism of these singular rock-hills, however much one might be in advance of another, I took out my compass and found that they lay northwest and southeast, the rock being on its edge, and sharp edges they were. This one, to speak from memory, was perhaps a third of a mile in length, but quite narrow, rising gradually from the northwest to the height of about eighty feet, but steep on the southeast end. The southwest side was as steep as an ordinary roof, or as we could safely climb; the northeast was an abrupt precipice from which you could jump clean to the bottom, near which the river flowed; while the

level top of the ridge, on which you walked along,
was only from one to three or four feet in width.
For a rude illustration, take the half of a pear
cut in two lengthwise, lay it on its flat side, the
stem to the northwest, and then halve it vertically
in the direction of its length, keeping the southwest half. Such was the general form.

There was a remarkable series of these great
rock-waves revealed by the burning; breakers,
as it were. No wonder that the river that found
its way through them was rapid and obstructed
by falls. No doubt the absence of soil on these
rocks, or its dryness where there was any, caused
this to be a very thorough burning. We could
see the lake over the woods, two or three miles
ahead, and that the river made an abrupt turn
southward around the northwest end of the
cliff on which we stood, or a little above us, so
that we had cut off a bend, and that there was
an important fall in it a short distance below
us. I could see the canoe a hundred rods behind, but now on the opposite shore, and supposed that the Indian had concluded to take
out and carry round some bad rapids on that
side, and that that might be what he had beckoned to me for; but after waiting a while I
could still see nothing of him, and I observed
to my companion that I wondered where he was,
though I began to suspect that he had gone
inland to look for the lake from some hill-top

on that side, as we had done. This proved to be the case; for after I had started to return to the canoe, I heard a faint halloo, and descried him on the top of a distant rocky hill on that side. But as, after a long time had elapsed, I still saw his canoe in the same place, and he had not returned to it, and appeared in no hurry to do so, and, moreover, as I remembered that he had previously beckoned to me, I thought that there might be something more to delay him than I knew, and began to return northwest, along the ridge, toward the angle in the river. My companion, who had just been separated from us, and had even contemplated the necessity of camping alone, wishing to husband his steps, and yet to keep with us, inquired where I was going; to which I answered, that I was going far enough back to communicate with the Indian, and that then I thought we had better go along the shore together, and keep him in sight.

When we reached the shore, the Indian appeared from out the woods on the opposite side, but on account of the roar of the water it was difficult to communicate with him. He kept along the shore westward to his canoe, while we stopped at the angle where the stream turned southward around the precipice. I again said to my companion, that we would keep along the shore and keep the Indian in sight. We started to do so, being close together, the Indian behind

us having launched his canoe again, but just
then I saw the latter, who had crossed to our
side, forty or fifty rods behind, beckoning to me,
and I called to my companion, who had just
disappeared behind large rocks at the point of
the precipice, three or four rods before me, on
his way down the stream, that I was going to
help the Indian a moment. I did so, — helped
get the canoe over a fall, lying with my breast
over a rock, and holding one end while he received it below, — and within ten or fifteen
minutes at most I was back again at the point
where the river turned southward, in order to
catch up with my companion, while Polis glided
down the river alone, parallel with me. But to
my surprise, when I rounded the precipice,
though the shore was bare of trees, without rocks,
for a quarter of a mile at least, my companion
was not to be seen. It was as if he had sunk
into the earth. This was the more unaccountable to me, because I knew that his feet were,
since our swamp walk, very sore, and that he
wished to keep with the party; and besides,
this was very bad walking, climbing over or
about the rocks. I hastened along, hallooing
and searching for him, thinking he might be
concealed behind a rock, yet doubting if he had
not taken the other side of the precipice, but the
Indian had got along still faster in his canoe,
till he was arrested by the falls, about a quarter

of a mile below. He then landed, and said that we could go no farther that night. The sun was setting, and on account of falls and rapids, we should be obliged to leave this river and carry a good way into another farther east. The first thing then was to find my companion, for I was now very much alarmed about him, and I sent the Indian along the shore down stream, which began to be covered with unburnt wood again just below the falls, while I searched backward about the precipice which we had passed. The Indian showed some unwillingness to exert himself, complaining that he was very tired, in consequence of his day's work, that it had strained him very much getting down so many rapids alone; but he went off calling somewhat like an owl. I remembered that my companion was near-sighted, and I feared that he had either fallen from the precipice, or fainted and sunk down amid the rocks beneath it. I shouted and searched above and below this precipice in the twilight till I could not see, expecting nothing less than to find his body beneath it. For half an hour I anticipated and believed only the worst. I thought what I should do the next day, if I did not find him, what I *could* do in such a wilderness, and how his relatives would feel, if I should return without him. I felt that if he were really lost away from the river there, it would be a desperate undertaking to find him;

and where were they who could help you? What would it be to raise the country where there were only two or three camps, twenty or thirty miles apart, and no road, and perhaps nobody at home? Yet we must try the harder, the less the prospect of success.

I rushed down from this precipice to the canoe in order to fire the Indian's gun, but found that my companion had the caps. I was still thinking of getting it off when the Indian returned. He had not found him, but he said that he had seen his tracks once or twice along the shore. This encouraged me very much. He objected to firing the gun, saying that if my companion heard it, which was not likely, on account of the roar of the stream, it would tempt him to come toward us, and he might break his neck in the dark. For the same reason we refrained from lighting a fire on the highest rock. I proposed that we should both keep down the stream to the lake, or that I should go at any rate, but the Indian said, "No use, can't do anything in the dark; come morning, then we find 'em. No harm, — he make 'em camp. No bad animals here, no gristly bears, such as in California, where he's been, — warm night, — he well off as you and I." I considered that if he was well he could do without us. He had just lived eight years in California, and had plenty of experience with wild beasts and wilder men, was peculiarly accustomed to make journeys of great length, but if he were sick or dead, he was near where we were. The darkness in the woods was by this so thick that it alone decided the question. We must camp where we were. I knew that he had his knapsack, with blankets and matches, and, if well, would fare no worse than we, except that he would have no supper nor society.

This side of the river being so encumbered with rocks, we crossed to the eastern or smoother shore, and proceeded to camp there, within two or three rods of the falls. We pitched no tent, but lay on the sand, putting a few handfuls of grass and twigs under us, there being no evergreen at hand. For fuel we had some of the charred stumps. Our various bags of provisions had got quite wet in the rapids, and I arranged them about the fire to dry. The fall close by was the principal one on this stream, and it shook the earth under us. It was a cool, because dewy, night; the more so, probably, owing to the nearness of the falls. The Indian complained a good deal, and thought afterward that he got a cold there which occasioned a more serious illness. We were not much troubled by mosquitoes at any rate. I lay awake a good deal from anxiety, but, unaccountably to myself, was at length comparatively at ease respecting him. At first I had apprehended the worst, but now I had little doubt but that I should find him in the morning. From time to time I fancied that I heard his voice calling through the roar of the falls from the opposite side of the river; but it is doubtful if we could have heard him across the stream there. Sometimes I doubted whether the Indian had really seen his tracks, since he manifested an unwillingness to make much of a search, and then my anxiety returned.

It was the most wild and desolate region we had camped in, where, if anywhere, one might expect to meet with befitting inhabitants, but I heard only the squeak of a night-hawk flitting over. The moon in her first quarter, in the fore part of the night, setting over the bare rocky hills, garnished with tall, charred, and hollow stumps or shells of trees, served to reveal the desolation.

THURSDAY, July 30.

I aroused the Indian early this morning to go in search of our companion, expecting to find him within a mile or two, farther down the stream. The Indian wanted his breakfast first, but I reminded him that my companion had had neither breakfast nor supper. We were obliged first to carry our canoe and baggage over into another stream, the main East Branch, about three-fourths of a mile distant, for Webster

Stream was no farther navigable. We went twice over this carry, and the dewy bushes wet us through like water up to the middle; I hallooed in a high key from time to time, though I had little expectation that I could be heard over the roar of the rapids, and moreover we were necessarily on the opposite side of the stream to him. In going over this portage the last time, the Indian, who was before me with the canoe on his head, stumbled and fell heavily once, and lay for a moment silent, as if in pain. I hastily stepped forward to help him, asking if he was much hurt, but after a moment's pause, without replying, he sprang up and went forward. He was all the way subject to taciturn fits, but they were harmless ones.

We had launched our canoe and gone but little way down the East Branch, when I heard an answering shout from my companion, and soon after saw him standing on a point where there was a clearing a quarter of a mile below, and the smoke of his fire was rising near by. Before I saw him I naturally shouted again and again, but the Indian curtly remarked, "He hears you," as if once was enough. It was just below the mouth of Webster Stream. When we arrived, he was smoking his pipe, and said that he had passed a pretty comfortable night, though it was rather cold, on account of the dew.

It appeared that when we stood together the

previous evening, and I was shouting to the
Indian across the river, he, being near-sighted,
had not seen the Indian nor his canoe, and when
I went back to the Indian's assistance, did not
see which way I went, and supposed that we
were below and not above him, and so making
haste to catch up, he ran away from us. Having
reached this clearing, a mile or more below our
camp, the night overtook him, and he made a
fire in a little hollow, and lay down by it, in his
blanket, still thinking that we were ahead of
him. He thought it likely that he had heard
the Indian call once the evening before, but mistook it for an owl. He had seen one botanical
rarity before it was dark, — pure white *Epilobium angustifolium* amidst the fields of pink
ones, in the burnt lands. He had already stuck
up the remnant of a lumberer's shirt, found on
the point, on a pole by the water-side, for a
signal, and attached a note to it, to inform us
that he had gone on to the lake, and that if he
did not find us there, he would be back in a
couple of hours. If he had not found us soon,
he had some thoughts of going back in search
of the solitary hunter whom we had met at Telos
Lake, ten miles behind, and, if successful, hire
him to take him to Bangor. But if this hunter
had moved as fast as we, he would have been
twenty miles off by this time, and who could
guess in what direction? It would have been

like looking for a needle in a hay-mow, to search for him in these woods. He had been considering how long he could live on berries alone.

We substituted for his note a card containing our names and destination, and the date of our visit, which Polis neatly enclosed in a piece of birch-bark to keep it dry. This has probably been read by some hunter or explorer ere this.

We all had good appetites for the breakfast which we made haste to cook here, and then, having partially dried our clothes, we glided swiftly down the winding stream toward Second Lake.

As the shores became flatter with frequent gravel and sand bars, and the stream more winding in the lower land near the lake, elms and ash trees made their appearance; also the wild yellow lily (*Lilium Canadense*), some of whose bulbs I collected for a soup. On some ridges the burnt land extended as far as the lake. This was a very beautiful lake, two or three miles long, with high mountains on the southwest side, the (as our Indian said) *Nerlumskeechticook*, i. e. Dead-Water Mountain. It appears to be the same called Carbuncle Mountain on the map. According to Polis, it extends in separate elevations all along this and the next lake, which is much larger. The lake, too, I think, is called by the same name, or perhaps with the addition of *gamoc* or *mooc*. The morning was a bright one, and perfectly still and serene, the lake as smooth as glass, we making the only ripple as we paddled into it. The dark mountains about it were seen through a glaucous mist, and the brilliant white stems of canoe-birches mingled with the other woods around it. The wood-thrush sang on the distant shore, and the laugh of some loons, sporting in a concealed western bay, as if inspired by the morning, came distinct over the lake to us, and, what was remarkable, the echo which ran round the lake was much louder than the original note; probably because, the loon being in a regularly curving bay under the mountain, we were exactly in the focus of many echoes, the sound being reflected like light from a concave mirror. The beauty of the scene may have been enhanced to our eyes by the fact that we had just come together again after a night of some anxiety. This reminded me of the Ambejijis Lake on the West Branch, which I crossed in my first coming to Maine. Having paddled down three-quarters of the lake, we came to a standstill, while my companion let down for fish. A white (or whitish) gull sat on a rock which rose above the surface in mid-lake not far off, quite in harmony with the scene; and as we rested there in the warm sun, we heard one loud crushing or crackling sound from the forest, forty or fifty rods distant, as of a stick broken by the foot of some large animal. Even this was an interesting incident there. In the midst of our dreams of giant lake-trout, even then supposed to be nibbling, our fisherman drew up a diminutive red perch, and we took up our paddles again in haste.

It was not apparent where the outlet of this lake was and while the Indian thought it was in one direction, I thought it was in another. He said, "I bet you fourpence it is there," but he still held on in my direction, which proved to be the right one. As we were approaching the outlet, it being still early in the forenoon, he suddenly exclaimed, "Moose! moose!" and told us to be still. He put a cap on his gun, and standing up in the stern, rapidly pushed the canoe straight toward the shore and the moose. It was a cow-moose, about thirty rods off, standing in the water by the side of the outlet, partly behind some fallen timber and bushes, and at that distance she did not look very large. She was flapping her large ears, and from time to time poking off the flies with her nose from some part of her body. She did not appear much alarmed by our neighborhood, only occasionally turned her head and looked straight at us, and then gave her attention to the flies again. As we approached nearer, she got out of the water, stood higher and regarded us more suspiciously. Polis pushed the canoe steadily forward in the shallow water, and I for a moment forgot the

moose in attending to some pretty rose-colored
Polygonums just rising above the surface, but
the canoe soon grounded in the mud eight or
ten rods distant from the moose, and the Indian
seized his gun and prepared to fire. After standing still a moment, she turned slowly, as usual,
so as to expose her side, and he improved this
moment to fire, over our heads. She thereupon
moved off eight or ten rods at a moderate pace,
across a shallow bay, to an old standing-place
of hers, behind some fallen red maples, on the
opposite shore, and there she stood still again
a dozen or fourteen rods from us, while the
Indian hastily loaded and fired twice at her, without her moving. My companion, who passed him
his caps and bullets, said that Polis was as excited as a boy of fifteen, that his hand trembled,
and he once put his ramrod back upside down.
This was remarkable for so experienced a hunter.
Perhaps he was anxious to make a good shot
before us. The white hunter had told me that
the Indians were not good shots, because they
were excited, though he said that we had got a
good hunter with us.

The Indian now pushed quickly and quietly
back and a long distance round, in order to get
into the outlet, — for he had fired over the neck
of a peninsula between it and the lake, — till
we approached the place where the moose had
stood, when he exclaimed, "She is a goner,"

and was surprised that we did not see her as soon as he did. There, to be sure, she lay perfectly dead, with her tongue hanging out, just where she had stood to receive the last shots, looking unexpectedly large and horse-like, and we saw where the bullets had scarred the trees.

Using a tape, I found that the moose measured just six feet from the shoulder to the tip of the hoof, and was eight feet long as she lay. Some portions of the body, for a foot in diameter, were almost covered with flies, apparently the common fly of our woods, with a dark spot on the wing, and not the very large ones which occasionally pursued us in mid-stream, though both are called moose-flies.

Polis, preparing to skin the moose, asked me to help him find a stone on which to sharpen his large knife. It being all a flat alluvial ground where the moose had fallen, covered with red maples, etc., this was no easy matter, we searched far and wide, a long time, till at length I found a flat kind of slate-stone, and soon after he returned with a similar one, on which he soon made his knife very sharp.

While he was skinning the moose, I proceeded to ascertain what kind of fishes were to be found in the sluggish and muddy outlet. The greatest difficulty was to find a pole. It was almost impossible to find a slender, straight pole ten or twelve feet long in those woods. You might search half an hour in vain. They are commonly spruce, arbor-vitæ, fir, etc., short, stout, and branchy, and do not make good fish-poles, even after you have patiently cut off all their tough and scraggy branches. The fishes were red perch and chivin.

The Indian having cut off a large piece of sirloin, the upper lip and the tongue, wrapped them in the hide, and placed them in the bottom of the canoe, observing that there was "one man," meaning the weight of one. Our load had previously been reduced some thirty pounds, but a hundred pounds were now added, a serious addition, which made our quarters still more narrow, and considerably increased the danger on the lakes and rapids, as well as the labor of the carries. The skin was ours, according to custom, since the Indian was in our employ, but we did not think of claiming it. He being a skilful dresser of moose-hides, would make it worth seven or eight dollars to him, as I was told. He said that he sometimes earned fifty or sixty dollars in a day at them; he had killed ten moose in one day, though the skinning and all took two days. This was the way he had got his property. There were the tracks of a calf thereabouts, which he said would come "by, by," and he could get it if we cared to wait, but I cast cold water on the project.

We continued along the outlet toward Grand

Lake, through a swampy region, by a long, winding, and narrow dead-water, very much choked up by wood, where we were obliged to land sometimes in order to get the canoe over a log. It was hard to find any channel, and we did not know but we should be lost in the swamp. It abounded in ducks, as usual. At length we reached Grand Lake, which the Indian called *Matungamook*.

At the head of this we saw, coming in from the southwest, with a sweep apparently from a gorge in the mountains, Trout Stream, or *Uncardnerheese*, which name, the Indian said, had something to do with mountains.

We stopped to dine on an interesting high rocky island, soon after entering Matungamook Lake, securing our canoe to the cliffy shore. It is always pleasant to step from a boat on to a large rock or cliff. Here was a good opportunity to dry our dewy blankets on the open sunny rock. Indians had recently camped here, and accidentally burned over the western end of the island, and Polis picked up a gun-case of blue broadcloth, and said that he knew the Indian it belonged to, and would carry it to him. His tribe is not so large but he may know all its effects. We proceeded to make a fire and cook our dinner amid some pines, where our predecessors had done the same, while the Indian busied himself about his moose-hide on the shore. for he said

that he thought it a good plan for one to do all
the cooking, i. e. I suppose if that one were not
himself. A peculiar evergreen overhung our
fire, which at first glance looked like a pitch
pine (*P. rigida*), with leaves little more than an
inch long, spruce-like, but we found it to be the
Pinus Banksiana, — "Banks's, or the Labrador Pine," also called Scrub Pine, Gray Pine,
etc., a new tree to us. These must have been
good specimens, for several were thirty or thirty-
five feet high. Richardson found it forty feet
high and upward, and states that the porcupine
feeds on its bark. Here also grew the Red Pine
(*Pinus resinosa*).

I saw where the Indians had made canoes in a
little secluded hollow in the woods, on the top of
the rock, where they were out of the wind, and
large piles of whittlings remained. This must
have been a favorite resort for their ancestors,
and, indeed, we found here the point of an arrow-
head, such as they have not used for two centuries
and now know not how to make. The Indian,
picking up a stone, remarked to me, "That
very strange lock (rock)." It was a piece of
hornstone, which I told him his tribe had probably brought here centuries before to make
arrow-heads of. He also picked up a yellowish
curved bone by the side of our fireplace and
asked me to guess what it was. It was one of the
upper incisors of a beaver, on which some party

had feasted within a year or two. I found also most of the teeth, and the skull, etc. We here dined on fried moose-meat.

One who was my companion in my two previous excursions to these woods, tells me that when hunting up the Caucomgomoc, about two years ago, he found himself dining one day on moose-meat, mud-turtle, trout, and beaver, and he thought that there were few places in the world where these dishes could easily be brought together on one table.

After the almost incessant rapids and falls of the Madunkchunk (Height-of-land, or Webster Stream), we had just passed through the dead-water of Second Lake, and were now in the much larger dead-water of Grand Lake, and I thought the Indian was entitled to take an extra nap here. Ktaadn, near which we were to pass the next day, is said to mean "Highest Land." So much geography is there in their names. The Indian navigator naturally distinguishes by a name those parts of a stream where he has encountered quick water and forks, and again, the lakes and smooth water where he can rest his weary arms, since those are the most interesting and more arable parts to him. The very sight of the *Nerlumskeechticook*, or Dead-Water Mountains, a day's journey off over the forest, as we first saw them, must awaken in him pleasing memories. And not less interesting is it to the white traveller, when he is crossing a placid lake in these out-of-the-way woods, perhaps thinking that he is in some sense one of the earlier discoverers of it, to be reminded that it was thus well known and suitably named by Indian hunters perhaps a thousand years ago.

Ascending the precipitous rock which formed this long narrow island, I was surprised to find that its summit was a narrow ridge, with a precipice on one side, and that its axis of elevation extended from northwest to southeast, exactly like that of the great rocky ridge at the commencement of the Burnt Ground, ten miles northwesterly. The same arrangement prevailed here, and we could plainly see that the mountain ridges on the west of the lake trended the same way. Splendid large harebells nodded over the edge and in the clefts of the cliff, and the blue-berries (*Vaccinium Canadense*) were for the first time really abundant in the thin soil on its top. There was no lack of them henceforward on the East Branch. There was a fine view hence over the sparkling lake, which looked pure and deep, and had two or three, in all, rocky islands in it. Our blankets being dry, we set out again, the Indian as usual having left his gazette on a tree. This time it was we three in a canoe, my companion smoking. We paddled southward down this handsome lake, which appeared to extend nearly as far east as south, keeping near the western shore, just outside a small island, under the dark *Nerlumskeechticook* Mountain. For I had observed on my map that this was the course. It was three or four miles across it. It struck me that the outline of this mountain on the southwest of the lake, and of another beyond it, was not only like that of the huge rock waves of Webster Stream, but in the main like Kineo, on Moosehead Lake, having a similar but less abrupt precipice at the southeast end; in short, that all the prominent hills and ridges hereabouts were larger or smaller Kineos, and that possibly there was such a relation between Kineo and the rocks of Webster Stream.

The Indian did not know exactly where the outlet was, whether at the extreme southwest angle or more easterly, and had asked to see my plan at the last stopping-place, but I had forgotten to show it to him. As usual, he went feeling his way by a middle course between two probable points, from which he could diverge either way at last without losing much distance. In approaching the south shore, as the clouds looked gusty, and the waves ran pretty high, we so steered as to get partly under the lee of an island, though at a great distance from it.

I could not distinguish the outlet till we were almost in it, and heard the water falling over the dam there.

Here was a considerable fall, and a very substantial dam, but no sign of a cabin or camp. The hunter whom we met at Telos Lake had told us that there were plenty of trout here, but at this hour they did not rise to the bait, only cousin trout, from the very midst of the rushing waters. There are not so many fishes in these rivers as in the Concord.

While we loitered here, Polis took occasion to cut with his big knife some of the hair from his moose-hide, and so lightened and prepared it for drying. I noticed at several old Indian camps in the woods the pile of hair which they had cut from their hides.

Having carried over the dam, he darted down the rapids leaving us to walk for a mile or more, where for the most part there was no path, but very thick and difficult travelling near the stream. At length he would call to let us know where he was waiting for us with his canoe, when, on account of the windings of the stream, we did not know where the shore was, but he did not call often enough, forgetting that we were not Indians. He seemed to be very saving of his breath, — yet he would be surprised if we went by, or did not strike the right spot. This was not because he was unaccommodating, but a proof of superior manners. Indians like to get along with the least possible communication and ado. He was really paying us a great compliment all the while, thinking that we preferred a hint to a kick.

At length, climbing over the willows and fallen trees, when this was easier than to go round or under them, we overtook the canoe, and glided down the stream in smooth but swift water for several miles. I here observed again, as at Webster Stream, and on a still larger scale the next day, that the river was a smooth and regularly inclined plane down which we coasted. As we thus glided along we started the first black ducks which we had distinguished.

We decided to camp early to-night, that we might have ample time before dark; so we stopped at the first favorable shore, where there was a narrow gravelly beach on the western side, some five miles below the outlet of the lake. It was an interesting spot, where the river began to make a great bend to the east, and the last of the peculiar moose-faced *Nerlumskeechticook* Mountains not far southwest of Grand Lake rose dark in the northwest a short distance behind, displaying its gray precipitous southeast side, but we could not see this without coming out upon the shore.

Two steps from the water on either side, and you come to the abrupt bushy and rooty if not turfy edge of the bank, four or five feet high, where the interminable forest begins, as if the stream had but just cut its way through it.

It is surprising on stepping ashore anywhere into this unbroken wilderness to see so often,

at least within a few rods of the river, the marks
of the axe, made by lumberers who have either
camped here, or driven logs past in previous
springs. You will see perchance where, going
on the same errand that you do, they have cut
large chips from a tall white-pine stump for their
fire. While we were pitching the camp and
getting supper, the Indian cut the rest of the hair
from his moose-hide, and proceeded to extend it
vertically on a temporary frame between two
small trees, half a dozen feet from the opposite
side of the fire, lashing and stretching it with
arbor-vitæ bark, which was always at hand, and
in this case was stripped from one of the trees it
was tied to. Asking for a new kind of tea, he
made us some, pretty good, of the checkerberry
(*Gaultheria procumbens*), which covered the
ground, dropping a little bunch of it tied up with
cedar bark into the kettle; but it was not quite
equal to the *Chiogenes*. We called this therefore Checkerberry-tea Camp.

I was struck with the abundance of the *Linnæa borealis*, checkerberry, and *Chiogenes hispidula*, almost everywhere in the Maine woods.
The wintergreen (*Chimaphila umbellata*) was
still in bloom here, and *Clintonia* berries were
abundant and ripe. This handsome plant is one
of the most common in that forest. We here
first noticed the moose-wood in fruit on the
banks. The prevailing trees were spruce (com-

monly black), arbor-vitæ, canoe-birch, (black ash and elms beginning to appear,) yellow birch, red maple, and a little hemlock skulking in the forest. The Indian said that the white-maple punk was the best for tinder, that yellow-birch punk was pretty good, but hard. After supper he put on the moose tongue and lips to boil, cutting out the *septum*. He showed me how to write on the under side of birch bark, with a black-spruce twig, which is hard and tough and can be brought to a point.

The Indian wandered off into the woods a short distance just before night, and, coming back, said, "Me found great treasure — fifty, sixty dollars' worth." "What's that?" we asked. "Steel traps, under a log, thirty or forty, I did n't count 'em. I guess Indian work — worth three dollars apiece." It was a singular coincidence that he should have chanced to walk to and look under that particular log, in that trackless forest.

I saw chivin and chub in the stream when washing my hands, but my companion tried in vain to catch them. I also heard the sound of bull-frogs from a swamp on the opposite side, thinking at first that they were moose; a duck paddled swiftly by; and sitting in that dusky wilderness, under that dark mountain, by the bright river which was full of reflected light, still I heard the wood-thrush sing, as if no higher

civilization could be attained. By this time the
night was upon us.

You commonly make your camp just at sundown, and are collecting wood, getting your
supper, or pitching your tent while the shades
of night are gathering around and adding to the
already dense gloom of the forest. You have
no time to explore or look around you before it
is dark. You may penetrate half a dozen rods
farther into that twilight wilderness, after some
dry bark to kindle your fire with, and wonder
what mysteries lie hidden still deeper in it, say
at the end of a long day's walk; or you may run
down to the shore for a dipper of water, and get
a clearer view for a short distance up or down
the stream, and while you stand there, see a fish
leap, or duck alight in the river, or hear a wood-
thrush or robin sing in the woods. That is as
if you had been to town or civilized parts. But
there is no sauntering off to see the country,
and ten or fifteen rods seems a great way from
your companions, and you come back with the
air of a much travelled man, as from a long
journey, with adventures to relate, though you
may have heard the crackling of the fire all the
while, — and at a hundred rods you might be
lost past recovery, and have to camp out. It is
all mossy and *moosey*. In some of those dense
fir and spruce woods there is hardly room for
the smoke to go up. The trees are a *standing*

night, and every fir and spruce which you fell is
a plume plucked from night's raven wing. Then
at night the general stillness is more impressive
than any sound, but occasionally you hear the
note of an owl farther or nearer in the woods,
and if near a lake, the semi-human cry of the
loons at their unearthly revels.

To-night the Indian lay between the fire and
his stretched moose-hide, to avoid the mosquitoes.
Indeed, he also made a small smoky fire of damp
leaves at his head and his feet, and then as usual
rolled up his head in his blanket. We with our
veils and our wash were tolerably comfortable,
but it would be difficult to pursue any sedentary
occupation in the woods at this season: you cannot see to read much by the light of a fire through
a veil in the evening, nor handle pencil and paper.
well with gloves or anointed fingers.

On the mainland were Norway pines, indicating a new geological formation, and it was such
a dry and sandy soil as we had not noticed before.

As we approached the mouth of the East
Branch, we passed two or three huts, the first
sign of civilization after Hunt's, though we saw
no road as yet; we heard a cow-bell, and even
saw an infant held up to a small square window
to see us pass, but apparently the infant and the
mother that held it were the only inhabitants
then at home for several miles. This took the
wind out of our sails, reminding us that we were

travellers surely, while it was a native of the soil, and had the advantage of us. Conversation flagged. I would only hear the Indian, perhaps, ask my companion, "You load my pipe?" He said that he smoked alder bark for medicine. On entering the West Branch at Nickertow it appeared much larger than the East. Polis remarked that the former was all gone and lost now, that it was all smooth water hence to Old-town, and he threw away his pole which was cut on the Umbazookskus. Thinking of the rapids, he said once or twice, that you would n't catch him to go East Branch again; but he did not by any means mean all that he said.

Things are quite changed since I was here eleven years ago. Where there were but one or two houses, I now found quite a village, with saw-mills, and a store (latter was locked, but its contents were so much the more safely stored), and there was a stage-road to Mattawamkeag, and the rumor of a stage. Indeed, a steamer had ascended thus far once, when the water was very high. But we were not able to get any sugar, only a better shingle to lean our backs against.

We camped about two miles below Nickertow, on the south side of the West Branch, covering with fresh twigs the withered bed of a former traveller, and feeling that we were now in a settled country, especially when in the evening we heard an ox sneeze in its wild pasture across the river. Wherever you land along the frequented part of the river, you have not far to go to find these sites of temporary inns, the withered bed of flattened twigs, the charred sticks, and perhaps the tent-poles. And not long since, similar beds were spread along the Connecticut, the Hudson, and the Delaware, and longer still ago by the Thames and Seine, and they now help to make the soil where private and public gardens, mansions and palaces are. We could not get fir twigs for our bed here, and the spruce was harsh in comparison, having more twig in proportion to its leaf, but we improved it somewhat with hemlock. The Indian remarked as before, "Must have hard wood to cook moose-meat," as if that were a maxim, and proceeded to get it. My companion cooked some in California fashion, winding a long string of the meat round a stick and slowly turning it in his hand before the fire. It was very good. But the Indian, not approving of the mode, or because he was not allowed to cook it his own way, would not taste it. After the regular supper we attempted to make a lily soup of the bulbs which I had brought along, for I wished to learn all I could before I got out of the woods. Following the Indian's directions, for he began to be sick, I washed the bulbs carefully, minced some moose-meat and some pork, salted and boiled all together, but we had not patience to try the experiment fairly, for he said it must be boiled till the roots were completely softened so as to thicken the soup like flour; but though we left it on all night, we found it dried to the kettle in the morning, and not yet boiled to a flour. Perhaps the roots were not ripe enough, for they commonly gather them in the fall. As it was, it was palatable enough, but it reminded me of the Irishman's limestone broth. The other ingredients were enough alone. The Indian's name for these bulbs was *Sheepnoc*. I stirred the soup by accident with a striped maple or moose-wood stick, which I had peeled, and he remarked that its bark was an emetic.

He prepared to camp as usual between his moose-hide and the fire, but it beginning to rain suddenly, he took refuge under the tent with us, and gave us a song before falling asleep.

FRIDAY, July 31.

The Indian said, "You and I kill moose last night, therefore use 'em best wood. Always use hard wood to cook moose-meat." His "best wood" was rock maple. He cast the moose's lip into the fire, to burn the hair off, and then rolled it up with the meat to carry along. Observing that we were sitting down to breakfast without any pork, he said, with a very grave look, "Me want some fat," so he was told that he might have as much as he would fry.

We had smooth but swift water for a considerable distance, where we glided rapidly along, scaring up ducks and kingfishers. But as usual, our smooth progress erelong came to an end, and we were obliged to carry canoe and all about half a mile down the right bank, around some rapids or falls. It required sharp eyes sometimes to tell which side was the carry, before you went over the falls, but Polis never failed to land us rightly. The raspberries were particularly abundant and large here, and all hands went to eating them, the Indian remarking on their size.

Often on bare rocky carries the trail was so indistinct that I repeatedly lost it, but when I walked behind him I observed that he could keep it almost like a hound, and rarely hesitated, or, if he paused a moment on a bare rock, his eye immediately detected some sign which would have escaped me. Frequently *we* found no path at all at these places, and were to him unaccountably delayed. He would only say it was "ver strange."

We had heard of a Grand Fall on this stream, and thought that each fall we came to must be it, but after christening several in succession with this name, we gave up the search. There were more Grand or Petty Falls than I can remember.

I cannot tell how many times we had to walk

on account of falls or rapids. We were expecting all the while that the river would take a
final leap and get to smooth water, but there was
no improvement this forenoon. However, the
carries were an agreeable variety. So surely
as we stepped out of the canoe and stretched
our legs we found ourselves in a blueberry and
raspberry garden, each side of our rocky trail
around the falls being lined with one or both.
There was not a carry on the main East Branch
where we did not find an abundance of both
these berries, for these were the rockiest places,
and partially cleared, such as these plants prefer,
and there had been none to gather the finest
before us.

In our three journeys over the carries, for we
were obliged to go over the ground three times
whenever the canoe was taken out, we did full
justice to the berries, and they were just what
we wanted to correct the effect of our hard bread
and pork diet. Another name for making a
portage would have been going a berrying. We
also found a few *Amelanchier*, or *service* berries,
though most were abortive, but they held on
rather more generally than they do in Concord.
The Indian called them *Pemoymenuk*, and said
that they bore much fruit in some places. He
sometimes also ate the northern wild red cherries,
saying that they were good medicine, but they
were scarcely edible.

We bathed and dined at the foot of one of these carries. It was the Indian who commonly reminded us that it was dinner-time, sometimes even by turning the prow to the shore. He once made an indirect but lengthy apology, by saying that we might think it strange, but that one who worked hard all day was very particular to have his dinner in good season. At the most considerable fall on this stream, when I was walking over the carry, close behind the Indian, he observed a track on the rock, which was but slightly covered with soil, and, stooping, muttered "caribou." When we returned, he observed a much larger track near the same place, where some animal's foot had sunk into a small hollow in the rock, partly filled with grass and earth, and he exclaimed with surprise, "What that?" "Well, what is it?" I asked. Stooping and laying his hand in it, he answered with a mysterious air, and in a half whisper, "Devil [that is, Indian Devil, or cougar] lodges about here — very bad animal — pull 'em *locks* all to pieces." "How long since it was made?" I asked. "To-day or yesterday," said he. But when I asked him afterwards if he was sure it was the devil's track, he said he did not know. I had been told that the scream of a cougar was heard about Ktaadn recently, and we were not far from that mountain.

We spent at least half the time in walking to-day, and the walking was as bad as usual, for the Indian being alone, commonly ran down far below the foot of the carries before he waited for us. The carry-paths themselves were more than usually indistinct, often the route being revealed only by the countless small holes in the fallen timber made by the tacks in the drivers' boots, or where there *was* a slight trail we did not find it. It was a tangled and perplexing thicket, through which we stumbled and threaded our way, and when we had finished a mile of it, our starting-point seemed far away. We were glad that we had not got to walk to Bangor along the banks of this river, which would be a journey of more than a hundred miles. Think of the denseness of the forest, the fallen trees and rocks, the windings of the river, the streams emptying in and the frequent swamps to be crossed. It made you shudder. Yet the Indian from time to time pointed out to us where he had thus crept along day after day when he was a boy of ten, and in a starving condition. He had been hunting far north of this with two grown Indians. The winter came on unexpectedly early, and the ice compelled them to leave their canoe at Grand Lake, and walk down the bank. They shouldered their furs and started for Oldtown. The snow was not deep enough for snow-shoes, or to cover the inequalities of the ground. Polis was soon too weak to carry any burden; but he managed to catch one otter. This was the most they all had to eat on this journey, and he remembered how good the yellow-lily roots were, made into a soup with the otter oil. He shared this food equally with the other two, but being so small he suffered much more than they. He waded through the Mattawamkeag at its mouth, when it was freezing cold and came up to his chin, and he, being very weak and emaciated, expected to be swept away. The first house which they reached was at Lincoln, and thereabouts they met a white teamster with supplies, who seeing their condition gave them as much of his load as they could eat. For six months after getting home he was very low, and did not expect to live, and was perhaps always the worse for it.

We could not find much more than half of this day's journey on our maps (the "Map of the Public Lands of Maine and Massachusetts," and "Colton's Railroad and Township Map of Maine," which copies the former). By the maps there was not more than fifteen miles between camps, at the outside, and yet we had been busily progressing all day, and much of the time very rapidly.

For seven or eight miles below that succession of "Grand" falls, the aspect of the banks as well as the character of the stream was changed. After passing a tributary from the northeast, perhaps Bowlin Stream, we had good swift smooth water, with a regular slope, such as I have described. Low, grassy banks and muddy shores began. Many elms, as well as maples, and more ash trees overhung the stream, and supplanted the spruce.

My lily-roots having been lost when the canoe was taken out at a carry, I landed late in the afternoon, at a low and grassy place amid maples, to gather more. It was slow work grubbing them up amid the sand, and the mosquitoes were all the while feasting on me. Mosquitoes, black flies, etc., pursued us in mid-channel, and we were glad sometimes to get into violent rapids, for then we escaped them.

A red-headed woodpecker flew across the river, and the Indian remarked that it was good to eat. As we glided swiftly down the inclined plane of the river, a great cat-owl launched itself away from a stump on the bank, and flew heavily across the stream, and the Indian, as usual, imitated its note. Soon the same bird flew back in front of us, and we afterwards passed it perched on a tree. Soon afterward a white-headed eagle sailed down the stream before us. We drove him several miles, while we were looking for a good place to camp, for we expected to be overtaken by a shower, — and still we could distinguish him by his white tail, sailing away from time to time, from some tree by the shore still farther down the stream. Some shecorways, being surprised by us, a part of them dived, and we passed directly over them, and could trace their course here and there by a bubble on the surface, but we did not see them come up. Polis detected once or twice what he called a "tow" road, an indistinct path leading into the forest. In the mean while we passed the mouth of the Seboois on our left. This did not look so large as our stream, which was indeed the main one. It was some time before we found a camping-place, for the shore was either too grassy and muddy, where mosquitoes abounded, or too steep a hillside. The Indian said that there were but few mosquitoes on a steep hillside. We examined a good place, where somebody had camped a long time; but it seemed pitiful to occupy an old site, where there was so much room to choose, so we continued on. We at length found a place to our minds, on the west bank, about a mile below the mouth of the Seboois, where, in a very dense spruce wood above a gravelly shore, there seemed to be but few insects. The trees were so thick that we were obliged to clear a space to build our fire and lie down in, and the young spruce trees that were left were like the wall of an apartment rising around us. We were obliged to pull ourselves up a steep bank to get there. But the place which you have selected for your camp, though never so rough and grim, begins at once to have its attractions, and becomes a very centre of civilization to you: "Home is home, be it never so homely."

It turned out that the mosquitoes were more numerous here than we had found them before, and the Indian complained a good deal, though he lay, as the night before, between three fires and his stretched hide. As I sat on a stump by the fire, with a veil and gloves on trying to read, he observed, "I make you candle," and in a minute he took a piece of birch bark about two inches wide and rolled it hard, like an allumette fifteen inches long, lit it, and fixed it by the other end horizontally in a split stick three feet high, stuck it in the ground, turning the blazing end to the wind, and telling me to snuff it from time to time. It answered the purpose of a candle pretty well.

I noticed, as I had done before, that there was a lull among the mosquitoes about midnight, and that they began again in the morning. Nature is thus merciful. But apparently they need rest as well as we. Few if any creatures are equally active all night. As soon as it was light I saw, through my veil, that the inside of the tent about our heads was quite blackened with myriads, each one of their wings when flying, as has been calculated, vibrating some three thousand times in a minute, and their combined hum was almost as bad to endure as their stings. I had an uncomfortable night on this account, though I am not sure that one succeeded in his attempt to sting me. We did not suffer so much from insects on this excursion as the statements of some who have explored these woods in midsummer led us to anticipate. Yet I have no doubt that at some seasons and in some places they are a much more serious pest. The Jesuit Hierome Lalemant, of Quebec, reporting the death of Father Reni Menard, who was abandoned, lost his way, and died in the woods, among the Ontarios near Lake Superior, in 1661, dwells chiefly on his probable sufferings from the attacks of mosquitoes when too weak to defend himself, adding that there was a frightful number of them in those parts, "and so insupportable," says he, "that the three Frenchmen who have made that voyage affirm that there was no other means of defending one's self but to run always without stopping, and it was even necessary for two of them to be employed in driving off these creatures while the third wanted to drink, otherwise he could not have done it." I have no doubt that this was said in good faith.

August 1.

I caught two or three large red chivin (*Leuciscus pulchellus*) early this morning, within twenty feet of the camp, which, added to the moose-tongue, that had been left in the kettle boiling over night, and to our other stores, made a sumptuous breakfast. The Indian made us some hemlock tea instead of coffee, and we were not obliged to go as far as China for it; indeed, not quite so far as for the fish. This was tolerable, though he said it was not strong enough. It was interesting to see so simple a dish as a kettle of water with a handful of green hemlock sprigs in it, boiling over the huge fire in the open air, the leaves fast losing their lively green color, and know that it was for our breakfast.

We were glad to embark once more, and leave some of the mosquitoes behind. We had passed the *Wassataquoik* without perceiving it. This, according to the Indian, is the name of the main East Branch itself, and not properly applied to this small tributary alone, as on the maps.

We found that we had camped about a mile above Hunt's, which is on the east bank, and is the last house for those who ascend Ktaadn on this side.

We also had expected to ascend it from this point, but omitted it on account of the chafed feet of one of my companions. The Indian, however, suggested that perhaps he might get a pair of moccasins at this place, and that he could walk very easily in them without hurting his feet, wearing several pairs of stockings, and he said beside that they were so porous that when you had taken in water it all drained out again in a little while. We stopped to get some sugar, but found that the family had moved away, and the house was unoccupied, except temporarily by some men who were getting the hay. They told me that the road to Ktaadn left the river eight miles above; also that perhaps we could get some sugar at Fisk's, fourteen miles below. I do not remember that we saw the mountain at all from the river. I noticed a seine here stretched on the bank, which probably had been used to catch salmon. Just below this, on the west bank, we saw a moose-hide stretched, and with it a bear-skin, which was comparatively very small. I was the more interested in this sight, because it was near here that a townsman of ours, then quite a lad, and alone, killed a large bear some years ago. The Indian said that they belonged to Joe Aitteon, my last guide, but how he told I do not know. He was probably hunting near, and had left them for the day. Finding that we were going directly to Oldtown, he regretted that he had not taken more of the moose-meat to his family, saying that in a short time, by drying it, he could have made it so light as to have brought away the greater part, leaving the bones. We once or twice inquired after the lip, which is a famous tit-bit, but he said, "That go Oldtown for my old woman; don't get it every day."

Maples grew more and more numerous. It was lowering, and rained a little during the forenoon, and, as we expected a wetting, we stopped early and dined on the east side of a small expansion of the river, just above what are probably called Whetstone Falls, about a dozen miles below Hunt's. There were pretty fresh moose-tracks by the water-side. There were singular long ridges hereabouts, called "horse-backs," covered with ferns. My companion having lost his pipe asked the Indian if he could not make him one. "O yer," said he, and in a minute rolled up one of birch-bark, telling him to wet the bowl from time to time. Here also he left his gazette on a tree.

We carried round the falls just below, on the west side. The rocks were on their edges, and very sharp. The distance was about three fourths of a mile. When we had carried over one load, the Indian returned by the shore, and I by the path; and though I made no particular haste, I was nevertheless surprised to find him at the other end as soon as I. It was remarkable how easily he got along over the worst ground. He said to me, "I take canoe and you take the rest, suppose you can keep along with me?" I thought that he meant, that while he ran down the rapids I should keep along the shore, and be ready to assist him from time to time, as I had done before; but as the walking would be very bad,

I answered, "I suppose you will go too fast for me, but I will try." But I was to go by the path, he said. This I thought would not help the matter, I should have so far to go to get to the river-side when he wanted me. But neither was this what he meant. He was proposing a race over the carry, and asked me if I thought I could keep along with him by the same path, adding that I must be pretty smart to do it. As his load, the canoe, would be much the heaviest and bulkiest, though the simplest, I thought that I ought to be able to do it, and said that I would try. So I proceeded to gather up the gun, axe, paddle, kettle, frying-pan, plates, dippers, carpets, etc., etc., and while I was thus engaged he threw me his cow-hide boots. "What, are these in the bargain?" I asked. "O yer," said he; but before I could make a bundle of my load I saw him disappearing over a hill with the canoe on his head; so, hastily scraping the various articles together, I started on the run, and immediately went by him in the bushes, but I had no sooner left him out of sight in a rocky hollow, than the greasy plates, dippers, etc., took to themselves wings, and while I was employed in gathering them up again, he went by me; but hastily pressing the sooty kettle to my side, I started once more, and soon passing him again, I saw him no more on the carry. I do not mention this as anything of a feat, for it was but poor running on my part, and he was obliged to move with great caution for fear of breaking his canoe as well as his neck. When he made his appearance, puffing and panting like myself, in answer to my inquiries where he had been, he said, "Rocks (locks) cut 'em feet," and laughing added, "O, me love to play sometimes." He said that he and his companions when they came to carries several miles long used to try who would get over first; each perhaps with a canoe on his head. I bore the sign of the kettle on my brown linen sack for the rest of the voyage.

We made a second carry on the west side, around some falls about a mile below this. It rained hard in the night and spoiled another box of matches for us, which the Indian had left out, for he was very careless; but, as usual, we had so much the better night for the rain, since it kept the mosquitoes down.

SUNDAY, August 2, —

Was a cloudy and unpromising morning. One of us observed to the Indian, "You did not stretch your moose-hide last night, did you, Mr. Polis?" Whereat he replied, in a tone of surprise, though perhaps not of ill humor: "What you ask me that question for? Suppose I stretch 'em, you see 'em. May be your way talking, may be all right, no Indian way." I had observed that he did not wish to answer the same question more than once, and was often silent when it was put again for the sake of certainty, as if he were moody. Not that he was incommunicative, for he frequently commenced a long-winded narrative of his own accord, — repeated at length the tradition of some old battle, or some passage in the recent history of his tribe in which he had acted a prominent part, from time to time drawing a long breath, and resuming the thread of his tale, with the true story-teller's leisureliness, perhaps after shooting a rapid, — prefacing with "we-ll-by-by," etc., as he paddled along. Especially after the day's work was over, and he had put himself in posture for the night, he would be unexpectedly sociable, exhibit even the *bonhommie* of a Frenchman, and we would fall asleep before he got through his periods.

Nickertow is called eleven miles from Mattawamkeag by the river. Our camp was, therefore, about nine miles from the latter place.

The Indian was quite sick this morning with the colic. I thought that he was the worse for the moose-meat he had eaten.

We reached the Mattawamkeag at half past eight in the morning, in the midst of a drizzling rain, and after buying some sugar set out again.

The Indian growing much worse, we stopped in the north part of Lincoln to get some brandy

for him, but failing in this, an apothecary recommended Brandreth's pills, which he refused to
take, because he was not acquainted with them.
He said to me, "Me doctor — first study my
case, find out what ail 'em — then I know what
to take." We dropped down a little farther,
and stopped at mid-forenoon on an island and
made him a dipper of tea. Here too we dined
and did some washing and botanizing, while he
lay on the bank. In the afternoon we went on
a little farther, though the Indian was no better.
"*Burntibus*," as he called it, was a long smooth
lake-like reach below the Five Islands. He said
that he owned a hundred acres somewhere up
this way. As a thunder shower appeared to be
coming up, we stopped opposite a barn on the
west bank, in Chester, about a mile above
Lincoln. Here at last we were obliged to spend
the rest of the day and night, on account of our
patient, whose sickness did not abate. He lay
groaning under his canoe on the bank, looking
very woe-begone, yet it was only a common case
of colic. You would not have thought, if you
had seen him lying about thus, that he was the
proprietor of so many acres in that neighborhood, was worth $6,000, and had been to Wash-
ington. It seemed to me that, like the Irish, he
made a greater ado about his sickness than a
Yankee does, and was more alarmed about himself. We talked somewhat of leaving him with

his people in Lincoln, — for that is one of their homes, — and taking the stage the next day, but he objected on account of the expense, saying, "Suppose me well in morning, you and I go Oldtown by noon."

As we were taking our tea at twilight, while he lay groaning still under his canoe, having at length found out "what ail him," he asked me to get him a dipper of water. Taking the dipper in one hand, he seized his powder-horn with the other, and pouring into it a charge or two of powder, stirred it up with his finger, and drank it off. This was all he took to-day after breakfast beside his tea.

To save the trouble of pitching our tent, when we had secured our stores from wandering dogs, we camped in the solitary half-open barn near the bank, with the permission of the owner, lying on new-mown hay four feet deep. The fragrance of the hay, in which many ferns, etc., were mingled, was agreeable, though it was quite alive with grasshoppers which you could hear crawling through it. This served to graduate our approach to houses and feather-beds. In the night some large bird, probably an owl, flitted through over our heads, and very early in the morning we were awakened by the twittering of swallows which had their nests there.

We started early before breakfast, the Indian being considerably better, and soon glided by Lincoln, and after another long and handsome lake-like reach, we stopped to breakfast on the west shore, two or three miles below this town.

We frequently passed Indian Islands with their small houses on them. The Governor, Aitteon, lives in one of them, in Lincoln.

The Penobscot Indians seem to be more social, even, than the whites. Ever and anon in the deepest wilderness of Maine you come to the log-hut of a Yankee or Canada settler, but a Penobscot never takes up his residence in such a solitude. They are not even scattered about on their islands in the Penobscot, which are all within the settlements, but gathered together on two or three, — though not always on the best soil, — evidently for the sake of society. I saw one or two houses not now used by them, because, as our Indian Polis said, they were too solitary.

The small river emptying in at Lincoln is the Matanancook, which also, we noticed, was the name of a steamer moored there. So we paddled and floated along, looking into the mouths of rivers. When passing the Mohawk Rips, or, as the Indian called them, "Mohog lips," four or five miles below Lincoln, he told us at length the Indian said that there was an island opposite its mouth which was called *Olarmon*. That in old times, when visitors were coming to Old-town, they used to stop there to dress and fix up or paint themselves. "What is that which ladies used?" he asked. Rouge? Red vermilion? "Yer," he said, "that is *larmon*, a kind of clay or red paint, which they used to get here."

We decided that we too would stop at this island, and fix up our inner man, at least, by dining.

It was a large island with an abundance of hemp-nettle, but I did not notice any kind of red paint there. The Olarmon River, at its mouth at least, is a dead stream. There was an-other large island in that neighborhood, which the Indian called "*Soogle*" (i. e. Sugar) Island.

About a dozen miles before reaching Oldtown he inquired, "How you like 'em your pilot?" But we postponed an answer till we had got quite back again.

The *Sunkhaze*, another short dead stream, comes in from the east two miles above Old-town. There is said to be some of the best deer ground in Maine on this stream. Asking the meaning of this name, the Indian said, "Sup-pose you are going down Penobscot, just like we, and you see a canoe come out of bank and go along before you, but you no see 'em stream. That is *Sunkhaze*."

the story of a fight between his tribe and the Mohawks there, anciently, — how the latter were overcome by stratagem, the Penobscots using concealed knives, — but they could not for a long time kill the Mohawk chief, who was a very large and strong man, though he was attacked by several canoes at once, when swim-ming alone in the river.

From time to time we met Indians in their canoes, going up river. Our man did not com-monly approach them, but exchanged a few words with them at a distance in his tongue. These were the first Indians we had met since leaving the *Umbazookskus*.

At Piscataquis Falls, just above the river of that name, we walked over the wooden railroad on the eastern shore, about one and a half miles long, while the Indian glided down the rapids. The steamer from Oldtown stops here, and pas-sengers take a new boat above. Piscataquis, whose mouth we here passed, means "branch." It is obstructed by falls at its mouth, but can be navigated with batteaux or canoes above through a settled country even to the neighborhood of Moosehead Lake, and we had thought at first of going that way. We were not obliged to get out of the canoe after this on account of falls or rapids, nor, indeed, was it quite necessary here. We took less notice of the scenery to-day, because we were in quite a settled country. The river became broad and sluggish, and we saw a blue heron winging its way slowly down the stream before us.

We passed the Passadumkeag River on our left and saw the blue *Olamon* mountains at a distance in the southeast. Hereabouts our Indian told us at length the story of their contention with the priest respecting schools. He thought a great deal of education and had recommended it to his tribe. His argument in its favor was, that if you had been to college and learnt to calculate, you could "keep 'em property, — no other way." He said that his boy was the best scholar in the school at Oldtown, to which he went with whites. He himself is a Protestant, and goes to church regularly in Oldtown. According to his account, a good many of his tribe are Protestants, and many of the Catholics also are in favor of schools. Some years ago they had a schoolmaster, a Protestant, whom they liked very well. The priest came and said that they must send him away, and finally he had such influence, telling them that they would go to the bad place at last if they retained him, that they sent him away. The school party, though numerous, were about giving up. Bishop Fenwick came from Boston and used his influence against them. But our Indian told his side that they must not give up, must hold on, they were the strongest. If they

gave up, then they would have no party. But they answered that it was "no use, priest too strong, we'd better give up." At length he persuaded them to make a stand.

The priest was going for a sign to cut down the liberty-pole. So Polis and his party had a secret meeting about it; he got ready fifteen or twenty stout young men, "stript 'em naked, and painted 'em like old times," and told them that when the priest and his party went to cut down the liberty-pole, they were to rush up, take hold of it and prevent them, and he assured them that there would be no war, only a noise, "no war where priest is." He kept his men concealed in a house near by, and when the priest's party were about to cut down the liberty-pole, the fall of which would have been a death-blow to the school party, he gave a signal, and his young men rushed out and seized the pole. There was a great uproar, and they were about coming to blows, but the priest interfered, saying, "No war, no war," and so the pole stands, and the school goes on still.

We thought that it showed a good deal of tact in him, to seize this occasion and take a stand on it; proving how well he understood those with whom he had to deal.

The Olamon River comes in from the east in Greenbush a few miles below the Passadumkeag. When we asked the meaning of this name

He had previously complimented me on my paddling, saying that I paddled "just like anybody," giving me an Indian name which meant "great paddler." When off this stream he said to me, who sat in the bows, "Me teach you paddle." So turning toward the shore he got out, came forward and placed my hands as he wished. He placed one of them quite outside the boat, and the other parallel with the first, grasping the paddle near the end, not over the flat extremity, and sold me to slide it back and forth on the side of the canoe. This, I found, was a great improvement which I had not thought of, saving me the labor of lifting the paddle each time, and I wondered that he had not suggested it before. It is true, before our baggage was reduced we had been obliged to sit with our legs drawn up, and our knees above the side of the canoe, which would have prevented our paddling thus, or perhaps he was afraid of wearing out his canoe, by constant friction on the side.

I told him that I had been accustomed to sit in the stern, and lifting my paddle at each stroke, getting a pry on the side each time, and I still paddled partly as if in the stern. He then wanted to see me paddle in the stern. So, changing paddles, for he had the longer and better one, and turning end for end, he sitting flat on the bottom and I on the crossbar, he began to paddle very hard, trying to turn the canoe, looking over his shoulder and laughing, but finding it in vain he relaxed his efforts, though we still sped along a mile or two very swiftly. He said that he had no fault to find with my paddling in the stern, but I complained that he did not paddle according to his own directions in the bows.

Opposite the Sunkhaze is the main boom of the Penobscot, where the logs from far up the river are collected and assorted.

As we drew near to Oldtown I asked Polis if he was not glad to get home again; but there was no relenting to his wildness, and he said, "It makes no difference to me where I am." Such is the Indian's pretence always.

We approached the Indian Island through the narrow strait called "Cook." He said, "I 'xpect we take in some water there, river so high, — never see it so high at this season. Very rough water there, but short; swamp steamboat once. Don't you paddle till I tell you, then you paddle right along." It was a very short rapid. When we were in the midst of it he shouted "paddle," and we shot through without taking in a drop.

Soon after the Indian houses came in sight, but I could not at first tell my companion which of two or three large white ones was our guide's. He said it was the one with blinds.

We landed opposite his door at about four in

the afternoon, having come some forty miles this day. From the Piscataquis we had come remarkably and unaccountably quick, probably as fast as the stage or the boat, though the last dozen miles was dead water.

Polis wanted to sell us his canoe, said it would last seven or eight years, or, with care, perhaps ten; but we were not ready to buy it.

We stopped for an hour at his house, where my companion shaved with his razor, which he pronounced in very good condition. Mrs. P. wore a hat and had a silver brooch on her breast, but she was not introduced to us. The house was roomy and neat. A large new map of Old-town and the Indian Island hung on the wall, and a clock opposite to it. Wishing to know when the cars left Oldtown, Polis's son brought one of the last Bangor papers, which I saw was directed to "Joseph Polis," from the office.

This was the last that I saw of Joe Polis. We took the last train, and reached Bangor that night.

APPENDIX

APPENDIX

I. TREES

THE prevailing trees (I speak only of what I saw) on the east and west branches of the Penobscot and on the upper part of the Allegash were the fir, spruce (both black and white), and arbor-vitæ, or "cedar." The fir has the darkest foliage, and, together with the spruce, makes a very dense "black growth," especially on the upper parts of the rivers. A dealer in lumber with whom I talked called the former a weed, and it is commonly regarded as fit neither for timber nor fuel. But it is more sought after as an ornamental tree than any other evergreen of these woods except the arbor-vitæ. The black spruce is much more common than the white. Both are tall and slender trees. The arbor-vitæ, which is of a more cheerful hue, with its light-green fans, is also tall and slender, though sometimes two feet in diameter. It often fills the swamps.

Mingled with the former, and also here and there forming extensive and more open woods by themselves, indicating, it is said, a better soil, were canoe and yellow birches (the former was always at hand for kindling a fire, — we saw no small white-birches in that wilderness), and sugar and red maples.

The Aspen (*Populus tremuloides*) was very common on burnt grounds. We saw many straggling white pines, commonly unsound trees, which had therefore been skipped by the choppers; these were the largest trees we saw; and we occasionally passed a small wood in which this was the prevailing tree; but I did not notice nearly so many of these trees as I can see in a single walk in Concord. The speckled or hoary alder (*Alnus incana*) abounds everywhere along the muddy banks of rivers and lakes, and in swamps. Hemlock could commonly be found for tea, but was nowhere abundant. Yet F. A. Michaux states that in Maine, Vermont, and the upper part of New Hampshire, etc., the hemlock forms three fourths of the evergreen woods, the rest being black spruce. It belongs to cold hillsides.

The elm and black ash were very common along the lower and stiller parts of the streams, where the shores were flat and grassy or there were low gravelly islands. They made a pleasing variety in the scenery, and we felt as if nearer home while gliding past them.

The above fourteen trees made the bulk of the woods which we saw.

The larch (Juniper), beech, and Norway pine (*Pinus resinosa*, red pine) were only occasionally seen in particular places. The *Pinus Banksiana* (gray or Northern scrub-pine), and a single small red oak (*Quercus rubra*) only, are on islands in Grand Lake, on the East Branch.

The above are almost all peculiarly Northern trees, and found chiefly, if not solely, on mountains southward.

II.   FLOWERS AND SHRUBS

It appears that in a forest like this the great majority of flowers, shrubs, and grasses are confined to the banks of the rivers and lakes, and to the meadows, more open swamps, burnt lands, and mountain-tops; comparatively very few indeed penetrate the woods. There is no such dispersion even of wild-flowers as is commonly supposed, or as exists in a cleared and settled country. Most of our wild-flowers, so called may be considered as naturalized in the localities where they grow. Rivers and lakes are the great protectors of such plants against the aggressions of the forest, by their annual rise and fall keeping open a narrow strip where these more delicate plants have light and space in which to grow. They are the *protegés* of the rivers. These narrow and straggling bands and isolated groups are, in a sense, the pioneers of civilization. Birds, quadrupeds, insects, and man also, in the main, follow the flowers, and the latter in his turn makes more room for them and for berry-bearing shrubs, birds, and small quadrupeds. One settler told me that not only black-berries and raspberries, but mountain-maples came in, in the clearing and burning.

Though plants are often referred to primitive woods as their locality, it cannot be true of very many, unless the woods are supposed to include such localities as I have mentioned. Only those which require but little light, and can bear the drip of the trees, penetrate the woods, and these have commonly more beauty in their leaves than in their pale and almost colorless blossoms.

The prevailing flowers and conspicuous small plants of the *woods*, which I noticed, were: *Clintonia borealis*, *Linnæa*, checkerberry (*Gaultheria procumbens*), *Aralia nudicaulis* (wild sarsaparilla), great round-leaved orchis, *Dalibarda repens*, *Chiogenes hispidula* (creeping snow-berry), *Oxalis acetosella* (common wood-sorrel), *Aster acuminatus*, *Pyrola secunda* (one-sided pyrola), *Medeola Virginica* (Indian cucumber-root), small *Circæa* (enchanter's nightshade), and perhaps *Cornus Canadensis* (dwarfed cornel).

Of these, the last of July, 1858, only the *Aster acuminatus* and great round-leaved *orchis* were conspicuously in bloom.

The most common flowers of the *river* and *lake shores* were: *Thalictrum cornuti* (meadow-rue), *Hypericum ellipticum, mutilum* and *Canadense* (St. John's-wort), horsemint, horehound, *Lycopus Virginicus* and *Europæus,* var. *sinuatus* (bugle-weed), *Scutellaria galericulata* (skull-cap), *Solidago lanceolata* and *squarrosa*, East Branch (golden-rod), *Diplopappus umbellatus* (double-bristled aster), *Aster radula, Cicuta maculata* and *bulbifera* (water-hemlock), meadow-sweet, *Lysimachia stricta* and *ciliata* (loose-strife), *Galium trifidum* (small bed-straw), *Lilium Canadense* (wild yellow-lily), *Platanthera peramœna* and *psycodes* (great purple orchis and small purple-fringed orchis), *Mimulus ringens* (monkey-flower), dock (water), blue flag, *Hydrocotyle Americana* (marsh pennywort), *Sanicula Canadensis?* (black snake-root), *Clematis Virginiana?* (common virgin's-bower), *Nasturtium palustre* (marsh cress), *Ranunculus recurvatus* (hooked crowfoot), *Asclepias incarnata* (swamp milkweed), *Aster Tradescanti* (Tradescant's aster), *Aster miser*, also *longifolius, Eupatorium purpureum* apparently, lake shores (Joe-Pye-weed), *Apocynum Cannabinum* East Branch (Indian hemp), *Polygonum cilinode* (bind-weed), and others. Not to mention among inferior orders wool-grass and the sensitive fern.

In the water, *Nuphar advena* (yellow pond-lily) some *potamogetons* (pond-weed), *Sagittaria variabilis* (arrow-head), *Sium lineare?* (water-parsnip).

Of these, those conspicuously in flower the last of July,

1857, were: rue, *Solidago lanceolata* and *squarrosa, Diplopappus umbellatus, Aster radula, Lilium Canadense,* great and small purple orchis, *Mimulus ringens,* blue flag, virgin's-bower, etc.

The characteristic flowers in *swamps* were: *Rubus triflorus* (dwarf raspberry), *Calla palustris* (water-arum), and *Sarracenia purpurea* (pitcher-plant). On *burnt grounds: Epilobium angustifolium,* in full bloom (great willow-herb), and *Erechthites hieracifolia* (fire-weed). On *cliffs: Campanula rotundifolia* (harebell), *Cornus Canadensis* (dwarf cornel), *Arctostaphylos uva-ursi* (bearberry), *Potentilla tridentata* (mountain cinquefoil), *Pteris aquilina* (common brake). At *old camps, carries, and loggingpaths: Cirsium arvense* (Canada thistle), *Prunella vulgaris* (common self-heal), clover, herd's-grass, *Achillea millefolium* (common yarrow), *Leucanthemum vulgare* (white-weed), *Aster macrophyllus, Halenia deflexa,* East Branch (spurred gentian), *Antennaria margaritacea* (pearly everlasting), *Actæa rubra* and *alba,* wet carries (red and white cohosh), *Desmodium Canadense* (tick-trefoil), sorrel.

The handsomest and most interesting flowers were the great purple orchises, rising ever and anon, with their great purple spikes perfectly erect, amid the shrubs and grasses of the shore. It seemed strange that they should be made to grow there in such profusion, seen of moose and moose-hunters only, while they are so rare in Concord. I have never seen this species flowering nearly so late with us, or with the small one.

The prevailing underwoods were: *Dirca palustris* (moose-wood), *Acer spicatum* (mountain maple), *Viburnum lantanoides* (hobble-bush), and frequently *Taxus baccata,* var. *Canadensis* (American yew).

The prevailing shrubs and small trees along the shore were: *osier rouge* and alders (before mentioned); sallows, or small willows, of two or three kinds, as *Salix humilis*, *rostrata*, and *discolor?*, *Sambucus Canadensis* (black elder), rose, *Viburnum opulus* and *nudum* (cranberry-tree and withe-rod), *Pyrus Americana* (American mountain-ash), *Corylus rostrata* (beaked hazel-nut), *Diervilla trifida* (bush-honeysuckle), *Prunus Virginiana* (choke-cherry), *Myrica gale* (sweet-gale), *Nemopanthes Canadensis* (mountain holly), *Cephalanthus occidentalis* (button-bush), *Ribes prostratum*, in some places (fetid currant).

More particularly of shrubs and small trees in *swamps:* some willows, *Kalmia glauca* (pale laurel), *Ledum latifolium* and *palustre* (Labrador tea), *Ribes lacustre* (swamp gooseberry), and in one place *Betula pumila* (low birch). At *camps and carries:* raspberry, *Vaccinium Canadense* (Canada blueberry), *Prunus Pennsylvanica* also along shore (wild red cherry), *Amelanchier Canadensis* (shad-bush), *Sambucus pubens* (red-berried elder). Among those peculiar to the *mountains* would be the *Vaccinium vitis idæa* (cow-berry).

Of plants commonly regarded as *introduced* from Europe, I observed at Ansel Smith's clearing, Chesuncook, abundant in 1857; *Ranunculis acris* (buttercups), *Plantago major* (common plantain), *Chenopodium album* (lamb's-quarters), *Capsella bursa-pastoris*, 1853 (shepherd's-purse), *Spergula arvensis*, also, north shore of Moosehead, in 1853, and elsewhere, 1857 (corn-spurrey), *Taraxacum dens-leonis* — regarded as indigenous by Gray, but evidently introduced there — (common dandelion), *Polygonum Persicaria* and *hydropiper*, by a logging-path in woods at Smith's (lady's thumb and smart-weed), *Rumex acetosella*, common at carries (sheep-sorrel), *Trifolium pratense*, 1853, and carries frequent (red clover), *Leucanthemum vulgare*, carries (white weed), *Phleum pratense*, carries, 1853–7 (herd's-grass), *Verbena hastata* (blue vervain), *Cirsium arvense*, abundant at camps, 1857 (Canada thistle), *Rumex crispus?*, West Branch, 1853? (curled dock), *Verbascum thapsus*, between Bangor and lake, 1853 (common mullein).

It appears that I saw about a dozen plants which had accompanied man as far into the woods as Chesuncook, and had naturalized themselves there, in 1853. Plants begin thus early to spring by the side of a logging-path, — a mere vista through the woods, which can only be used in the winter, on account of the stumps and fallen trees, — which at length are the roadside plants in old settlements. The pioneers of such are planted in part by the first cattle, which cannot be summered in the woods.

III. LIST OF PLANTS

THE following is a list of the plants which I noticed in the Maine woods, in the years of 1853 and 1857. (Those marked * not in woods.)

1. THOSE WHICH ATTAINED THE HEIGHT OF TREES

Alnus incana (speckled or hoary alder), abundant along streams, etc.

Thuja occidentalis (American arbor-vitæ), one of the prevailing.

Fraxinus sambucifolia (black ash), very common, especially near dead water. The Indian spoke of "yellow ash" as also found there.

Populus tremuloides (American aspen), very common, especially on burnt lands, almost as white as birches.

Populus grandidentata (large toothed aspen), perhaps two or three.

Fagus ferruginea (American beech), not uncommon, at least on the West Branch (saw more in 1846).

Betula papyracea (canoe birch), prevailing everywhere and about Bangor.

Betula excelsa (yellow birch), very common.

Betula lenta (black birch), on the West Branch in 1853.

Betula alba (American white birch), about Bangor only.

Ulmus Americana (American or white elm), West Branch and low down the East Branch, i. e. on the lower and alluvial part of the river, very common.

Larix Americana (American or black larch), very common on the Umbazookskus, some elsewhere.

Abies Canadensis (hemlock-spruce), not abundant, some on the West Branch, and a little everywhere.

Acer saccharinum (sugar maple), very common.

Acer rubrum (red or swamp maple), very common.

Acer dasycarpum (white or silver maple), a little low on East Branch and in Chesuncook woods.

Quercus rubra (red oak), one on an island in Grand Lake, East Branch, and, according to a settler, a few on the east side of Chesuncook Lake; a few also about Bangor in 1853.

Pinus strobus (white pine), scattered along, most abundant at Heron Lake.

Pinus resinosa (red pine), Telos and Grand Lake, a little afterwards here and there.

Abies balsamea (balsam fir), perhaps the most common tree, especially in the upper parts of rivers.

Abies nigra (black or double spruce), next to the last the most common, if not equally common, and on mountains.

Abies alba (white or single spruce), common with the last along the rivers.

Pinus Banksiana (gray or Northern scrub-pine), a few on an island in Grand Lake.

Twenty-three in all (23).

2. SMALL TREES AND SHRUBS

Prunus depressa (dwarf-cherry), on gravel bars, East Branch, near Hunt's, with green fruit, obviously distinct from the *pumila* of river and meadows.

Vaccinium corymbosum (common swamp blueberry), Bucksport.

Vaccinium Canadense (Canada blueberry), carries and rocky hills everywhere as far south as Bucksport.

Vaccinium Pennsylvanicum (dwarf-blueberry?), Whetstone Falls.

Betula pumila (low birch), Mud Pond Swamp.

Prinos verticillata (black alder, '57), now placed with *Ilex* by Gray, 2d ed.

Cephalanthus occidentalis (button bush).

Prunus Pennsylvanica (wild red cherry), very common at camps, carries, etc., along rivers; fruit ripe August 1, 1857.

Prunus Virginiana (choke-cherry), river-side, common.

Cornus alternifolia (alternate-leaved cornel), West Branch, 1853.

Ribes prostratum (fetid currant), common along streams, on Webster Stream.

Sambucus Canadensis (common elder), common along river-sides.

Sambucus pubens (red-berried elder), not quite so common, road-sides toward Moosehead, and on carries afterward, fruit beautiful.

Ribes lacustre (swamp-gooseberry), swamps, common, Mud Pond Swamp and Webster Stream; not ripe July 29, 1857.

Corylus rostrata (beaked hazel-nut), common.

Taxus baccata, var. *Canadensis* (American yew), a common under-shrub at an island in West Branch and Chesuncook woods.

Viburnum lantanoides (hobble-bush), common, especially in Chesuncook woods; fruit ripe in September, 1853, not in July, 1857.

Viburnum opulus (cranberry-tree), on West Branch; one in flower still, July 25, 1857.

Viburnum nudum (withe-rod), common along rivers.

Kalmia glauca (pale laurel), swamps, common, as at Moosehead carry and Chamberlain swamp.

Kalmia angustifolia (lamb-kill), with *Kalmia glauca.*

Acer spicatum (mountain maple), a prevailing underwood.

Acer striatum (striped maple), in fruit July 30, 1857; green the first year; green, striped with white, the second; darker, the third, with dark blotches.

Cornus stolonifera (red-osier dogwood), prevailing shrub on shore of West Branch; fruit still white in August, 1857.

Pyrus Americana (American mountain ash), common along shores.

Amelanchier Canadensis (shad-bush), rocky carries, etc.; considerable fruit in 1857.

Rubus strigosus (wild red raspberry), very abundant, burnt grounds, camps, and carries, but not ripe till we got to Chamberlain dam and on East Branch.

Rosa Carolina (swamp-rose), common on the shores of lakes, etc.

Rhus typhina* (stag-horn sumac).

Myrica gale (sweet-gale), common.

Nemopanthes Canadensis (mountain holly), common in low ground, Moosehead carry, and on Mount Kineo.

Cratægus (*coccinea?* scarlet-fruited thorn), not uncommon; with hard fruit in September, 1853.

Salix (near to *petiolaris*, petioled willow), very common in Umbazookskus meadows.

Salix rostrata (long-beaked willow), common.

Salix humilis (low bush-willow), common.

Salix discolor (glaucous willow ?).

Salix lucida (shining willow), at island in Heron Lake.

Dirca palustris (moose-wood), common.

In all, 38.

3. SMALL SHRUBS AND HERBACEOUS PLANTS

Agrimonia Eupatoria (common agrimony), not uncommon.

Circæa Alpina (enchanter's nightshade), very common in woods.

Nasturtium palustre (marsh cress), var. *hispidum*, common as at A. Smith's.

Aralia hispida (bristly sarsaparilla), on West Branch, both years.

Aralia nudicaulis (wild sarsaparilla), Chesuncook woods.

Sagittaria variabilis (arrow-head), common at Moosehead and afterward.

Arum triphyllum (Indian turnip), now *arisæma*, Moosehead carry in 1853.

Asclepias incarnata (swamp milk-weed), Umbazookskus River and after, redder than ours, and a different variety from our var. *pulchra*.

Aster acuminatus (pointed-leaved aster), the prevailing aster in woods, not long open on South Branch July 31st; two or more feet high.

Aster macrophyllus (large-leaved aster), common, and the whole plant surprisingly fragrant, like a medicinal herb, just out at Telos Dam July 29, 1857, and after to Bangor and Bucksport; bluish flower (in woods on Pine Stream and at Chesuncook in 1853).

Aster radula (rough-leaved aster), common, Moosehead carry and after.

Aster miser (petty aster), in 1853 on West Branch and common on Chesuncook shore.

Aster longifolius (willow-leaved blue aster), 1853, Moosehead and Chesuncook shores.

Aster cordifolius (heart-leaved aster), 1853, West Branch.

Aster Tradescanti (Tradescant's aster), 1857. A narrow-leaved one Chesuncook shore, 1853.

Aster, *longifolius* like, with small flowers West Branch, 1853.

Aster puniceus (rough-stemmed aster), Pine Stream.

Diplopappus umbellatus (large *diplopappus* aster), common along river.

Arctostaphylos uva-ursi (bear-berry), Kineo, etc., 1857.

Polygonum cilinode (fringe-jointed false buckwheat), common.

Bidens cernua (bur-marigold), 1853, West Branch.

Ranunculus acris (buttercups), abundant at Smith's dam, Chesuncook, 1853.

Rubus triflorus (dwarf-raspberry), low grounds and swamps, common.

Utricularia vulgaris* (greater bladder-wort), Pushaw.

Iris versicolor (larger blue-flag), common Moosehead, West Branch, Umbazookskus, etc.

Sparganium (bur-reed).

Calla palustris (water-arum), in bloom July 27, 1857, Mud Pond Swamp.

Lobelia cardinalis (cardinal-flower), apparently common, but out of bloom August, 1857.

Cerastium nutans (clammy wild chickweed?).

Gaultheria procumbens (checkerberry), prevailing everywhere in woods along banks of rivers.

Stellaria media* (common chickweed), Bangor.

Chiogenes hispidula (creeping snowberry), very common in woods.

Cicuta maculata (water-hemlock).

Cicuta bulbifera (bulb-bearing water-hemlock), Penobscot and Chesuncook shore, 1853.

Galium trifidum (small bed-straw), common.

Galium Aparine (cleavers?), Chesuncook, 1853.

Galium, one kind on Pine Stream, 1853.

Trifolium pratense (red-clover), on carries, etc.

Actæa spicata, var. *alba* (white cohosh), Chesuncook woods 1853, and East Branch 1857.

Actæa var. *rubra* (red cohosh), East Branch 1857.

Vaccinium vitis-idæa (cow-berry), Ktaadn, very abundant.

Cornus Canadensis (dwarf-cornel), in woods Chesuncook 1853; just ripe at Kineo July 24, 1857, common; still in bloom, Moosehead carry September 16, 1853.

Medeola Virginica (Indian cucumber-root), West Branch and Chesuncook woods.

Dalibarda repens (Dalibarda), Moosehead carry and after, common. In flower still, August 1, 1857.

Taraxacum dens-leonis (common dandelion), Smith's 1853, only there. Is it not foreign?

Diervilla trifida (bush honeysuckle), very common.

Rumex hydrolapathum? (great water-dock), in 1857; noticed it was large seeded in 1853, common.

Rumex crispus? (curled-dock), West Branch 1853.

Apocynum cannabinum (Indian hemp), Kineo, *Bradford*, and East Branch 1857, at Whetstone Falls.

Apocynum androsœmifolium (spreading dogbane) Kineo, *Bradford*.

Clintonia borealis (Clintonia), all over woods; fruit just ripening July 25, 1857.

A lemna (duckweed), Pushaw 1857.

Elodea Virginica (marsh St. John's-wort), Moosehead 1853.

Epilobium angustifolium (great willow-herb), great fields on burnt lands; some white at Webster Stream.

Epilobium coloratum (purple-veined willow-herb), once in 1857.

Eupatorium purpureum (Joe-Pye-weed), Heron, Moosehead and Chesuncook lake-shores, common.

Allium (onion), a new kind to me in bloom, without bulbs above, on rocks near Whetstone Falls? East Branch.

Halenia deflexa (spurred gentian), carries on East Branch, common.

Geranium Robertianum (Herb Robert).

Solidago lanceolata (bushy golden-rod), very common.

Solidago, one of the three-ribbed, in both years.

Solidago thyrsoidea (large mountain golden-rod), one on Webster Stream.

Solidago squarrosa (large-spiked golden-rod), the most common on East Branch.

Solidago altissima (rough hairy golden-rod), not uncommon both years.

Coptis trifolia (three-leaved gold-thread).

Smilax herbacea (carrion-flower), not uncommon both years.

*Spiræa tomentosa** (hardhack), Bangor.

Campanula rotundifolia (harebell), cliffs Kineo, Grand Lake, etc.

Hieracium (hawk-weed), not uncommon.

Veratrum viride (American white hellebore).

Lycopus Virginicus (bugle-weed), 1857.

Lycopus Europæus (water-horehound), var. *sinuatus,* Heron Lake shore.

Chenopodium album (lamb's-quarters), Smith's.

Mentha Canadensis (wild mint), very common.

Galeopsis tetrahit (common hemp-nettle), Olarmon Isle, abundant, and below, in prime August 3, 1857.

Houstonia cærulea (bluets), now *Oldenlandia* (Gray, 2d ed.), 1857.

Hydrocotyle Americana (marsh pennywort), common.

Hypericum ellipticum (elliptical-leaved St. John's-wort), common.

Hypericum mutilum (small St. John's-wort), both years, common.

Hypericum Canadense (Canadian St. John's-wort), Moosehead Lake and Chesuncook shores, 1853.

Trientalis Americana (star-flower), Pine Stream, 1853.

Lobelia inflata (Indian tobacco).

Spiranthes cernuus (ladies' tresses), Kineo and after.

Nabalus (rattlesnake root), 1857; *altissimus* (tall white lettuce), Chesuncook woods, 1853.

Antennaria margaritacea (pearly everlasting), common, Moosehead, Smith's, etc.

Lilium Canadense (wild yellow lily), very common and large, West and East Branch; one on East Branch, 1857, with strongly revolute petals, and leaves perfectly smooth beneath, but not larger than the last, and apparently only a variety.

Linnæa borealis (Linnæa), almost everywhere in woods.

Lobelia Dortmanna (water-lobelia), pond in Bucksport.

Lysimachia ciliata (hairy-stalked loosestrife), very common, Chesuncook shore and East Branch.

Lysimachia stricta (upright loosestrife), very common.

Microstylis ophioglossoides (adder's-mouth), Kineo.

Spiræa salicifolia (common meadow-sweet), common.

Mimulus ringens (monkey-flower), common, lake-shores, etc.

Scutellaria galericulata (skullcap), very common.

Scutellaria lateriflora (mad-dog skullcap), Heron Lake, 1857, Chesuncook, 1853.

Platanthera psycodes (small purple-fringed orchis), very common, East Branch and Chesuncook, 1853.

Platanthera fimbriata (large purple-fringed orchis), very common, West Branch and Umbazookskus, 1857.

Platanthera orbiculata (large round-leaved orchis), very common in woods, Moosehead and Chamberlain carries, Caucomgomoc, etc.

Amphicarpæa monocea (hog peanut).

Aralia racemosa (spikenard), common, Moosehead carry, Telos Lake, etc., and after; out about August 1, 1857.

Plantago major (common plantain), common in open land at Smith's in 1853.

Pontederia cordata* (pickerel-weed), only near Oldtown, 1857.

Potamogeton (pond-weed), not common.

Potentilla tridentata (mountain cinquefoil), Kineo.

Potentilla Norvegica (cinquefoil), Heron Lake shore and Smith's.

Polygonum amphibium (water-persicaria), var. *aquaticum*, Second Lake.

Polygonum Persicaria (lady's-thumb), log-path, Chesuncook, 1853.

Nuphar advena (yellow pond-lily), not abundant.

Nymphœa odorata (sweet water-lily), a few in West Branch, 1853.

Polygonum hydropiper (smart-weed), log-path, Chesuncook.

Pyrola secunda (one-sided pyrola), very common, Caucomgomoc.

Pyrola elliptica (shin-leaf), Caucomgomac River.

Ranunculus Flammula (spearwort, var. *reptans*).

Ranunculus recurvatus (hooked crowfoot), Umbazookskus landing, etc.

Typha latifolia* (common cat-tail or reedmace), extremely abundant between Bangor and Portland.

Sanicula Marylandica (black snake-root), Moosehead carry and after.

Aralia nudicaulis (wild sarsaparilla).

Capsella bursa-pastoris (shepherd's-purse), Smith's, 1853.

Prunella vulgaris (self-heal), very common everywhere.

Erechthites hieracifolia (fireweed), 1857, and Smith's open land, 1853.

Sarracenia purpurea (pitcher-plant), Mud Pond swamp.

Smilacina bifolia (false Solomon's-seal), 1857, and Chesuncook woods, 1853.

Smilacina racemosa (false spikenard?), Umbazookskus carry (July 27, 1853).

Veronica scutellata (marsh speedwell).

Spergula arvensis (corn spurrey), 1857, not uncommon, 1853, Moosehead and Smith's.

Fragaria (strawberry), 1853 Smith's, 1857 Bucksport.

Thalictrum Cornuti (meadow-rue), very common, especially along rivers, tall, and conspicuously in bloom in July, 1857.

Cirsium arvense (Canada thistle), abundant at camps and highway sides in the north of Maine.

Cirsium muticum (swamp-thistle), well in bloom Webster Stream, August 31.

Rumex acetosella (sheep-sorrel), common by river and log-paths, as Chesuncook log-path.

Impatiens fulva (spotted touch-me-not).

Trillium erythrocarpum (painted trillium), common West Branch and Moosehead carry.

Verbena hastata (blue vervain).

Clematis Virginiana (common virgin's-bower), common on river banks, feathered in September, 1853, in bloom July, 1857.

Leucanthemum vulgare (white-weed).

Sium lineare (water-parsnip), 1857, and Chesuncook shore, 1853.

Achillea millefolium (common yarrow), by river and log-paths, and Smith's.

Desmodium Canadense (Canadian tick-trefoil), not uncommon.

Oxalis acetosella (common wood-sorrel), still out July 25, 1853, at Moosehead carry and after.

Oxalis stricta (yellow wood-sorrel), 1853, at Smith's and his wood-path.

Liparis liliifolia (tway-blade), Kineo, *Bradford*.

Uvularia grandiflora (large-flowered bellwort), woods common.

Uvularia sessilifolia (sessile-leaved bellwort), Chesun cook woods, 1853.

In all, 145.

4. OF LOWER ORDER.

Scirpus Eriophorum (wool-grass), very common, especially on low islands. A coarse grass, four or five feet high, along the river.

Phleum pratense (herd's-grass), on carries, at camps and clearings.

Equisetum sylvaticum (sylvatic horse-tail).

Pteris aquilina (brake), Kineo and after.

Onoclea sensibilis (sensitive-fern), very common along the river sides; some on the gravelly shore of Heron Lake Island.

Polypodium Dryopteris (brittle polypody).

Woodsia Ilvensis (rusty Woodsia), Kineo.

Lycopodium lucidulum (toothed club-moss).

Usnea (a parmeliaceous lichen), common on various trees.

IV. LIST OF BIRDS

A very small hawk at Great Falls, on Webster Stream.

Haliætus leucocephalus (white-headed or bald-eagle), at Ragmuff, and above and below Hunt's, and on pond below Mattawamkeag.

Pandion haliætus (fish-hawk or osprey), heard, also seen on East Branch.

Bubo Virginianus (cat-owl), near Camp Island, also above mouth of Schoonis, from a stump back and forth, also near Hunt's on a tree.

Icterus phœniceus (red-winged blackbird), Umbazook-skus River.

Corvus Americanus (American crow), a few, as at outlet of Grand Lake; a peculiar cawing.

Fringilla Canadensis (tree-sparrow), think I saw one on Mount Kineo July 24, which behaved as if it had a nest there.

Garrulus cristatus (blue-jay).

Parus atricapillus (chicadee), a few.

Muscicapa tyrannus (king-bird).

Muscicapa Cooperii (olive-sided fly-catcher), everywhere a prevailing bird.

Muscicapa virens (wood pewee), Moosehead, and I think beyond.

Muscicapa ruticila (American redstart), Moosehead.

Vireo olivaceus (red-eyed vireo), everywhere common.

Turdus migratorius (red-breasted robin), some everywhere.

Turdus melodus (wood-thrush), common in all the woods.

Turdus Wilsonii (Wilson's thrush), Moosehead and beyond.

Turdus aurocapillus (golden-crowned thrush or oven-bird), Moosehead.

Fringilla albicollis (white-throated sparrow), Kineo and after, apparently nesting; the prevailing bird early and late.

Fringilla melodia (song-sparrow), at Moosehead or beyond.

Sylvia pinus (pine warbler), one part of voyage.

Muscicapa acadica (small pewee), common.

Trichas Marylandica (Maryland yellow-throat), every-where.

Coccyzus Americanus? (yellow-billed cuckoo), common.

Picus erythrocephalus (red-headed woodpecker), heard and saw; and good to eat.

Sitta Carolinensis? (white-breasted American nuthatch), heard.

Alcedo alcyon (belted kingfisher), very common.

Caprimulgus Americanus (night-hawk).

Tetrao umbellus (partridge), Moosehead carry, etc.

Tetrao cupido? (pinnated grouse), Webster Stream.

Ardea cœrulea (blue heron), lower part of Penobscot.

Totanus macularius (spotted sandpiper or peetweet), everywhere.

Larus argentatus? (herring-gull), Heron Lake on rocks, and Chamberlain. Smaller gull on Second Lake.

Anas obscura (dusky or black duck), once in East Branch.

Anas sponsa (summer or wood duck), everywhere.

Fuligula albicola (spirit duck or dipper), common.

Colymbus glacialis (great Northern diver or loon), in all the lakes. A swallow; the night-warbler? once or twice.

Mergus Merganser (buff-breasted merganser or sheldrake), common on lakes and rivers.

V. QUADRUPEDS

A bat on West Branch; beaver skull at Grand Lake; Mr. Thatcher ate beaver with moose on the Caucomgomoc. A musk-rat on the last stream; the red squirrel is common in the depths of the woods; a dead porcupine on Chamberlain road; a cow moose and tracks of calf; skin of a bear, just killed.

VI. OUTFIT FOR AN EXCURSION

The following will be a good outfit for one who wishes to make an excursion of *twelve* days into the Maine woods in July, with a companion, and one Indian for the same purposes that I did.

Wear, — a check shirt, stout old shoes, thick socks, a neck ribbon, thick waistcoat, thick pants, old Kossuth hat, a linen sack.

Carry, — in an India-rubber knapsack, with a large flap, two shirts (check), one pair thick socks, one pair drawers, one flannel shirt, two pocket-handkerchiefs, a light India-rubber coat or a thick woollen one, two bosoms and collars to go and come with, one napkin, pins, needles, thread, one blanket, best gray, seven feet long.

Tent, — six by seven feet, and four feet high in middle, will do; veil and gloves and insect-wash, or, better, mosquito-bars to cover all at night; best pocket-map, and perhaps description of the route; compass; plant-book and red blotting-paper; paper and stamps, botany, small pocket spy-glass for birds, pocket microscope, tape-measure, insect-boxes.

Axe, full size if possible, jackknife, fish-lines, two only apiece, with a few hooks and corks ready, and with pork for bait in a packet, rigged; matches (some also in a small vial in the waistcoat pocket); soap, two pieces; large knife and iron spoon (for all); three or four old news-papers, much twine, and several rags for dishcloths; twenty feet of strong cord, four-quart tin pail for kettle, two tin dippers, three tin plates, a fry-pan.

Provisions. — Soft hardbread, twenty-eight pounds; pork, sixteen pounds; sugar, twelve pounds; one pound black tea or three pounds coffee, one box or a pint of salt, one quart Indian meal, to fry fish in; six lemons, good to correct the pork and warm water; perhaps two or three pounds of rice, for variety. You will probably get some berries, fish, etc., beside.

A gun is not worth the carriage, unless you go as hunters. The pork should be in an open keg, sawed to fit; the sugar, tea or coffee, meal, salt, etc., should be put in separate water-tight India-rubber bags, tied with a leather string; and all the provisions, and part of the rest of the baggage, put into two large India-rubber bags, which have been proved to be water-tight and durable. Expense of pre-ceding outfit is twenty-four dollars.

An Indian may be hired for about one dollar and fifty cents per day, and perhaps fifty cents a week for his canoe (this depends on the demand). The canoe should be a strong and tight one. This expense will be nineteen dollars.

Such an excursion need not cost more than twenty-five

dollars apiece, starting at the foot of Moosehead, if you already possess or can borrow a reasonable part of the outfit. If you take an Indian and canoe at Oldtown, it will cost seven or eight dollars more to transport them to the lake.

VII. A LIST OF INDIAN WORDS.

1. *Ktaadn*, said to mean *Highest Land*, Rale puts for *Mt. Pemadene;* for *Grai, pierre à aiguiser, Kitadaügan.* (v. Potter.)

Mattawamkeag, place where two rivers meet. (Indian of carry.) (v. Williamson's History of Maine, and Willis.)

Molunkus.

Ebeeme, rock.

Noliseemack; other name, Shad Pond.

Kecunnilessu, chicadee.

Nipsquecohossus, woodcock.

Skuscumonsuk, kingfisher. Has it not the pl. termination *uk* here, or *suk?* } Joe.

Wassus, bear, *aouessous.* Rale.

Lunxus, Indian-devil.

Upahsis, mountain-ash.

Moose, (is it called, or does it mean, wood-eater? *mous*, Rale.

Katahdinauguoh, said to mean mountains about Ktaadn

Ebemena, tree-cranberry. *Ibibimin, nar,* red, bad fruit. Rale. } Joe.

Wighiggin, a bill or writing, *aouixigan,* "*Livre, lettre, peinture, ceinture.*" Rale. } Indian of carry.

Sebamook, Large-bay Lake, *Peqouasebem;* add *ar* for plural, *lac* or *étang.* Rale. *Ouaüri-naügamek, anse dans un lac.* Rale. *Mspame*, large water. Polis. } Nicholai.

Sebago and *Sebec*, large open water.

Chesuncook, place where many streams empty in. (v. Willis and Potter.) } Tahmunt, etc.

Caucomgomoc, Gull Lake. (*Caucomgomoc*, the lake; *caucomgomoc-took*, the river, Polis.)

Pammadumcook.

Kenduskieg, Little Eel River. (v. Willis.) Nicholai.

Penobscot, Rocky River. *Puapeskou*, stone. (Rale v. Springer). } Indian of carry.

Umbazookskus, meadow stream. (Much-meadow river, Polis.)

Millinocket, place of Islands.

Souneunk, that runs between Mountains.

Aboljacarmegus, Smooth-ledge Falls and Dead-water. } Nicholai.

Aboljacarmeguscook, the river there.

Muskiticook, Dead Stream. (Indian of carry.) *Meski-kou*, or *Meskikouikou*, a place where there is grass. (Rale.) *Muskéeticook*, Dead water. (Polis.)

Mattahumkeag, Sand-creek Pond.

Piscataquis, branch of a river. } Nicholai.

Shecorways, sheldrakes.

Naramekechus, peetweet. } Polis.

Medawisla, loon.

Orignal, Moosehead Lake. (Montresor.)

Chor-chor-que, usnea.

Adelungquamooktum, wood-thrush.

Bematruichtik, high land generally. (*Mt. Pemadené*, Rale.) } Polis.

Maquoxigil, bark of red osier, Indian tobacco.

Kineo, *flint* (Williamson; old Indian hunter). (Hodge.)

Artoosoqu', phosphorescence.

Subekoondark, white spruce.

Skusk, black spruce.

Beskabekuk, the "Lobster Lake" of maps.

Beskabekuk shishtook, the dead water below the island.

Paytaytequick, Burnt-Ground Stream, what Joe called *Ragmuff*.

Nonlangyis, the name of a dead-water between the last and Pine Stream.

Karsaootuk, Black River (or Pine Stream). *Mkazéouighen*, black. Rale.

} Polis.

Michigan, fimus. Polis applied it to a sucker, or a poor, good-for-nothing fish. *Fiante (?) mitsegan*, Rale. (Pickering puts the ? after the first word.)

Cowosnebagosar, Chiogenes hispidula, means, grows where trees have rotted.

Pockadunkquaywayle, echo. *Pagadaükoueouérré.* Rale.

} Polis.

Bororquasis, moose-fly.

Nerlumskeechtcook (or *quoik?*), (or *skeetcook*), Dead water, and applied to the mountains near.

Apmoojeuegamook, lake that is crossed.

Allegash, hemlock-bark. (v. Willis.)

Paytaywecongomec, Burnt-Ground Lake, *Telos.*

Madunkehunk, Height-of-land Stream (Webster Stream).

Madunkehunk-gamooc, Height-of-land Lake.

Matungamooc, Grand Lake.

} Polis.

Uncardnerheese, Trout Stream.

Wassataquoik (or *-cook*), Salmon River, East Branch. (v. Willis.)

Pemoymenuk, Amelanchier berries, "*Pemou-aimin, nak,* a black fruit. Rale." Has it not here the plural ending?

Sheepnoc, Lilium Canadense bulbs. "*Sipen, nak,* white, larger than *penak.*" Rale.

Paytgumkiss, Petticoat (where a small river comes into the Penobscot below Nickatow).

Burntibus, a lake-like reach in the Penobscot.

} Polis.

Passadumkeag, "where the water falls into the Penobscot above the falls." (Williamson.) *Paüsidaükioui* is, *au dessus de la montagne.* Rale.

Olarmon, or *larmon,* (Polis) red paint. "Vermilion, paint, *Ouramaü.*" Rale.

Sunkhaze, "See canoe come out; ho, see 'em stream." (Polis.) The mouth of a river, according to Rale, is *Saüghedétegoue.* The place where one stream empties into another, thus, ᕯ is *saüktaüoui.* (v. Willis.)

Tomhegan Br. (at Moosehead). "*Hatchet, temahigan.*" Rale.

Nickatow, "*Nicketaoutegué,* or *Niketoutegoue, rivière qui fourche.*" Rale.

2. From WILLIAM WILLIS, on the Language of the Abnaquies. Maine Hist. Coll., Vol. IV.

Abalajako-megus (river near Ktaadn).

Aitteon (name of a pond and sachem).

Apmogenegamook (name of a lake).

Allagash (a bark camp). Sockbasin, a Penobscot, told

him, "The Indians gave this name to the lake from the fact of their keeping a hunting-camp there."

Bamonewengamock, head of Allagash, Cross Lake. (Sockbasin.)

Chesuncook, Big Lake.   (Sockbasin.)

Caucongamock (a lake).

Ebeeme, mountains that have plums on them.   (Sockbasin.)

Ktaadn.   Sockbasin pronounces this Ka-tah-din, and said it meant "large mountain or large thing."

Kenduskeag (the place of Eels).

Kineo (flint), mountain on the border, etc.

Metawamkeag, a river with a smooth gravelly bottom. (Sockbasin.)

Metanawcook.

Millinoket, a lake with many islands in it. (Sockbasin.)

Matakeunk (river).

Molunkus (river).

Nicketow, Neccotoh, where two streams meet ("Forks of the Penobscot").

Negas (Indian village on the Kenduskeag).

Orignal (Montresor's name for Moosehead Lake).

Ponguongamook, Allagash, name of a Mohawk Indian killed there.   (Sockbasin.)

Penobscot, *Penobskeag*, French *Pentagoet*, etc.

Pougohwaken (Heron Lake).

Pemadumcook (lake).

Passadumkeag, where water goes into the river above falls.   (Williamson.)

Ripogenus (river).

Sunkhaze (river), Dead water.

Souneunk.

Seboomook. Sockbasin says this word means "the shape of a Moose's head, and was given to the lake," etc. *Howard* says differently.

Seboois, a brook, a small river. (Sockbasin.)

Sebec (river).

Sebago (great water).

Telos (lake).

Telasiuis (lake).

Umbagog (lake), doubled up; so called from its form. (Sockbasin.)

Umbazookskus (lake).

Wassatiquoik, a mountain river. (Sockbasin).

Judge C. E. Potter of Manchester, New Hampshire, adds in November, 1855: —

"*Chesuncook.* This is formed from *Chesunk,* or *Schunk,* (a goose), and *Auke* (a place), and means 'The Goose Place.' Chesunk, or Schunk, is the sound made by the wild geese when flying."

Ktaadn. This is doubtless a corruption of *Kees* (high), and *Auke* (a place).

Penobscot, Penapse (stone, rock-place), and *Auke* (place).

Suncook, Goose-place, *Schunk-auke.*

The Judge says that *schoot* means to rush, and hence *schoodic* from this and *auke* (a place where water rushes), and that *schoon* means the same; and that the Marble-head people and others have derived the words *scoon* and *scoot* from the Indians, and hence schooner; refers to a Mr. Chute.